W9-ARK-214

The *Unofficial*

DOWNTON ABBEY COOKBOOK

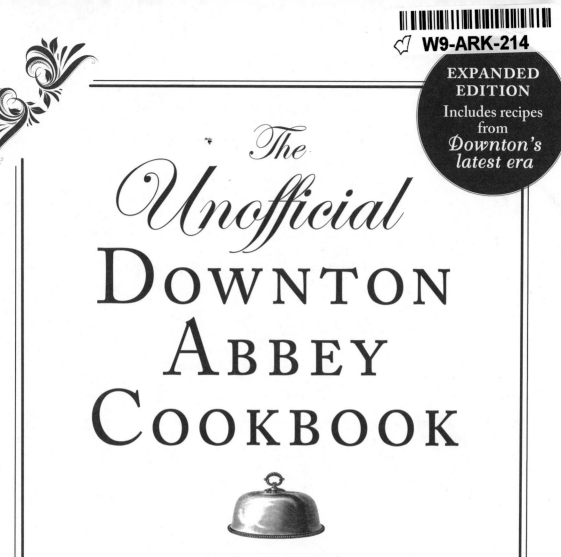

From LADY MARY'S CRAB CANAPÉS *to* DAISY'S MOUSSE AU CHOCOLAT

~~~ *More Than 150 Recipes* ~~~

from UPSTAIRS AND DOWNSTAIRS

Emily Ansara Baines

Aadamsmedia

AVON, MASSACHUSETTS

Published by
Adams Media, a division of F+W Media, Inc.
57 Littlefield Street, Avon, MA 02322. U.S.A.
www.adamsmedia.com

ISBN 10: 1-4405-8291-2
ISBN 13: 978-1-4405-8291-2
eISBN 10: 1-4405-8292-0
eISBN 13: 978-1-4405-8292-9

Printed in the United States of America.

10   9   8   7   6   5   4   3   2   1

Library of Congress Cataloging-in-Publication Data
Baines, Emily Ansara.
   The unofficial Downton Abbey cookbook / Emily Ansara Baines. -- Expanded edition.
      pages cm
   Includes bibliographical references and index.
   ISBN-13: 978-1-4405-8291-2 (pb : alk. paper)
   ISBN-10: 1-4405-8291-2 (pb : alk. paper)
   ISBN-13: 978-1-4405-8292-9 (ebook)
   ISBN-10: 1-4405-8292-0 (ebook)
   1. Cooking. 2. Cooking, English. 3. Great Britain--Social life and customs. 4. Downton Abbey (Television
program) I. Title.
   TX714.B33354 2014
   641.5941--dc23
                                    2014027506

Always follow safety and common sense cooking protocol while using kitchen utensils, operating ovens and stoves, and handling uncooked food. If children are assisting in the preparation of any recipe, they should always be supervised by an adult.

Many of the designations used by manufacturers and sellers to distinguish their products are claimed as trademarks. Where those designations appear in this book and Adams Media was aware of a trademark claim, the designations have been printed with initial capital letters.

Images © Clipart.com, iStockphoto.com/SelenaMaiskaia, Dover Publications.

This book is available at quantity discounts for bulk purchases.
For information, please call 1-800-289-0963.

For my parents.

Acknowledgments

As always, infinite love and thanks to my friends and family. Mom and Dad, without your constant support—physical and emotional—this book could not exist. Thank you for loving me. Thank you for believing in me. And, of course, big hugs to my little brother Chris, for all the advice and for supporting me in your own way.

I must thank my beloved Spencer Balliet, who makes my heart feel warm on even the coldest of nights. Thank you for being my best friend as well as my greatest love. You always make me smile. I love you more than any words can say. But let me start with this: I love you more than Diet Coke.

Thanks, as always, to my agent, the spectacular Danielle Chiotti and all the crew at Upstart Crow Literary, along with Brendan O'Neill and the entire team over at Adams Media. Without you guys this book would quite literally never be published. Thank you for the handholding and ingenious edits.

My friends, other family, you know who you are—thank you for being there. Keagan, Laura, Alice, Cory, Jas, Stella, Vince, Nick, all of you—thank you. I owe you an eight-course meal. Spencer can cook it.

As always, I would like to thank Aimee Bender, who is a role model for me not just as a writer, but as a human being.

And, of course, thank you Julian Fellowes, Carnival Films, WGBH Boston, and everyone involved in the making of *Downton Abbey*. What you have created is an inspiration to us all.

Contents

Chapter 4 FOURTH AND FIFTH COURSES: JUICY JOINTS AND SUCCULENT STEAKS 79

Chapter 5 SIXTH COURSE: RESPLENDENT ROASTS, GORGEOUS GAME, AND ACCOMPANYING SALADS 95

Chapter 6 SEVENTH COURSE: THE NECESSARY VEGETABLE 117

Chapter 7 THE FINISHING TOUCH: SWEETS AND DESSERTS 131

Chapter 8   TEA AT DOWNTON ABBEY 167

Part 2
SUSTENANCE FOR THE STAFF 191

Chapter 9   HEARTY BREAKFASTS TO START THE WORK DAY 193

Chapter 10   A QUICK LUNCH BETWEEN BUSINESS 203

Chapter 11 DOWNSTAIRS SUPPER 221

Chapter 12 DESSERTS FOR THE SERVANTS' SWEET TOOTH 247

Introduction

Downton Abbey, the grand estate synonymous with opulence, exists in a time of great change. Wars begin and end, economies crash, beloved characters pass on, and social structures are turned on their heads. And yet, through it all the grandeur and generosity of the Crawley home remains strong, as shown through the sumptuous offerings cooked by Mrs. Patmore and served by Mr. Carson. Everyone at Downton Abbey, from kitchen maids Daisy and Ivy to the Countess of Grantham herself, takes intense pride in a well-serviced dinner, no matter what disaster may be occurring in the world or an individual's personal life. That's just good manners! Indeed, the Countess of Grantham and her daughters plan their parties down to the very last detail. The knowledgeable—and proper—hostess accounts for every single minute of her guests' stay. Of course, once the freedom of automobile transportation becomes commonly available in the 1920s, guests can frequent the estate at their will—but they still always return in time for tea and dinner!

The technological innovations of the 1920s weren't just regulated to vehicles: Poor Mrs. Patmore fights a raging battle with the industrial improvements seemingly foisted upon her kitchen—ones like Daisy's beloved electric mixer, or the refrigerator the Countess of Grantham keeps requesting Mrs. Patmore approve. Yet, as Martha Levinson declares, "Come war and peace Downton still stands—and the Crawleys are still in it!" Thus, this cookbook embraces the classic, albeit extravagant, *Service à la Russe*, the French table service enjoyed by all who dined at Downton Abbey. This required the butler and the footmen to bring each course out (the number of courses ranges from eight to thirteen depending on the occasion and time period) sequentially rather than all at once. A typical *Service à la Russe* consisted of the following menu:

- *Hors d'oeuvre variés* (often oysters or caviar)
- Two soups (one thick, one clear)
- Two kinds of fish (one boiled, the other fried)
- An entrée
- The joint, a.k.a. a large piece of meat cooked in one piece
- The sorbet
- Roast and salad
- Vegetables
- A hot dessert
- Ice cream and wafers
- Fresh and dry fruits
- Coffee and liqueurs

Often, additional "removes" or "refreshers" (such as sorbet) were added in between the heavier courses. Cheese was often served with the fruits and before the coffee and liqueurs.

Most of these courses are represented by a chapter full of recipes that you can serve at your own dinner party—with or without Mr. Carson and Mrs. Hughes—with an additional chapter for that most British of meals: afternoon tea. With these recipes as a guide, you can sample delicious upper-class delights such as Steak Chasseur, Crispy Roast Duck with Blackberry Sauce, and Lord Grantham's American Italian: Risotto alla Milanese. With only a rudimentary understanding of nutrition but a great appreciation for taste, even vegetables were soaked in butter. Potatoes Lyonnaise, Pommes de Terre Sarladaise, Cucumbers à la Poulette, and Baked and Buttery Balsamic Asparagus with Sea Salt were more butter and cream than vegetable, and perhaps more saccharine than the sweetest of the many desserts offered at Downton: desserts such as Raspberry Meringue Pie, Sussex Pond Pudding, and Upstairs Downstairs Christmas Plum Pudding to their far fancier French counterparts such as Grand Gougères and Daisy's Mousse au Chocolat. In addition, you'll find historical facts, course pairings, tips for table seating, and etiquette guidelines, which will allow you to host not only a realistic Edwardian dinner service, but a successful party as well.

Meanwhile, while the servants were not granted extravagant meals in the *Service à la Russe* style, they nonetheless enjoyed a very filling breakfast, lunch, and dinner—with perhaps a tea thrown in for good measure. In Part 2, you'll find a sampling of the filling dishes that Mr. Carson, Mrs. Hughes, Thomas, Anna, Daisy, and the rest of the Downton Abbey staff enjoyed, such as Classic Steak and Kidney Pie; Chicken, Leek, and Caerphilly Cheese Pie for St. David's Day; and Magnificent Mutton Stew. While not as ornate, these dishes are certainly filling and are ones that both you and your family could enjoy before, during, or after a long workday.

So, while the world of *Downton Abbey* no longer exists, with these recipes you can recreate it, and live one day as a lady, the next as a lady's maid. As the saying goes, you are what you eat. Enjoy! And bon appétit! (Just don't forget your manners or you'll be sure to hear about it from the Dowager Countess.)

Part 1

DINING WITH THE CRAWLEYS

For the Crawleys, dining at Downton Abbey was done with a sense of sophistication and style—even if the family was dining alone—and, in this part, you'll learn how to dine like those living "upstairs." Each chapter denotes a specific course featured in a typical *Downton Abbey* dinner, granting you the freedom to mix and match courses and their recipes to your—and your guests'—palates. You'll also find step-by-step guidance for and recipes to serve at a proper afternoon tea. All chapters offer etiquette tips, to which you should pay great heed before hosting your first event. After all, you don't want to offend any prospective suitors!

Chapter 1

HORS D'OEUVRES VARIÉS

The hors d'oeuvres, or appetizers, set the scene and subsequently the entire mood of a formal dinner party. Thus, it should come as no surprise that both Mrs. Patmore and the Countess of Grantham would take their hors d'oeuvres very seriously—as would their guests. If the dinner invitation suggested an 8 P.M. dinner, it was expected that guests would arrive a half-hour early so they could take part in idle chitchat and share news while drinking cocktails and munching on these offerings. After all, many an episode of *Downton Abbey* begins with the Crawleys fighting or insinuating or laughing among themselves as they drink and snack before Carson announces dinner. An entire argument or proposal could occur in the time it would take for the Dowager Countess to finish her caviar.

Hors d'oeuvres started to become more of an expected and accepted offering in the early to mid 1900s. Indeed, the idea of eating food as a way to whet the appetite started in Russia, where guests partook of caviar, herring, anchovies, and other salty food in a separate room before dinner. Russia was also the birthplace of the *Service à la Russe* (a.k.a. "in the Russian style of dining"). While the Earl of Grantham might not like to be associated with Russia, he would not balk at the chance to show off his opulence and his ability to provide not just an extravagant meal but an extravagant array of snacks (expensive caviar and decadent oysters were standard offerings). Sometimes, however, depending on the number of people and the lateness of the hour, hors d'oeuvres would be served at the dinner table with the guests already seated. But no matter where the hors d'oeuvres were served, they would be served with Chablis—and at Downton Abbey you know they'd also be served with a wry sense of humor and plenty of witty repartee.

Grilled Oysters with Lemon Garlic Butter

As oysters and caviar were the most common appetizers offered before a large meal, the Earl and Countess of Grantham—along with their children—would know not to eat oysters with their fingers but with a fork. After all, one incorrect move and the Dowager Countess would have a field day complaining about her family's manners.

YIELDS 4–6 SERVINGS

1¼ cups unsalted butter

2 tablespoons finely grated Parmesan cheese

1 tablespoon finely grated Pecorino Romano cheese

1 tablespoon minced parsley leaves

1 tablespoon fresh lemon juice

1 teaspoon lime juice

2 teaspoons minced garlic

1 teaspoon minced chives

1 teaspoon minced shallot

1 teaspoon kosher salt

1 teaspoon sugar

½ teaspoon cayenne pepper

25 shucked oysters, half of each shell reserved and washed

1. Mix together all ingredients other than oysters in a large bowl, then place mixture on a piece of plastic wrap, rolling it to form a stiff log. Freeze until firm.
2. Move oven rack to middle of oven. Preheat oven to 350°F.
3. Place washed oyster shells on a baking sheet. Top each shell with one oyster. Remove the butter log from the freezer and unwrap, slicing it into 25 rounds. Place each round on top of an oyster.
4. Put oysters in oven and cook about 10–15 minutes until they are cooked through, curled around the edges with bubbling butter. Do not overcook. To test for doneness, tap oyster shell. If hollow-sounding, then the oyster is done.

TIMES GONE BY

In the decade preceding World War I, Lady Jeune, Baroness St. Helier, a well-known socialite and self-proclaimed "modern woman," revolted against what she saw as extravagance and outdated customs. She proclaimed, "No dinner should consist of more than eight dishes: soup, fish, entrée, joint, game, sweet, hors d'oeuvres, and perhaps an ice; but each dish should be perfect of its kind." Luckily, this dish counts as an hors d'oeuvre and makes the cut!

Smoked Salmon Mousse

A more "modern" appetizer that the Dowager Countess would both detest for its modernity and enjoy for its taste, this is a take on the better known dessert mousses and jellies. However, we can rest assured that Mrs. Patmore would not offer this modern mousse on the night that the Dowager Countess first meets Matthew Crawley—the dear Dowager Countess is in a bad enough mood already.

YIELDS 10–12 SERVINGS

Unsalted butter for
  greasing mold
1 envelope unflavored
  gelatin
¼ cup cold water
½ cup boiling water
½ cup mayonnaise
2 tablespoons lemon juice
4 drops hot sauce
½ teaspoon paprika
1 teaspoon sea salt
2 cups poached salmon,
  flaked into minute pieces
2 tablespoons capers,
  drained
1 cup whipped cream

1. Grease a 6-cup fish mold with butter.
2. Soften the gelatin in cold water. Add the ½ cup boiling water and stir well, making sure to thoroughly dissolve gelatin.
3. Let cool thoroughly, then stir in mayonnaise, lemon juice, hot sauce, paprika, and sea salt. Mix well. Fold in the salmon bits and capers. Add the whipped cream and continue folding until everything is well combined.
4. Pour the mousse into the mold, then cover with plastic wrap and chill in the refrigerator overnight.
5. Unmold the mousse onto a large plate and serve.

Suggested Pairings

Although it would be difficult to get some of these ingredients in England back in the early 1900s, try serving this dish with sliced avocados, celery sticks, olives, and baguette slices.

The Countess of Grantham's Moules en Sauce

This French recipe, enjoyed frequently by those visiting the Breton coast, would be a fancy, yet easy-to-make appetizer that the Countess of Grantham would offer when Matthew Crawley and his mother first visit, as it is sure to please even those whom she has yet to really know.

YIELDS 4 SERVINGS

½ cup light Bacardi rum

1 cup dry white wine

2 tablespoons unsalted butter

2 large onions, sliced into rings

2 stalks celery, chopped

1 clove garlic, minced

⅛ teaspoon cayenne pepper

8 cups mussels, cleaned and debearded

2 bay leaves

2 sprigs fresh thyme

Kosher salt and freshly ground black pepper to taste

½ cup heavy cream

Thyme, for garnish

1. In a small bowl, mix together rum and wine and set aside.
2. Melt butter over medium-low heat in a large saucepan. Add onions, celery, garlic, and cayenne pepper. Stir occasionally until the onions are transparent.
3. Place mussels in pan and stir. Once the mussels begin to release their juice, pour the wine-rum mixture over them. Stir in bay leaves and thyme, then add kosher salt and freshly ground black pepper. Cook for an additional 10 minutes, stirring frequently.
4. Once the mussels have opened, add 2 large tablespoons of the cream into the sauce. Pour mussels and sauce into bowls, then add another tablespoon of cream and thyme for garnish.

Etiquette Lessons

To clean your mussels, be sure to discard any mussels that are broken or open. Before cooking, soak your mussels in water for 20–25 minutes. To remove a mussel's beard, hold the mussel in one hand, then cover the other hand with a dishcloth. Grasp the beard with the dishcloth and yank towards the hinge edge of the mussel, *not* towards the opening end of the mussel. Place debearded mussels in another bowl of clean, cold water and use a firm brush to scrub off any remaining sand or attachments on mussels.

Zesty Mussels in Tomato Garlic Sauce

It was typical in Edwardian times to serve Chablis along with mussel hors d'oeuvres. As many a night at Downton Abbey could erupt thanks to the "hot" tempers of its inhabitants, and as this is a spicier mussel appetizer than The Countess of Grantham's *Moules en Sauce* (see recipe in this chapter), it's no wonder that wine would serve as both the drink of choice and one of the main ingredients in this spicy dish.

YIELDS 2–4 SERVINGS

1 cup white wine

1 cup tomato-and-clam juice cocktail

1 (14.5-ounce) can diced tomatoes in garlic and olive oil

4 cloves garlic, chopped

½ teaspoon crushed red pepper flakes

1 pound mussels, cleaned and debearded

4 tablespoons unsalted butter

1. In a large pot, combine wine, tomato-and-clam juice cocktail, diced tomatoes, garlic, and red pepper flakes. Bring to a boil and add mussels.
2. Cover and continue to boil for 6–8 minutes or until all the mussels have opened. Discard any closed mussels.
3. Remove mussels from liquid and keep warm. Pour off liquid, leaving only about 2 cups. Do not discard garlic if possible. Boil the 2 cups until it reduces to about 1½ cups.
4. Stir in butter until butter has melted and sauce has thickened. Serve mussels with sauce. Also try serving with sourdough bread to soak up extra sauce.

TIMES GONE BY

In seventeenth- and eighteenth-century France, the bourgeoisie—the middle class—were far stricter about manners than the nobility. As there was no king standing nearby to enforce the rules of etiquette, the bourgeoisie saw it as up to them to impose and dictate the rules of civility, which means that they could be considered even worse snobs than their more prestigious counterparts.

Potatoes with Caviar and Crème Fraîche

With another reliable hors d'oeuvres standby, the Countess of Grantham would be sure to wow even the cynical Matthew Crawley with this simple, yet nonetheless delicious treat. After all, if the hostess of Downton could offer such a decadent treat as a mere appetizer, Matthew Crawley would quickly become aware that he is entering a whole other world—one with impeccable food to go with those impeccable manners.

YIELDS 4–6 SERVINGS

2 dozen fingerling potatoes, washed and halved lengthwise

1 cup extra-virgin olive oil, divided

2 tablespoons fresh rosemary

2 teaspoons pink Himalayan sea salt

1 teaspoon freshly ground black pepper

½ teaspoon thyme

1 cup crème fraîche

1 (3-ounce) jar high-quality caviar (such as Osetra caviar)

Fresh chives, minced, for garnish

1. Preheat oven to 350°F.
2. In a large bowl, toss potatoes with ⅔ cup of the olive oil, the rosemary, pink Himalayan sea salt, and pepper.
3. Coat a small pan with remaining olive oil. Place potatoes in pan cut-side down. Bake potatoes in preheated oven for 45 minutes–1 hour or until potatoes are tender on the inside and golden on the outside.
4. Let the potatoes cool slightly, then place on a serving platter.
5. In a small bowl, stir thyme into crème fraîche.
6. Spread each potato with a ½ teaspoon of crème fraîche mix and a ½ teaspoon of caviar. Garnish with chives.

Suggested Pairings

For a different taste, try replacing the black caviar with red caviar. While not quite as expensive and subsequently not as fancy, this will provide your guests with an unusual flavor that they are likely not used to tasting at fancy Edwardian dinner parties.

Lady Mary's Crab Canapés

While the Countess of Grantham might offer the Potatoes with Caviar and Crème Fraîche (see recipe in this chapter) or her eponymous *Moules en Sauce* (see recipe in this chapter), she would likely offer more than one appetizer, including these delicious yet light crab canapés. However, Lady Mary, upon learning her entire inheritance is lost to a total stranger, would match the namesake of this dish by acting quite "crabby."

YIELDS 8–10 SERVINGS,
48 CANAPÉS

48 mini-toasts such as
   Pride of France
¼ cup unsalted butter,
   melted
1½ cups canned crabmeat
⅓ cup mayonnaise
½ cup cream cheese
1 cup grated Parmesan
   cheese
4 scallions, finely chopped
1 tablespoon Old Bay
   seasoning
1 teaspoon sea salt
1 dash Tabasco sauce
1 teaspoon fresh lemon
   juice
½ teaspoon white pepper

1. Preheat oven to 375°F.
2. Slather individual toasts with melted butter, thoroughly coating each toast. Place toasts on a lightly oiled baking sheet and toast in oven for 1–2 minutes.
3. In a large bowl, blend together crabmeat, mayonnaise, and cream cheese. Once evenly blended, stir in Parmesan cheese, followed by scallions, Old Bay seasoning, sea salt, Tabasco sauce, lemon juice, and white pepper. Stir in more salt and pepper to taste.
4. Spread crabmeat mixture on individual toasts and arrange evenly on a baking sheet. Bake in the middle of preheated oven until puffed, about 10–15 minutes. Serve warm.

TIMES GONE BY

The term *canapé* comes from the French word for "couch." This makes sense if you look at the garnish as a person, sitting on a couch (the bread/pastry). Nonetheless, it is expected that a canapé be salty or spicy, as its job as an appetizer is to increase the guests' appetites.

The Crawley Sisters' Stuffed Mushrooms

While this is an Italian-based dish, its fun feel and mouthwatering texture make it a classic hors d'oeuvre that everyone—whether upstairs or downstairs—can get behind. While the perceived attitude of the Crawley sisters matches the stuffiness of the mushrooms, a deeper look inside shows that they have warm, perhaps even gooey, hearts—just like these appetizers!

YIELDS 12 STUFFED MUSHROOMS

12 whole, fresh mushrooms

1 tablespoon extra-virgin olive oil

1 tablespoon unsalted butter

¼ cup chopped green onions

1½ tablespoons minced garlic

1 dash Worcestershire sauce

1 (8-ounce) package cream cheese, softened

½ cup fresh Parmesan cheese, shredded

1 teaspoon kosher salt

½ teaspoon freshly ground black pepper

¼ teaspoon onion powder

½ teaspoon ground cayenne pepper

1 cup Italian seasoned bread crumbs

The Crawley Sisters' Stuffed Mushrooms
(continued)

1. Preheat oven to 350°F. Thoroughly grease a medium or large baking sheet.
2. Carefully clean mushrooms, removing stems. Chop stems extremely fine.
3. In a large skillet over medium heat, melt olive oil and butter. Add chopped mushroom stems, chopped green onions, and minced garlic, followed by 1 dash Worcestershire sauce. Cook garlic and mushrooms until all moisture has evaporated, being careful to not burn the garlic. Set aside and let cool.
4. When garlic, onion, and mushroom-stem mixture is no longer hot to the touch, stir in cream cheese, Parmesan cheese, salt, pepper, onion powder, and cayenne pepper. Mixture will be thick and difficult to stir.
5. Fill mushroom caps with a good amount of stuffing. Sprinkle top of each mushroom cap's stuffing with Italian bread crumbs. Arrange mushroom caps on prepared baking sheet.
6. Bake mushrooms in preheated oven for 20–25 minutes or until mushrooms are extremely hot and liquid starts to form. Cool slightly and serve.

TIMES GONE BY

The extravagant Crawleys actually owe frugality for this delicious dish. It was through a lack of ingredients—but a surplus of mushrooms—that Italian chefs and farmers first came up with the concept of stuffed mushrooms. As the nineteenth century wore on, and Italian restaurants realized that many patrons preferred fancy food to the food you may associate with red-and-white-checkered tablecloths, they started offering stuffed mushrooms delicately arranged on plates and filled with a wide range of vegetables and cheeses. Before the Italians could say *Buon appetito*, these delicacies were flying off the table and into their patrons' mouths!

Upstairs Anchovy-Onion Tarts

While this tart is a delicious and unique appetizer offering, it's likely that Lady Mary would stay away from this particular hors d'oeuvre, as it would give her bad breath—and then the charming Pamuk might never want to kiss her.

YIELDS 10–12 TARTS

For Pastry
1¼ cups all-purpose flour

¾ cup unsalted butter, chopped into cubes

1 teaspoon kosher salt

3 tablespoons cold water

For Filling
2 tablespoons extra-virgin olive oil

4 tablespoons unsalted butter

3 large onions, sliced

1 teaspoon chopped fresh sage

1 (2-ounce) tube anchovy paste

2 cloves garlic chopped

½ teaspoon sugar

4 tablespoons tomato paste

2 teaspoons chopped fresh thyme

Upstairs Anchovy-Onion Tarts

(continued)

1. **To make pastry:** In a large bowl and using your fingers, blend together flour, butter, and salt, kneading until mixture resembles coarse bread crumbs. Add cold water, stirring until fully incorporated. Once again using your hands, squeeze together a small amount of dough—if it does not hold together, add more water a few teaspoons at a time. Be careful not to overwork mixture.

2. Turn dough out onto a lightly floured surface. Divide dough into four equal-sized portions, using the palms of your hands to evenly distribute fat in dough. Gather dough back together, pressing into a ball, then flatten one more time into one 5-inch disk. Wrap in plastic wrap and chill for at least 1 hour or until firm.

3. **To make filling:** Heat olive oil and butter in a large skillet over medium heat. Stir in onions and sage. Cook onions, stirring occasionally, for 35–40 minutes or until carmelized onions are soft and golden brown.

4. Preheat oven to 375°F.

5. In a medium-sized bowl, stir together anchovy paste, garlic, sugar, tomato paste, and thyme.

6. Roll out chilled dough on a lightly floured surface until dough is a 12- to 13-inch disc. Place disc on a large, parchment paper–covered baking sheet.

7. Evenly spread tomato–anchovy paste mixture over dough, leaving a 1½- to 2-inch border along pastry edge. Arrange caramelized onions on top of tomato–anchovy paste mixture. Fold edges of pastry over. Bake pastry for 45–50 minutes or until golden brown. Serve warm, preferably presliced.

TIMES GONE BY

While the thicker nature of this snack might properly label it an entrée, hosts in the Edwardian era were allowed to vary their hors d'oeuvres offerings, especially if the appetizers in question were served at the table or even between meals. To ward off any questioning raised eyebrows, however, anchovies, a popular hors d'oeuvres standard, are added to this pastry.

Mrs. Patmore's Rosemary Oat Crackers

During the Crawley girls' childhoods and teenage years at Downton Abbey, it's likely that the Earl and Countess of Grantham would have offered their guests fancy homemade crackers, rather than those easily bought at a market. After all, what is the point of having a cook if she can't cook crackers? However, as the years wore on and ingredients became scarce thanks to the war, the Crawleys may have allowed Mrs. Patmore to use store-bought crackers as long as her other food continued to be excellent.

YIELDS 50–60 CRACKERS

2 cups old-fashioned rolled oats

1 teaspoon kosher salt

½ teaspoon freshly ground black pepper

1½ teaspoons chopped rosemary leaves

¼ teaspoon garlic powder

¼ cup plus 2 tablespoons all-purpose flour

¾ teaspoon baking powder

½ cup chopped unsalted butter

¼ cup whole milk

1. Preheat oven to 350°F.
2. Pulse oats in a food processor until chopped and fine. Add salt, pepper, rosemary, garlic powder, ¼ cup flour, baking powder, and butter. Pulse until mixture resembles coarse bread crumbs. Pour in milk and pulse until the ingredients combine to form a dough, approximately 45 seconds.
3. With a rolling pin, roll dough until it's ⅛-inch thick on a surface sprinkled with remaining flour. Cut about 50–60 squares. Place squares on lightly greased baking sheets and bake for about 15–20 minutes or until crackers are lightly browned on the bottom. Transfer crackers to a cooling rack and allow to cool completely before serving.

Etiquette Lessons

Invitations to a formal dinner should be sent at least seven to ten days before the event and should be replied to within a week of receipt. Unless there is illness, it is considered bad form to reject a dinner party invitation.

Caviar Cucumber Canapés

As it presents great flavor with little fuss, this elegant and simple hors d'oeuvre would likely impress the opinionated but well-meaning Lady Rosamund Painswick. Perhaps Lady Rosamund would offer these to Lady Mary while encouraging her to wait to answer Matthew's first marriage proposal, slyly suggesting that Lady Mary must prepare herself for a life of tiny yet nonetheless fantastic tastes.

YIELDS 4 SERVINGS

1 cup cream cheese
1 tablespoon fresh lemon
    juice
1 large English cucumber,
    cut into 15–20 slices
1 teaspoon kosher salt
½ teaspoon freshly ground
    pepper
4.5 ounces caviar

1. In a small bowl, thoroughly mix together cream cheese and lemon juice. (If cream cheese feels too thick, try adding 1 tablespoon of sour cream.)
2. Top cucumber slices with cream cheese and lemon juice mixture. Sprinkle with a bit of salt and pepper. Place a dollop of caviar on top of each cucumber slice, and serve.

Suggested Pairings

Nothing tastes better with caviar than champagne or Prosecco—though Lady Rosamund would never serve Prosecco to her guests when champagne is an option! If you'd like to diminish the salty flavor of the caviar, try serving some of Mrs. Patmore's Rosemary Oat Crackers (see recipe in this chapter) along with the cucumber slices, as the rosemary in the crackers will help lessen the intensity of the caviar taste.

Mushrooms Vol-au-Vent

When discussing the possibility of ending the harsh entail, the Dowager Countess would happily offer these filling French puff pastries to Matthew Crawley. As "Vol-au-Vent" translates to "blown by the wind," it's likely that the Dowager Countess (not to mention the Countess of Grantham) wishes that the entail could be easily blown away by a simple change in the weather! However, the ladies will have to make do with these delicious tarts, as Matthew can offer nothing but bad news.

YIELDS 4–6 SERVINGS

11 ounces frozen puff pastry, thawed but very cold

1 large egg, room temperature

1 tablespoon water

4 tablespoons unsalted butter

2 cloves garlic, diced

1 teaspoon fresh thyme

2 cups sliced mushrooms

4 tablespoons all-purpose flour

1 cup whole milk

¼ cup heavy cream

Kosher salt and freshly ground black pepper to taste

Mushrooms Vol-au-Vent

(continued)

1. On a clean, well-floured surface, roll out the pastry so it is ¼-inch thick. Using a 2½-inch pastry cutter, cut nine circles. Then, using a 1½-inch pastry cutter, make an indent (not all the way through) in the center of each pastry circle.

2. Place cut pastries on a baking sheet and cover. Chill in refrigerator for 30–45 minutes.

3. Preheat oven to 400°F.

4. In a small bowl, whisk together egg and water. Brush the tops of the pastry cases with the egg-water mixture.

5. Bake pastries in preheated oven for 40–45 minutes or until golden brown.

6. Cool pastry cases on a wire rack. Using a sharp knife, carefully remove lids and scoop out any uncooked filling.

7. In a large skillet over medium heat, melt butter. Stir in garlic and let simmer, stirring occasionally, for 3–5 minutes.

8. Add thyme and sliced mushrooms to butter-garlic mixture and cover. Let cook for an additional 3–5 minutes.

9. Remove lid and whisk in flour, cooking for 1 minute. Stir in milk and cream, and increase the heat. Let mixture boil for 15–20 seconds, then cover and reduce to a simmer for 3–5 minutes. Season with salt and pepper if desired.

10. Carefully fill prepared pastry cases with mushroom filling, then place pastry lids over the filling.

11. Lower oven temperature to 375°F. Cook pastries in oven for 10–15 minutes, watching carefully so they do not burn.

12. Remove pastries from oven and allow to cool slightly before serving.

Suggested Pairings

A high-quality crisp white wine such as a Chardonnay or Sauvignon Blanc would help the diners' palates pick up the sophisticated taste of the mushrooms.

Classic Oysters Rockefeller

While John D. Rockefeller had nothing to do with this dish, it was named for him because he was the richest man at the time, and the chef, Jules Alciatore—who took the original recipe to his grave—wanted to convey the richness of the sauce. It is likely that the American Countess of Grantham would make sure that Mrs. Patmore had a reliable recipe for this beloved—and fancy—American appetizer, making it possible for the Countess to have a taste of home when needed.

YIELDS 14–16 SERVINGS

48 fresh, unopened oysters, cleaned

2 cups pale ale beer

4 cloves garlic

4 teaspoons sea salt, divided

2 teaspoons freshly ground black pepper, divided

1 tablespoon Pernod

1 cup unsalted butter

1 large onion, chopped

2 cloves garlic, crushed

10 ounces fresh spinach, chopped

10 ounces Monterey jack cheese, shredded

10 ounces Fontina cheese, shredded

½ cup whole milk

1 teaspoon freshly ground black pepper

4 tablespoons fine bread crumbs

8 slices bacon, cooked and crumbled

Classic Oysters Rockefeller

(continued)

1. Place cleaned oysters in a large stockpot. Add beer, followed by enough water to cover oysters. Add garlic, 2 teaspoons of the sea salt, and 1 teaspoon of the pepper. Bring liquid to a boil, then drain oysters and set aside.

2. Once oysters have cooled, break off and discard the top shell. Splash each oyster with a little bit of Pernod, saving ½ tablespoon for future use. Arrange oysters evenly on a baking sheet.

3. Preheat oven to 400°F.

4. Melt butter in a large saucepan over medium heat. Stir in onion and garlic, and cook until onions are soft and translucent, about 5–7 minutes. Reduce heat to low and stir in spinach, followed by the Monterey jack and Fontina cheeses. Stirring frequently, cook until cheese melts. Add milk, followed by remaining 2 teaspoons sea salt and remaining 1 teaspoon pepper.

5. Spoon sauce over each oyster. Sprinkle oysters again with remaining Pernod. Sprinkle with bread crumbs and bacon.

6. Bake oysters until bubbly and golden, about 12–15 minutes. Remove from oven and serve.

TIMES GONE BY

While this recipe uses spinach, it's well known that authentic Oysters Rockefeller obtains its green sauce without the use of spinach, but rather from a mixture of parsley, celery, and scallions or chives. However, nobody knows the exact ratio of ingredients, and this fact, along with the likelihood that the original Oysters Rockefeller contained absinthe (which this recipe replaces with Pernod), a liquor that is illegal in several areas, makes duplicating real Oysters Rockefeller nearly impossible. This recipe, however, is a solid and extremely satisfying solution.

Crunchy Fig and Bleu Cheese Tarts

As any experienced chef would know, bleu cheese brings out the sweet taste of figs like no other ingredient. Thus, Mrs. Patmore would bake these delicious hors d'oeuvres that are simultaneously sweet and tart. Eaters beware, however: Nothing is as tart as the Crawley sense of humor!

YIELDS 4–6 SERVINGS

For Pastry
1 sheet frozen puff pastry, thawed

For Walnut Crunch
2 tablespoons honey

2 tablespoons sugar

2 tablespoons unsalted butter

½ teaspoon cinnamon

¼ teaspoon kosher salt

1 tablespoon heavy cream

¼ cup chopped toasted walnuts

For Figs
⅔ cup sugar

1 tablespoon lukewarm water

1 teaspoon kosher salt

12 fresh figs, halved lengthwise and stems removed

¼ cup unsalted butter

For Topping
6 ounces Stilton blue cheese, crumbled, room temperature

½ cup sweet port

Honey to taste

Crunchy Fig and Bleu Cheese Tarts

(continued)

1. Preheat oven to 350°F.
2. Roll out puff pastry sheet on a clean, lightly floured surface. Place puff pastry sheet in a well-greased baking pan and then place another sheet pan on top of puff pastry to prevent it from rising too much.
3. Bake puff pastry in preheated oven (with sheet pan still on top) for 5–8 minutes or until beginning to turn golden. Remove and set aside.
4. **To make walnut crunch:** In a medium-sized skillet, stir honey, sugar, butter, cinnamon, and salt over medium heat until butter melts. Cook mixture until it boils and reaches a deep golden brown, about 3–5 minutes. Stir in cream, followed by walnuts. Cook for an additional 2 minutes, then pour out over a sheet of heavy foil. Let cool completely, then chop walnut crunch into small pieces.
5. **To prepare figs:** Mix sugar, water, and salt in a heavy skillet over medium heat until sugar is evenly moist, adding more water if needed. Cook mixture until sugar turns golden, stirring occasionally, about 5 minutes. Place figs cut-side down in sugar mixture. Cook figs until they begin to release juice. Immediately add butter, swirling skillet to melt. Remove from heat and add port. Let figs marinate in port mixture for 5–10 minutes before removing figs to a plate to cool. Once again, bring syrup to a boil, whisking until smooth. Cool completely.
6. Using a 2- to 3-inch pastry cutter, cut out rounds of semi-baked puff pastry. Divide walnut mixture among rounds, then top with fig halves, cut-side up.
7. Bake tarts in preheated oven (still at 350°F) for 30 minutes or until golden brown. Remove from oven and let cool slightly.
8. Artfully arrange cheese on top of tarts, followed by the sweet port syrup. Drizzle with honey and serve.

Suggested Pairings

If you choose to serve this dish as a dessert rather than as an appetizer, try pairing these pastries with a delicious yet full-bodied dessert wine such as a Riesling, Moscato, or Chianti. Be careful, however, as Moscato can be an especially sweet wine, and, depending on the brand, can easily overpower, rather than complement, the bleu cheese.

Chapter 2

First and Second Courses: Soups and Fish

Prior to the advent of the *Service à la Russe* used at Downton Abbey, guests would enter the dining room to find their soup already placed on their assigned plates. Once the soup was eaten, the soup bowls would be removed and quickly replaced with fish and then basically a full meal in an attempt to prepare the appetite for the roast. However, with *Service à la Russe*, the soups and other dishes were served one after the other by Thomas and William in courses and not in large meals. In fact, two soups—one thick, one clear—would be offered, and it would be up to guests to decide which one—or both—they wanted to try. Offer one or many of the soups in this chapter at your next dinner party and see who wants what!

Velvety Cream of Mushroom Soup

What makes Mrs. Patmore's cream of mushroom soup so irresistible is its luxurious, velvety texture, which, after reading the famous and highly esteemed master chef Escoffier's treatise on French cooking, Mrs. Patmore would know could only be established by forming a delicious *velouté*—a mixture of a butter-flour roux with chicken stock—as the base.

<u>YIELDS 4–6 SERVINGS</u>

For Velouté

6 cups chicken stock

2 tablespoons unsalted butter

2 tablespoons all-purpose flour

For Soup

¼ cup unsalted butter

1 pound crimini or porcini mushrooms

2 shallots, minced

1 teaspoon kosher salt

½ teaspoon saffron

1 tablespoon brandy

3 egg yolks

½ cup heavy cream

1 teaspoon kosher salt

½ teaspoon white pepper

Velvety Cream of Mushroom Soup

(continued)

1. In a medium-sized pot, heat chicken stock to a light simmer.
2. In a separate pot over medium-high heat, heat 2 tablespoons unsalted butter until it starts to froth. Then stir in flour. Continually stirring, allow to cook for 3–5 minutes over medium heat. Do not let brown.
3. Whisk the warm stock into the roux and let simmer for 20–25 minutes, stirring frequently. It should slowly cook down by at least a third and be silky, or velvety, in appearance.
4. While the *velouté* simmers, make the mushroom base: In a sauté pan over medium heat, melt butter.
5. Finely mince the mushrooms and shallots, and add to pan. Then add 1 teaspoon salt. Simmer, covered, for several minutes or until shallots are translucent and the mushrooms lose their water.
6. In a very small dish, stir the saffron into the brandy, then add to mushroom base. Turn up the heat, then stir to combine. Stir until the brandy is nearly gone.
7. Using an immersion blender, purée the mushroom base.

8. Strain mushroom purée through a fine-mesh sieve, then add to *velouté*. Thoroughly stir together the two mixtures, then simmer for 15 minutes.
9. In a large bowl, beat together the egg yolks and heavy cream. Then ladle, a little at a time, some of the soup into the cream mixture. This allows you to slowly temper the eggs with the hot stock so nothing congeals. Once you have 5 ladles of soup in the cream mixture, pour it all back into the soup mixture and allow it to simmer for 10 minutes, but do not boil.

TIMES GONE BY

According to Chef Escoffier—commonly recognized as the finest master chef of the twenty-first century—*velouté* sauce, espagnole, béchamel, Hollandaise, and tomato sauces, are the so-called "five mother sauces" of classical cuisine. *Velouté* sauces are not usually used on their own; rather, their "daughter sauces," or sauces based on their mother counterparts, are created and used.

Unsinkable Cream of Barley Soup

Though this was one of the soups served on the *Titanic* on that infamous and tragic night, this dish would continue to be popular in Britain. As it is the death of the Earl of Grantham's heir on the *Titanic* that causes Matthew Crawley to enter the family's lives, serving this soup would likely lead to the sharing of many memories: some good, some bad.

YIELDS 4 SERVINGS

½ cup pearl barley

4½ cups reduced-sodium chicken broth, divided

1 tablespoon unsalted butter

1 tablespoon extra-virgin olive oil

4 medium shallots, minced

4 cups white mushrooms

4 stalks celery, chopped

1 tablespoon minced fresh sage

1 teaspoon sea salt

½ teaspoon freshly ground black pepper

2 tablespoons all-purpose flour

1 cup vermouth or dry white wine

½ cup sour cream

¼ cup heavy cream

½ cup minced fresh chives

Unsinkable Cream of Barley Soup
(continued)

1. In a small saucepan over high heat, bring pearl barley and 1½ cups of the broth to a boil. Cover, reduce heat, and simmer until tender, about 30–35 minutes.

2. In a dutch oven or large pot over medium-high heat, heat butter and oil. Add shallots and cook, stirring frequently, until softened, about 2 minutes. Add mushrooms, still stirring frequently, until they start to brown, about 10 minutes. Add celery, sage, sea salt, and pepper, and cook until vegetables begin to soften, about 5 minutes, stirring frequently. Then, sprinkle flour over vegetables and stir until flour is incorporated. Cook for about 1 minute. Mix in vermouth or white wine and cook and continue stirring until most of the alcohol has evaporated, about 1–2 minutes.

3. Pour in remaining broth and increase heat to high. Bring soup to a rolling boil, then reduce heat and simmer, stirring every 5 minutes, until the soup has thickened, about 25 minutes.

4. Add barley and cook, stirring occasionally, until soup is heated through, about 7 minutes. Mix in sour cream and heavy cream until thoroughly incorporated in soup. Dust with chives. Serve immediately or let chill in refrigerator overnight and then reheat to allow barley to fully soak in the flavors.

Etiquette Lessons

If a garnish doesn't come on top of your soup, you're expected to garnish it yourself. With the serving spoon, spoon a portion of the garnish directly onto your soup. Place any other garnishes only on your salad or bread plate. Once finished, put the serving spoon back on the garnish's underplate. And, of course, mind your manners and do not blow on your soup to cool it.

Mushroom Barley Soup

While this soup doesn't contain cream, it's nonetheless a filling option for the clear soup offering. Mrs. Patmore would likely offer this thin yet tasty soup on days when heavy conversation was expected, perhaps as a way to lighten the mood in the dining room.

YIELDS 4–6 SERVINGS

1½ cups barley
3½ cups water
2 tablespoons extra-virgin olive oil
2 medium onions, chopped
2 carrots, sliced
2 stalks celery, chopped
1 teaspoon ground thyme
1 (10-ounce) package sliced baby bella mushrooms
1 (10-ounce) package sliced Shiitake mushrooms
6 cups low-sodium vegetable broth
1 teaspoon kosher salt
½ teaspoon freshly ground black pepper

1. In a small saucepan, bring barley and water to a boil. Cover, reducing heat to low, and let simmer for 35–40 minutes or until tender.
2. Heat olive oil in a large saucepan over medium heat, then stir in the onions, carrots, and celery. Sprinkle in thyme, and sauté onions until translucent, about 15 minutes. Stir in all mushrooms, and cook for 10 minutes.
3. Pour vegetable broth into saucepan, and bring soup to a low boil over medium-high heat. Then reduce heat to low, and simmer for an additional 15 minutes. Stir in barley, and cook for an additional 5 minutes. Season with salt and pepper and serve.

Suggested Pairings

Follow this lighter soup with the heavier Filet Mignon with *Foie Gras* and Truffle Sauce (see Chapter 4). The light soup will help prepare your stomach—and your tastebuds—for the decadent meat dish.

Crisp Chestnut Soup

Chestnut soup, discussed in a popular eighteenth-century cookbook by Mrs. Hannah Glasse titled *The Art of Cookery Made Plain and Easy*, quickly became a staple in English kitchens. While this classic soup has gone through some changes since the mid-1700s with the advent of cooking-friendly technology like refrigerators and blenders, it would nonetheless be expected and enjoyed at the Downton estate.

YIELDS 4–6 SERVINGS

¼ cup unsalted butter
¾ cup finely chopped celery
½ cup finely chopped carrot
½ cup finely chopped white onion
6 cups chicken stock
2 whole cloves
1 teaspoon kosher salt
1 teaspoon ground sage
1 bay leaf
3 cups peeled, cooked, and crumbled whole chestnuts
¼ cup amaretto liqueur
½ cup heavy cream
Kosher salt and freshly ground black pepper to taste

1. In a medium-sized saucepan over low heat, melt butter. Stir in celery, carrot, and onion. Cover and let vegetables sweat for 15 minutes.
2. Pour chicken stock into saucepan, followed by cloves, salt, ground sage, and bay leaf. Bring mixture to a boil, then reduce heat and let simmer, covered, for 20 minutes. Add chestnuts and amaretto liqueur. Let simmer, covered, for an additional 5 minutes.
3. Remove soup from heat.
4. Purée soup in small batches, being extra careful as the soup is still hot. Allow to chill uncovered for ½ hour. Then store soup in refrigerator for at least 24 hours so flavors really thicken.
5. Remove soup from fridge, and reheat in a large saucepan over moderate heat. Stir in cream, and add salt and pepper to taste.

Suggested Pairings

Thanks to the use of sage, cloves, and chestnuts, this dish goes well with any turkey roast. Be careful not to serve a meal that's too heavy with this soup, however, as the dairy in this recipe already gives this small dish a solidity that other soups do not possess.

Creamy Butternut Squash Soup

Even Downton Abbey has its cold, damp evenings, and with such a large house one is sure to catch the shivers now and then. Fortunately this thick and creamy soup is sure to warm up the most frigid of guests! Perhaps Daisy, after witnessing the dead body of Pamuk, would see if there were any leftovers of this soup available to warm her chilled spirits.

YIELDS 4 SERVINGS

2 tablespoons unsalted
   butter
1 clove garlic, minced
2 medium onions, chopped
2 medium carrots,
   chopped
1 stalk celery, chopped
2 medium sweet potatoes,
   cubed
1 medium butternut
   squash, peeled, seeded,
   and cubed
1 (32-ounce) container
   chicken stock
1 teaspoon curry powder
½ teaspoon nutmeg
½ cup sour cream
Kosher salt and freshly
   ground black pepper to
   taste

1. Melt butter in a large pot over medium heat. Add garlic, onions, carrots, celery, sweet potatoes, and squash. Cook for 8–10 minutes or until lightly browned. Pour in enough chicken stock to fully cover the vegetables. Bring mixture to a boil, then reduce heat to low. Cover pot and let simmer for 45 minutes or until all vegetables are tender. Stir in curry powder and nutmeg.
2. Using an immersion blender, blend soup until smooth. Stir in sour cream, then salt and pepper to taste.

TIMES GONE BY

Downton Abbey was actually quite lucky to have Mrs. Patmore and her helper Daisy on staff. Thanks to the Industrial Revolution and World War I, new factory job openings lured many staff members away from their jobs at country estates. This in turn led to a rise in household management books, as many hostesses found themselves with inadequate staff.

Cream of Asparagus Soup

This is a classic soup, perfect for a springtime lunch or dinner at Downton Abbey. This soup, while cream-based, still possesses a light feel, and would not make the daughters of Downton feel too heavy when frolicking about in their springtime dresses while viewing churches with Matthew or attending a garden party.

YIELDS 4–6 SERVINGS

1½ pounds fresh asparagus
½ cup unsalted butter
1½ cups chopped yellow
 onion
1 teaspoon kosher salt
6 tablespoons all-purpose
 flour
1½ cups vegetable stock
3 cups whole milk, heated
1 teaspoon dried dill weed
1 teaspoon ground white
 pepper
2 tablespoons tamari sauce
⅓ cup sour cream

1. Break off and discard tough asparagus bottoms. Break off tips; set aside.
2. Heat butter in a medium skillet over medium heat. Stir in asparagus, onion, and 1 teaspoon of the salt. Cook for 10–12 minutes, stirring frequently.
3. Once onions are translucent, sprinkle with flour. Stir over very low heat for 6–8 minutes.
4. Slowly add vegetable stock, stirring constantly, until soup thickens. Let cool slightly.
5. Add milk. Using an immersion blender, purée soup until thoroughly smooth.
6. Gently heat soup, stirring in dill, white pepper, and tamari sauce. Do not let it boil!
7. In a small bowl, mix sour cream with 1 cup of the soup. Be sure to add soup very slowly so it doesn't curdle. Add mixture back into hot soup.
8. As soup heats, cook asparagus tips in boiling water until tender but still green. Add to soup.

Suggested Pairings

Try this with the Steak Chasseur (see Chapter 4) or Mrs. Patmore's Rosemary Oat Crackers (see Chapter 1). This soup will provide a solid base for the steak, and nothing beats dipping crackers in soup—especially when the crackers have a hint of rosemary!

Marvelous Mussel Soup

While mussels on their own were a popular hors d'oeuvre, this soup would be a creamy option only enjoyed by the most privileged of society. While Mrs. Patmore would know better than to offer a mussel soup after a mussel appetizer, it's likely that the prestige of mussels would be much appreciated by the Dowager Countess, so much so that the offering would be tempting.

YIELDS 4–6 SERVINGS

3 pounds raw mussels in shells

¼ cup unsalted butter

½ teaspoon paprika

6 green onions, finely chopped

6 celery stalks, chopped

4 sprigs parsley

1 cup dry white wine

1½ cups fish stock

2 cups heavy cream

Kosher salt to taste

Chopped parsley, for garnish

1. Make sure none of the mussels have opened. Clean mussels with a stiff brush under running water.
2. In a medium-sized saucepan, melt the butter. Add the paprika, green onions, and celery, and sauté, stirring, until they are soft but not brown. Add the mussels (still in their shells), parsley, wine, and fish stock. Bring mixture to a boil, then cover, reducing heat and simmering until the mussels open, about 8 minutes. Throw out any mussels that remain closed.
3. Using a slotted wooden spoon, remove mussels from the liquid. Strain liquid through a dampened cloth and measure. If liquid doesn't reach 4 cups, add additional fish stock. Return liquid to saucepan.
4. Remove the mussels from the open shells.
5. Add cream to the soup. Bring to a boil over high heat, then reduce heat slightly and boil until soup is reduced by about ¼. Lower heat to medium. Taste and add salt if needed. Add the mussels to the soup and cook until just heated through. Garnish with parsley.

Etiquette Lessons

In European, and especially in British, culture, saying "thank you" is one of the first expressions and lessons that children learn. In fact, in Britain there's a special word—"ta"—taught to children that works as both "please" and "thank you." That way, before an infant can properly pronounce "thank you," he or she can still express thanks.

Saxe-Coburg Soup

Queen Victoria's beloved consort, Prince Albert, loved Brussels sprouts. Some say this soup was developed for him; others say it was named for Queen Victoria's oldest son. Either way, the inhabitants of Downton Abbey could honor the royal family—and impress their own esteemed guests—by offering this soup as an option during the soup course.

YIELDS 4 SERVINGS

6 tablespoons unsalted butter

1½ pounds Brussels sprouts, trimmed, chopped, and blanched in boiling water for 2 minutes

1 large yellow onion, chopped

2 medium potatoes, peeled and diced

4 tablespoons flour

1 tablespoon white sugar

1½ cups heavy cream

1½ cups whole milk

4 cups vegetable stock

½ cup sherry

1. In a medium-large pot, melt butter over medium-low heat. Add the chopped Brussels sprouts, onion, and potatoes, then cover the pot and let sweat for 15 minutes. The vegetables should not color but should soften. Stir in the flour and sugar, and allow them to soften.
2. In a small pot, mix together cream and milk. Bring to a boil, then allow to cool slightly. Add milk mixture to soup, followed by vegetable stock and sherry.
3. Bring soup to a boil, then reduce heat to low and let simmer, partially covered, for 25–30 minutes or until the vegetables are incredibly tender.
4. Remove the soup and purée it in small batches with an immersion blender or food processor.
5. Serve the soup in a classic "no-handled" cream cup with saucer.

Suggested Pairings

Mini-toasts or Mrs. Patmore's Rosemary Oat Crackers (see Chapter 1) would go well with this soup, either for dunking or just as a simple side.

Partan Bree

Though this is a traditional Scottish recipe, it found its niche in many British households. Whether possessing a modest upbringing like Matthew Crawley or one of opulence like the children of the Dowager Countess, no aristocrat or guest would sneer at this delicious soup.

YIELDS 4–6 SERVINGS

2 cups milk

2 cups heavy cream

1 cup white rice

½ pound fresh cooked crabmeat

3 cups low-sodium chicken stock

Kosher salt and freshly ground black pepper to taste

Finely chopped chives, for seasoning

1. In a heavy saucepan, bring milk and 1 cup of the heavy cream to a boil. Add rice, and simmer until rice is well done. Remove from heat and add crabmeat.

2. Using an immersion blender or food processor, purée the soup. Return soup to a large saucepan and slowly stir in the chicken stock. Season with salt and pepper to taste, then add the last cup of cream. Pour into bowls and season with finely chopped chives.

TIMES GONE BY

While only two soups were served per meal at a fancy dinner party by the 1900s, in 1789 Princess Royal Charlotte hosted a ball that featured twenty tureens of different soups as the hot part of the supper. While it is doubtful that anyone had a full bowl of each soup, it would have been considered the height of good manners to try a little of each one.

Regal Brown Windsor Soup

This hearty soup was both nourishing and popular during the Victorian and Edwardian periods. In fact, Queen Victoria was especially fond of this soup, and it was often served at royal banquets. Mrs. Patmore would offer this soup with crusty bread to both staff and aristocrats alike.

YIELDS 4–6 SERVINGS

¼ cup unsalted butter

2 cups chopped yellow onions

1 large leek, chopped

2 large carrots, chopped

1½ pounds sirloin steak, cut into ½-inch cubes

1 tablespoon paprika

2 teaspoons kosher salt

2 teaspoons garlic powder

1½ teaspoons freshly ground black pepper

1 teaspoon onion powder

1 teaspoon cayenne pepper

1 teaspoon oregano

1 tablespoon all-purpose flour

4 cups good beef stock

1 bay leaf

1 teaspoon light brown sugar

1 tablespoon sweet vermouth

2 teaspoons Italian seasoning

¼ cup Madeira wine

4 sprigs rosemary

1. Melt butter in a large pot over medium-high heat. Add onions and cook for 3–5 minutes. Add the leek and carrots and cook, stirring frequently, until soft. Add the steak, and then add the paprika, salt, garlic powder, black pepper, onion powder, cayenne pepper, and oregano. Cook until steak is browned, about 5 minutes.

2. In a medium-sized bowl, combine flour with 2 tablespoons of the beef stock. Add to the pot and stir well. Add remaining beef stock, bay leaf, brown sugar, sweet vermouth, Italian seasoning, and Madeira wine. Stir well and bring mixture to a boil.

3. Lower the heat and simmer, partially uncovered, until meat is tender, about 1½ hours. Stir occasionally.

4. Discard bay leaf. Garnish soup with rosemary sprigs and serve immediately.

Etiquette Lessons

From the very start, it is a steadfast rule of politeness that no single person at a dinner party be shown favoritism. Though Lady Mary and Matthew Crawley often ignore this, there should be no whispering in dark corners and no showing a preference for the company of one particular individual. This is why at dinner a husband and wife are often separated, so they can include and make new friends.

Lady Mary's Spicy Mulligatawny Soup

Considering that a fair amount of British history deals with its colonization of India, it's no surprise that mulligatawny soup, with its Indian roots, became a part of the British culinary scene. Mulligatawny, or "Milagu Thanni," literally means "pepper water," and is a spicier option for one of the two soups served and enjoyed at a dinner, fancy or not. Considering Lady Mary's spicy personality, there's no doubt she'd enjoy this soup while in the midst of a fiery debate with Matthew!

YIELDS 6–8 SERVINGS

1 clove garlic, minced

¼ teaspoon cumin seeds, minced

4 whole cloves, finely crushed

1 tablespoon curry powder

½ teaspoon ground ginger

1 pinch cayenne pepper

½ cup unsalted butter

1 (4-pound) roasting chicken, cut into pieces

1 cup coarsely chopped chicken giblets

4 stalks celery, chopped

2 large onions, chopped

2 carrots, diced

1 leek, thinly sliced

11 cups chicken stock

Kosher salt and freshly ground black pepper to taste

1 cup long-grain rice

2 cups peeled, cored, and diced tart apples

1 cup plain yogurt

2 tablespoons fresh lemon juice

1 cup whipping cream, slightly warmed

Chopped fresh parsley for garnish

Lightly toasted sliced almonds for garnish

Lady Mary's Spicy Mulligatawny Soup
(continued)

1. In a medium-sized bowl, combine garlic and spices.
2. In a large, deep skillet, melt butter over medium-high heat. Add roasting chicken and sauté until lightly brown on all sides. Then add chicken giblets and sauté until cooked through.
3. Transfer chicken and giblets to stockpot. Drain all but 2 tablespoons of fat from the skillet. Add celery, onions, carrots, leek, and garlic-spice mixture to the stockpot, and stir well.
4. Pour 1 small ladle of chicken stock into the stockpot. Cook over low heat, stirring frequently, until vegetables are tender.
5. Stir in remaining stock, seasoning to taste with salt and pepper. Cover and simmer for 30 minutes.
6. Using a slotted wooden spoon, remove chicken and set aside. Add rice and simmer for an additional 15 minutes.
7. Once cool enough to touch, cut chicken into bite-sized pieces, removing bones and skin.
8. Return chicken to soup, then stir in apples and yogurt. Simmer for 15 minutes, skimming fat off top of soup if necessary.
9. Stir in lemon juice, followed by the whipping cream. Adjust seasoning to taste.
10. Pour soup into a heated tureen, and garnish with parsley and sliced almonds.

Etiquette Lessons

When eating soup, it is proper to hold your soup spoon in your right hand while scooping the soup away from yourself. The spoon should never be placed directly into the mouth, rather the soup should be gently tipped from the side of the spoon and poured into the mouth through an opening in the lips.

The Earl of Grantham's Green Turtle Soup

Due to the expense of importing the rare West Indian green turtle to England, serving turtle soup was a sign of great prestige. Thus, there's no doubt that the Earl and Countess of Grantham would try to impress their guests by serving this green turtle soup at important occasions, such as the Dowager Countess's birthday or a feast in honor of an engagement.

YIELDS 6 SERVINGS

1½ cups (3 sticks) unsalted butter, divided

2½ pounds turtle meat, diced

Kosher salt to taste

Fresh ground pepper to taste

2 medium white onions, diced

8 stalks celery, diced

10 cloves garlic, minced

3 red bell peppers, diced

1 tablespoon fresh thyme, ground

1 tablespoon oregano, ground

2 quarts beef stock

1 cup all-purpose flour

½ cup dry sherry

1 tablespoon hot sauce

⅓ cup Worcestershire sauce

½ cup lemon juice

1 cup tomato purée

½ cup chopped green onions

1 cup roughly chopped fresh spinach

6 large hard-boiled eggs, chopped

The Earl of Grantham's Green Turtle Soup

(continued)

1. In a large stockpot over medium to medium-high heat, melt ½ cup of the butter. Add turtle meat and brown. Season to taste with kosher salt and pepper. Cook for 20 minutes or until liquid is nearly gone.

2. Constantly stirring with a wooden spoon, add onions, celery, garlic, and bell peppers. Then add thyme and oregano, and sauté for around 20–25 minutes. Add beef stock, then bring soup to a boil. Let simmer for 25 minutes. Skim off any fat from the top.

3. As stock simmers, make the roux: In a small saucepan, melt remaining 1 cup butter over medium-low heat. Stirring with a wooden spoon, slowly add flour a few tablespoons at a time. Do not burn. Cook roux until it is pale in color and has a sand-like consistency, about 3–5 minutes. Set aside and let cool until soup is ready—roux should definitely be cool when added to soup.

4. Using a whisk, vigorously whisk roux into soup, adding a little at a time to prevent lumping. Simmer for about 20 minutes, stirring occasionally to prevent sticking.

5. Add sherry and bring soup to boil. Add hot sauce and Worcestershire sauce, then simmer for another 5 minutes. Skim off any fat or foam that comes to the top. Stir in lemon juice and tomato purée, then let simmer for another 5 minutes. Add green onions, spinach, and eggs, then allow to simmer for an additional 10 minutes and adjust seasoning to taste.

Times Gone By

In the mid- to late 1700s, confectioner Samuel Birch was the first to serve turtle soup in London, serving it with lemons, cayenne, and other condiments, with French bread on the side. Turtle soup later became so esteemed—yet so expensive to serve—that dishes such as Mock Turtle Soup (see Chapter 11) became a popular option, where a calf's head and plenty of Madeira was used in lieu of the turtle meat.

Mrs. Patmore's London Particular

The thick fogs that engulfed London until the mid- to late 1950s for which this soup is named would not be unknown to the Crawley family. Matthew, a London native, would especially enjoy this hearty ham and pea soup, as it would remind him of his childhood home.

YIELDS 4–6 SERVINGS

For Ham

1 smoked ham hock, soaked overnight in cold water

1 large onion, peeled and halved

2 stalks celery, chopped

4 peppercorns

1 bay leaf

3 sprigs fresh thyme

1 handful parsley

For Soup

1 pound green split peas, soaked overnight

½ cup unsalted butter

1 medium yellow onion, chopped

1 medium carrot, chopped

6 cups ham stock from ham in this recipe

Leftover boiled ham

Kosher salt and freshly ground black pepper, to taste

1. Rinse, then drain, soaked ham hock. Place ham hock, large onion, celery, peppercorns, bay leaf, thyme, and parsley in a large saucepan. Cover with water. Bring to a boil, then simmer, partially covered, for 2½ hours or until tender. Cool.
2. Strain ham stock through a fine-mesh sieve into a Tupperware or glass bowl with lid. Reserve the stock, and shred ham into bite-sized pieces. If stock is too spicy, dilute with some water.
3. Rinse soaked peas until water runs clear.
4. In a large saucepan or pot over medium-low heat, melt butter. Sauté the onion until it is soft and translucent. Add carrot, peas, and the stock. Bring soup to a boil, then reduce to a simmer, and skim off any fat floating at the top.
5. Simmer until the peas are very soft, about 45 minutes. Purée soup in small batches using an immersion or regular blender. If too thick, add more stock. Return soup to saucepan, add leftover ham, then heat through. Add salt and pepper, to taste. Serve in warm bowls, perhaps with chopped celery sprinkled on top.

Etiquette Lessons

Each great house—Downton Abbey included—was expected to throw at least one great garden party a year, preferably in August or September. Invitations were sent by the hostess weeks in advance, with the promise of tennis, croquet, or other amusements. If there was to be dancing at night, it was either done in a tent or under the moonlight on the lawn, perhaps illuminated by Chinese lanterns.

Alfred's Ritz-Approved Vichyssoise

As part of his test at The Ritz, Alfred is asked to make this chilled soup. Escoffier, the Ritz chef's muse, particularly loved this soup and would likely have required all of his prospective chefs to show their skill by creating it in his kitchen.

YIELDS 4–6 SERVINGS

2 tablespoons unsalted butter

2 leeks, chopped

1 large yellow onion, chopped

1 cup thinly sliced potatoes

Kosher salt and white pepper to taste

½ teaspoon dried thyme

½ teaspoon dried marjoram

2½ cups low-sodium chicken stock

1⅛ cups nonfat half-and-half

1 cup sour cream, for garnish

1 bunch chives, chopped, for garnish

1. Using a large stockpot, melt butter over low heat. Add chopped leeks and onion, cover, and let sweat for 10 minutes. Do not let them brown.
2. Add sliced potatoes and season with kosher salt and white pepper to taste. Add thyme and marjoram, stirring well, then more salt and white pepper as needed. Cover pot and continue to cook for another 10 minutes.
3. Add chicken stock and increase heat, bringing mixture to a boil. Reduce heat and cook, partially covered, for 25–30 minutes.
4. Purée in a blender or food processor until very, very smooth. Let cool, then chill thoroughly in fridge. Stir in half-and-half before serving. Garnish with sour cream and chives.

TIMES GONE BY

While Julia Child claimed that vichyssoise is American in origin, there is much debate regarding its birthplace. Louis Diat, a French chef at the Ritz Carlton in New York, claimed he reintroduced it to culinary society after remembering the cold potato leek soups of his childhood.

Lady Sybil's Poached Salmon with Creamy Hollandaise Sauce

The Earl of Grantham confronts Lady Sybil about her interest in feminism and politics one night over an uncomfortable dinner. Even this elegant fish dish cannot distract the rest of the family from the brewing storm of opinions. The spices used in this dish, while adding heat, are nothing compared to the hot tempers seething that night!

YIELDS 2 SERVINGS

5 tablespoons fresh lemon juice, divided

2 tablespoons extra-virgin olive oil

2 (6-ounce) skinless, boneless salmon fillets

2 teaspoons kosher salt, divided

½ teaspoon freshly ground black pepper

4 large egg yolks

1 tablespoon hot water

1 cup unsalted butter, cut into pieces

1 pinch cayenne pepper

Fresh parsley or chives, chopped, for garnish

Lady Sybil's Poached Salmon with Creamy Hollandaise Sauce

(continued)

1. Pour 4 tablespoons lemon juice and olive oil into a large pan that can easily fit both salmon fillets without much extra room. Add enough water to bring the water up to just below an inch. Season salmon fillets with salt and pepper, and add salmon to pan. Add enough water to cover salmon.

2. Heat salmon over medium-high heat until water is hot but not simmering, about 165°F. Poach until salmon is opaque and firm to the touch. Salmon should reach an internal temperature of 140°F.

3. In a small saucepan bring a few inches of water to a boil. Lower heat to medium-high, maintaining a gentle boil. In a metal bowl whisk together egg yolks and 1 tablespoon hot water, then place the bowl over, but not touching, the boiling water in the saucepan. Whisk constantly until yolks thicken and turn a light yellow, doubling in volume. Be careful not to scramble the yolks—it is okay to remove bowl from heat every now and then if necessary.

4. Once the egg yolks have thickened and doubled in volume, whisk in butter, a piece at a time, until it melts and mixes into the hollandaise sauce. Be sure to wait for each piece of butter to melt before adding the next one. Once all of the butter has been added, remove sauce from heat and whisk in the remaining lemon juice, cayenne pepper, and remaining teaspoon of salt.

5. Drain poached salmon and place fillets on individual dinner plates. Cover with hollandaise sauce. Sprinkle with parsley or chives and serve.

TIMES GONE BY

Some historians suggest that the rise of *grande cuisine* in England was due not to rising tastes among aristocrats such as the Earl of Grantham, but rather as a result of increased competition between restaurateurs. One way to attract more customers was by offering finer, perhaps more foreign food than that offered by competitors.

Daisy's Mustard Salmon with Lentils

If Daisy wanted to impress Mrs. Patmore with her cooking prowess, she would simply need to make this small but mighty salmon dish. Like Daisy herself, this salmon dish, with the help of the mustard, packs a surprising punch.

YIELDS 4 SERVINGS

For Mustard Sauce

¼ cup unsalted butter, softened

2 tablespoons chopped chives

1 tablespoon chopped tarragon

1 tablespoon Dijon mustard

2 teaspoons fresh lemon juice

1 teaspoon sugar

2 teaspoons kosher salt

1 teaspoon freshly ground black pepper

For Lentils

1 cup French green lentils

2 large carrots, chopped

2 cups water

2 cups vegetable broth

2 teaspoons fresh lemon juice

Salt and pepper, to taste

For Salmon

4 (6-ounce) skinless salmon fillets

1 teaspoon salt

½ teaspoon freshly ground black pepper

4 tablespoons unsalted butter

Daisy's Mustard Salmon with Lentils
(continued)

1. **To make mustard sauce:** In a small bowl, thoroughly mix together butter, chives, tarragon, Dijon mustard, lemon juice, sugar, salt, and pepper. Set aside.

2. **To make lentils:** In a heavy saucepan over high heat, bring lentils, carrots, water, and vegetable broth to a boil, then reduce heat and simmer, uncovered, until lentils are tender, about 25–30 minutes. Remove pan from heat and let stand for 5–7 minutes. Drain lentils, reserving 1 cup of the liquid.

3. Reheat drained lentils, carrots, and reserved liquid over medium heat, mixing in 4 tablespoons of mustard sauce. Stir until lentils are heated and butter is thoroughly mixed in. Add lemon juice, and salt and pepper to taste. Keep warm, covered.

4. **To prepare salmon:** Sprinkle salmon fillets with salt and pepper.

5. Heat butter in a large nonstick skillet over medium-high heat. Once butter has foamed, sauté salmon, flipping once, until salmon is cooked through and golden, about 8–10 minutes.

6. Serve salmon topped with remaining mustard sauce, over lentils and carrots.

Etiquette Lessons

There were usually two types of fish offered at a formal dinner party: one broiled, one lightly fried. This low-stress recipe would be a tempting choice for Mrs. Patmore to offer as her broiled option.

Baked Cod with Parmesan Bread Crumbs

While cod is the most popular choice for fish-and-chip dishes such as Spicy Pub Fish and Chips (see Chapter 10), it can also be used in a quite delicate, understated yet elegant fish dish. One can just imagine the Dowager Countess frowning at the unfamiliar texture of this dish, as she would be much more familiar with fish covered in sauce rather than bread crumbs!

YIELDS 4 SERVINGS

¼ cup Italian bread crumbs

4 tablespoons grated Parmesan cheese

1 tablespoon cornmeal

2 teaspoons extra-virgin olive oil

1 teaspoon Italian seasoning

¼ teaspoon garlic powder

1 teaspoon kosher salt

½ teaspoon freshly ground black pepper

4 (3- to 4-ounce) cod fillets

2 tablespoons mayonnaise

1 teaspoon lemon juice

1. Preheat oven to 425°F.
2. In a small bowl, mix together bread crumbs, Parmesan cheese, cornmeal, olive oil, Italian seasoning, garlic powder, salt, and pepper.
3. Grease the rack of a broiling pan. Place cod on the rack, folding under any thin edges. In a small bowl, whisk together the mayonnaise and lemon juice, then brush fillets with mayonnaise-and-lemon-juice mixture. Then spoon the crumb mixture evenly over top of fillets.
4. Bake fillets in preheated oven for 13–15 minutes or until the fish flakes easily when prodded with a fork. Fish should be opaque all the way through.

TIMES GONE BY

As Britain was a rather small island surrounded by a ready supply of fresh seafood, a great deal of fish was consumed during the Victorian era. In fact, oysters were once so readily available that they were used as a sausage filling in lieu of more expensive meat, and salmon was among the few fish the poor could afford. Nowadays, however, thanks to the rise in frozen fish, it has become a lot harder to find some of the lesser-known varieties of English fish . . . but if you are lucky, you might be able to hunt some down!

"Love Me Alfred" Fish Soufflé with Anchovy Sauce

Every soufflé consists of both a cream base and egg whites. The word "soufflé" is the past participle of the French word "souffler," or "to blow up." Poor Daisy would be aware of this when making this recipe. In her never-ending quest to win Alfred's love, a confident Daisy offers to show him how to make the sauce that goes along with this soufflé, but Alfred, who has no interest in cooking (at least for a little bit) once the Ritz turns him down, leaves a deflated Daisy in his wake. She'll just have to make this savory dish on her own, perhaps with some help from Ivy or Mrs. Patmore!

YIELDS 4 SERVINGS

For Fish Soufflé
4 tablespoons unsalted butter

2½ tablespoons all-purpose flour

½ teaspoon kosher salt

¾ cup whole milk, warmed

3 large eggs, separated

1 cup freshly grated Parmesan cheese

8 ounces fresh white fish fillet, steamed and de-boned

For Anchovy Sauce
¼ cup extra-virgin olive oil

2 medium yellow onions, finely chopped

2 cloves garlic, crushed

1 teaspoon brown sugar, preferably light brown

12 anchovies, or 1 (2-ounce) can in olive oil, chopped

1 tablespoon unsalted butter

⅛ teaspoon ground cloves

⅛ teaspoon ground nutmeg

1 tablespoon water

½ cup whole milk

"Love Me Alfred" Fish Soufflé with Anchovy Sauce

(continued)

1. Preheat oven to 400°F. Grease 4 soufflé dishes.
2. Melt butter in a medium saucepan over low heat. Add flour and salt and stir until smooth. Slowly add warmed milk to mixture, whisking continuously. Bring sauce to a boil, then cook, still stirring, for an additional 10 minutes.
3. Remove pan from heat. Transfer mixture to a large saucepan and beat in egg yolks one at a time. Stir in cheese until fully combined, then add the fish. Allow mixture to cool completely.
4. Meanwhile, in a large bowl, beat egg whites until soft peaks form. Gently fold ¼ of the egg whites into sauce at a time, adding until completely combined.
5. Pour into prepared soufflé dishes until dishes are about ¾ full. Be sure to leave room for the soufflés to expand.
6. Place soufflés in oven. Bake for 25 minutes at 400°F, then increase temperature to 450°F and bake for an additional 8 minutes, or until soufflés have fully risen and browned on top.
7. While cooking soufflés, make the anchovy sauce: Heat olive oil in a heavy saucepan. Stir in onion and garlic, cooking over low heat for 10 minutes or until translucent and mushy. Stir in brown sugar and let cook another minute. Add chopped anchovies, continuing to cook and stir until anchovies appear to "melt." Add butter, cloves, and nutmeg. Still stirring, cook for another minute before adding water. Gradually stir in milk. Once thoroughly combined, remove sauce from heat.
8. Serve sauce either alongside soufflés or drizzled atop, chef's choice.

Suggested Pairings

Spinach and Feta Salad with Fresh Beetroot (Chapter 5), British Brussels Sprouts with Chestnuts (Chapter 6), or the Baked and Buttery Balsamic Asparagus with Sea Salt (Chapter 6) would make an excellent side for this soufflé. Their fresh flavors perfectly balance the saltiness of the anchovies in the sauce.

Celebratory Salmon Coulibiac

Once Alfred begins his time at the prestigious London Ritz, he will no doubt be required to learn how to perfectly make this dish made popular by the great Escoffier. After all, this dish with its many layers and puff pastry shell makes for quite the *pièce de résistance* at dinner parties. While this dish is quite tricky to concoct, it is certainly one that can only help prove a chef like Alfred's prowess in the kitchen!

YIELDS 12–16 SERVINGS

2 sheets frozen puff pastry dough, thawed

1 egg yolk

1 tablespoon milk

3½ cups spinach, sautéed and mostly dry

¼ pound white mushrooms, sautéed and mostly dry

1 (4-pound) salmon fillet, preferably wild

Kosher salt and freshly ground black pepper to taste

2 large eggs, hard-boiled and chopped

1 large yellow onion, chopped

1 tablespoon chopped fresh dill leaves

1 teaspoon chopped fresh thyme

½ tablespoon chopped fresh parsley

Celebratory Salmon Coulibiac

(continued)

1. On two large baking sheets, roll out the puff pastry dough until it reaches ½-inch thickness. Set sheets aside in the fridge for 30 minutes. This will make the dough more malleable.

2. Preheat oven to 350°F.

3. Mix together egg yolk and milk in a small container to form a wash.

4. Lay one pastry sheet on a clean, lightly floured surface. Brush pastry sheet with half of the egg wash, then evenly spread spinach across, leaving a ½-inch border of pastry. Sprinkle mushrooms atop spinach.

5. Lay salmon on top of mushrooms. Season with salt and pepper. Be sure to leave a ½-inch border all around salmon/spinach/mushrooms.

6. Sprinkle chopped eggs and onion across salmon, followed by dill, thyme, and parsley.

7. Brush more egg wash across ½-inch border, then place the other pastry sheet on top of salmon and gently press the edges of the 2 sheets together so they seal tightly. Trim the edges and crimp with your fingers. The pastry can now be chilled on the baking sheet for 24 hours, if you're making this dish in advance. Otherwise, transfer the salmon to a sheet pan and bake for 30 minutes.

8. After 30 minutes, check salmon's temperature. When thermometer inserted in middle of salmon reads 125°F, remove from oven and let rest for an additional 15 minutes. Transfer salmon pastry to a cutting board and slice into 2-inch pieces. Serve warm.

TIMES GONE BY

This dish is Russian in origin, but it was so popular that Escoffier brought the dish to France and included recipes for it in his tome *Le Guide Culinaire*. And what was chic in France at that time would eventually be chic in London—specifically at The Ritz!

Chapter 3

THIRD COURSE: ELEGANT ENTRÉES

Entrées, in the *Service à la Russe* sense, meant anything that did not require carving with a knife. While the following dishes may seem like meals on their own, remember that, for the Downton Abbey set, this was just the third course out of an eight-course (or more) meal. However, entrées increased in importance over time, and in 1907 writer C. Herman Senn wrote: "Entrées are generally looked upon as the most essential part of the dinner . . . there can be no well-balanced dinner without an entrée course." It's likely that the Earl of Grantham would heartily agree with the importance of an entrée; however, whether that agreement is due to etiquette or hunger remains an unanswered question. The following entrées are incredibly rich, just like the company who consumes them.

Lobster Thermidor

Due to the incredibly expensive cost (not to mention intensive—and extensive—preparation) of lobster, this dish would only be served at Downton Abbey for the most regal of affairs when the family most wanted to impress, such as when the Earl of Grantham auditions future possible fiancés for Lady Mary.

YIELDS 4 SERVINGS

4 lemons, halved

2 onions, quartered

2 (1½-pound) lobsters

1 cup unsalted butter

½ cup all-purpose flour

¼ cup minced shallots

½ cup dry white wine

2 cups whole milk

2 cups heavy cream

Kosher salt and freshly ground black pepper to taste

2 tablespoons Dijon mustard

2 tablespoons chopped fresh tarragon

1 cup and 2 tablespoons grated Parmigiano-Reggiano cheese

1 pound bacon

2 cups julienned onions

½ cup green beans, blanched

2 teaspoons chopped garlic

Lobster Thermidor (continued)

1. Preheat oven to 375°F.
2. Bring a large stockpot of salted water containing the lemon halves and quartered onions to a boil. Add lobsters to boiling water and cook for 15 minutes.
3. Remove lobsters from water and place in an ice bath.
4. Melt butter in a large saucepan over medium-high heat, then form a roux by stirring in the flour. Add shallots and cook for 1 minute, then stir in the wine, milk, and heavy cream. Bring mixture to a boil, then lower to a simmer. Cook for 5 minutes or until the sauce is thick enough to thoroughly coat the back of a spoon. Season the sauce with salt and pepper. Do not be alarmed if this sauce is incredibly thick.
5. Remove sauce from heat and stir in the Dijon mustard and tarragon.
6. Free lobsters from ice bath and split each lobster in half. Remove the tail meat from the shells and gently crack the claws. Dice the tail meat, then fold into the sauce. Stir the 1 cup of grated cheese into the mixture.
7. Spoon mixture into lobster tails. Sprinkle remaining 2 tablespoons of the cheese over the lobsters. Place the now-filled lobsters on a large baking sheet in preheated oven. Bake lobsters for 10–15 minutes or until their tops are golden brown.
8. Meanwhile, in a well-oiled pan, heat bacon until crispy, about 10 minutes. Add julienned onions and sauté for another 5 minutes. Add the green beans and sauté for an additional 5 minutes. Season with salt and pepper, then mix in garlic.
9. Remove bacon, onions, and green beans from heat. Place mixture on serving plates, then top with lobsters.

Suggested Pairings

It was quite common for Lobster Thermidor to be served on a silver platter surrounded by Decadent Duchess Potatoes (see Chapter 6).

Lobster with Mornay Sauce

Lobster with Mornay Sauce is a rich dish for the most discerning of dinner guests. No matter what the Dowager Countess's mood may be, this dish would be sure to put a smile on her often-puckered face. The extravagance of this dish would render it appropriate for a celebration in honor of the Dowager Countess, perhaps after she wins the flower show, or maybe as a means of cheering her up after she lets Mr. Molesley's flowers take the prize.

YIELDS 4 SERVINGS

½ cup unsalted butter

1 pound lobster meat, diced

¼ cup all-purpose flour

1 cup low-sodium chicken broth

1½ cups heavy cream

1 teaspoon kosher salt

½ teaspoon ground white pepper

2 teaspoons sugar

½ cup freshly grated Gruyère cheese

½ cup freshly grated Parmesan cheese

1. Melt the butter in a medium-large saucepan over medium heat. Mix in lobster meat, cooking until opaque. Remove lobster from saucepan and set aside.
2. Reduce heat to low. Sprinkle flour in pan. Cook and stir for 3–5 minutes, making sure not to boil. Slowly stir in chicken broth, heavy cream, salt, pepper, and sugar. Simmer 7–10 minutes or until sauce thickens.
3. Stir in lobster and Gruyère and Parmesan cheeses. Continue cooking for an additional 5–7 minutes.

TIMES GONE BY

Mornay sauce (simply a béchamel sauce with cheese), while usually consisting of 1 part Gruyère and 1 part Parmesan cheeses, can also contain white Cheddar or even Emmental cheese. It would frequently be served on top of vegetables, though it can be served with lobster (such as in this dish), crab, or even shrimp. Or try this on asparagus!

Accolade-Winning Duck Confit

This is a time-consuming dish for which Mrs. Patmore would need at least two days' warning to properly prepare. That said, this dish would win her and her bosses many accolades from visiting guests, such as Sir Anthony Strallan—if he could turn away from Lady Edith long enough to eat! Sadly, in the end Lady Edith does not receive nearly as many accolades as this dish.

YIELDS 4–6 SERVINGS

3 tablespoons kosher salt
6 cloves garlic, minced
6 sprigs thyme
6 bay leaves
4 duck legs with thighs
4 duck wings, trimmed
Coarsely ground black
   pepper
4½ cups duck fat

1. Sprinkle 1 tablespoon salt on the bottom of a dish or glass container large enough to hold all pieces of duck in a single layer. Sprinkle half the garlic, thyme, and bay leaves over the salt. Place the duck, skin-side up, over the garlic and salt, then sprinkle with the remaining salt, garlic, thyme, bay leaves, and pepper. Cover and refrigerate for up to 2 days, but no more.
2. Preheat oven to 220°F.
3. Melt the duck fat in a small saucepan over medium-high heat. Brush salt and seasonings off the duck, then arrange the duck pieces in a single layer in a high-sided ovenproof dutch oven. Pour the duck fat over the duck pieces, fully immersing them in the liquid. Place duck in oven. Cook at a very low simmer until duck can be pulled easily from the bone, approximately 2½–3 hours. Remove confit from oven, then cool. Store duck in fat.

Suggested Pairings

A frequent pairing with this Duck Confit would be *Pommes de Terre Sarladaise* (see Chapter 6), translated as Potatoes Cooked in Duck Fat, and the Red Wine–Braised Red Cabbage with Apples (also in Chapter 6).

Seafood Crêpes with Mornay Sauce

A savory take on the classic crêpe, this is a decadent, albeit unusual, entrée to offer at dinner. This is the type of dish that would attract Lady Sybil due to its shock factor, as it would not be expected at a typical Downton Abbey dinner. Perhaps Mrs. Patmore would make this as a special treat before Sybil leaves for Ireland with her new husband.

YIELDS 4–6 SERVINGS

For Crêpes

1 cup whole milk

½ cup water

2 large eggs

¼ cup unsalted butter, melted

1 cup all-purpose flour

1 teaspoon sugar

½ teaspoon kosher salt

For Mornay Sauce

½ cup unsalted butter

4 tablespoons all-purpose flour

2 cups whole milk

¼ cup freshly grated Gruyère cheese

¼ cup dry white wine

½ cup heavy cream

1 large egg yolk, mixed into cream

Kosher salt and freshly ground white pepper to taste

For Seafood Mixture

¼ cup unsalted butter

1 medium yellow onion, chopped

½ pound baby bella mushrooms

1 cup cooked shrimp

1 cup cooked scallops

½ cup freshly grated Parmesan cheese

¼ cup freshly grated Gruyère cheese

2 tablespoons minced fresh parsley

1 teaspoon kosher salt

½ teaspoon ground white pepper

Seafood Crêpes with Mornay Sauce
(continued)

1. **First, make the crêpes:** In a large bowl, blend together milk and water. Whisk in eggs, followed by ⅛ cup of the melted butter, and the flour, sugar, and salt. Blend until smooth, then cover and let chill for 30 minutes.
2. Heat rest of butter in a medium-sized cooking pan. Add 2 tablespoons of batter mixture, and cook until lightly brown on bottom (about 1½–2 minutes). Flip crêpe and repeat with other side. Repeat with remaining batter. Place crêpes between pieces of parchment paper to stop them from sticking together, then set aside.
3. **Next, make sauce:** In a medium to large saucepan, melt butter over medium-low heat. Once melted, whisk in flour. Slowly add milk, stirring constantly until sauce thickens. Whisk in Gruyère cheese, followed by the white wine and cream-yolk mixture, and mix well. Season with salt and pepper, then remove from heat.
4. **Next, prepare the seafood mixture:** Preheat oven to 350°F and thoroughly grease a large, shallow baking dish.
5. In a large skillet over medium-high heat, melt butter and sauté chopped onion and mushrooms until onion is translucent and mushrooms are tender. Stir in shrimp and scallops, followed by ¾ cup of the Mornay sauce, the Parmesan and Gruyère cheeses, fresh parsley, salt, and white pepper. Stir until all ingredients are heated through.
6. Spoon 2–4 tablespoons of seafood mixture into the middle of each crêpe and roll up. Place crêpe seam-side down in greased baking dish. Repeat with remaining crêpes. Cover crêpes with remaining sauce. Bake for 15–20 minutes or until sauce bubbles.

Suggested Pairings

While crêpes are traditionally served with cider in Brittany, France, the birthplace of crêpes, that would not pair well with this savory (not to mention incredibly thick) entrée. Instead, try this with a crisp white wine or perhaps a gin and tonic—though that would never be allowed at Downton Abbey!

Sybil's Seafood Newburg

Perhaps the zestiest of Downton Abbey's offerings, this modern and spicy entrée would be different from what most Edwardians would expect—just like Lady Sybil's own personality! After all, not many Edwardian aristocrats would fall in love with—much less agree to marry—their chauffeur!

YIELDS 4–6 SERVINGS

For Newburg Sauce

4 tablespoons all-purpose flour

1 tablespoon paprika

1 teaspoon curry powder

¼ teaspoon nutmeg

⅛ teaspoon cayenne pepper

1 teaspoon kosher salt

¼ cup unsalted butter

1 shallot, minced

1 clove garlic, minced

2 cups whole milk

2 tablespoons tomato paste

½ cup dry sherry

For Seafood

4 cups water

2½ teaspoons kosher salt

2 teaspoons freshly ground black pepper

2 bay leaves

1 pound fresh scallops

½ pound lobster tail meat

1 pound large shrimp, peeled and deveined

Sybil's Seafood Newburg
(continued)

1. **First, make the Newburg sauce:** In a medium-sized bowl, combine flour, paprika, curry powder, nutmeg, cayenne pepper, and salt. Set aside.
2. In a large saucepan, melt butter over medium-low heat. Add minced shallot and garlic, and sauté until shallots begin to brown, about 2–3 minutes.
3. While shallots cook, mix together milk and tomato paste in a small saucepan over medium heat.
4. Stir flour mixture into the shallot-garlic mixture. Stir until all ingredients are well mixed in butter. Whisk in sherry until smooth. Stir in the milk-tomato mixture, whisking constantly, until the sauce is smooth yet thick. Remove from heat and cool. Do not refrigerate.
5. **Next, prepare the seafood:** Heat water, salt, pepper, and bay leaves in a large saucepan, bringing mixture to a boil. Add scallops and boil for 5 minutes. Remove scallops and set aside. Repeat with lobster meat and shrimp.
6. Add cooked shellfish to Newburg sauce and bring to a simmer over low heat. Serve hot, perhaps over pasta or rice.

TIMES GONE BY

Newburg sauce, while created at the American restaurant Delmonico's, is just fancy enough for Mrs. Patmore to use at her dinner table—but perhaps not when prestigious company is invited. Rumor has it that this sauce was originally known as Wenburg sauce, but Mr. Wenburg, after a fight with the proprietor of the restaurant, demanded that the sauce be renamed. The first three letters were flipped, and Newburg sauce was born.

Edwardian Chicken Tikka Masala

While it may seem strange to encounter an Indian dish during Edwardian times, this soup arrived on the British culinary scene around 1903, shortly after Edward VII was proclaimed Emperor of India. While there is great debate over the ethics of such a proclamation, the deliciousness of this dish was never in doubt. In fact, former Foreign Secretary Robin Cook made headlines in 2001 when he claimed in a speech that Chicken Tikka Masala was "a true British national dish." Whether this dish is more British than fish and chips or trifle remains to be seen—but if you are a fan of spice, like the daughters of Downton Abbey, don't shy away from this feast!

YIELDS 4 SERVINGS

For Chicken

1 cup plain yogurt

2 tablespoons lemon juice

2 teaspoons ground cumin

1 teaspoon ground cinnamon

2 teaspoons cayenne pepper

2 teaspoons freshly ground black pepper

1 teaspoon ground red pepper

1 tablespoon minced fresh ginger

½ teaspoon kosher salt

3 boneless, skinless chicken breasts, cut into bite-sized pieces

4 long skewers

For Sauce

1 tablespoon unsalted butter

1 clove garlic, minced

1 jalapeño pepper, minced

1 teaspoon ground coriander

1 teaspoon ground cumin

1 teaspoon paprika

1 teaspoon garam masala

½ teaspoon kosher salt

1 (8-ounce) can tomato sauce

1 cup heavy cream

¼ cup fresh cilantro, chopped

Edwardian Chicken Tikka Masala

(continued)

1. **To make chicken:** In a large metal bowl, thoroughly whisk yogurt, lemon juice, cumin, cinnamon, cayenne pepper, black pepper, red pepper, ginger, and ½ teaspoon salt. Stir in chicken, cover, and refrigerate for at least 1 hour. The longer you let the chicken marinate, the more tasty it will be.

2. Preheat a grill for high heat. Whether or not you soak your skewers is up to you. According to *Cook's Illustrated*, it is not necessary.

3. Lightly grease the grill grate. Skewer chicken, discarding marinade. Grill chicken until juices run clear, approximately 5 minutes per side.

4. **To make sauce:** Melt butter over medium-low heat in a large skillet. Sauté garlic and jalapeño for 1–2 minutes. Season with coriander, cumin, paprika, garam masala, and ½ teaspoon salt. Let simmer for 3–5 minutes, then stir in tomato sauce and heavy cream. Simmer on low heat about 25–30 minutes or until sauce thickens.

5. Remove chicken from skewers and add to sauce, thoroughly coating chicken pieces. Simmer for 5–7 minutes. Remove from skillet and sprinkle with cilantro. If desired, pair with basmati rice and naan. Use garlic naan for extra spice.

TIMES GONE BY

One of the most popular books on running a household in Victorian and Edwardian England, *Mrs. Beeton's Book of Household Management*, was published in 1861. Among its various cleaning tips, hostess guidelines, and oh-so-proper English recipes could be found a recipe similar to this one ... showing that even the unfairly stereotyped, stuffy Victorians didn't mind a bit of spice in their lives!

Crawley Family Chicken Breasts with Caper Cream Sauce

This dish combines the Edwardian love for capers/salty appetizers in a fancy entrée. As this is a relatively inexpensive yet still elegant dish to offer, this would be a staple for dinners at Downton Abbey when no guests are present.

YIELDS 4 SERVINGS

4 boneless, skinless
  chicken breasts
2 teaspoons lemon pepper
1 teaspoon sea salt
½ teaspoon freshly ground
  black pepper
2 teaspoons fresh dill
1½ teaspoons garlic
  powder
½ cup fresh lemon juice
4 tablespoons unsalted
  butter
1 clove garlic, diced
½ teaspoon sugar
2 tablespoons dry white
  wine
½ cup heavy cream
2 tablespoons capers,
  drained and rinsed

1. Thoroughly season chicken breasts with lemon pepper, sea salt, black pepper, dill, and garlic powder. Then marinate chicken breasts for at least 2 hours in lemon juice.
2. Melt butter in a large skillet over medium heat. Add garlic and sugar, and sauté for 5 minutes. Then place breasts in skillet and increase heat to medium-high. Turn chicken frequently until brown, about 5 minutes. Reduce heat to medium and cook breasts for 5–7 minutes or until breasts are cooked through. Remove chicken, cover with foil, and keep warm.
3. Increase heat to high, and whisk in wine and heavy cream. Whisk until mixture is reduced to a saucelike consistency, about 2–3 minutes. Remove from heat, then stir in capers. Pour sauce over chicken breasts and serve.

Suggested Pairings

For a different—yet nonetheless caper-filled—sauce, Mrs. Patmore could serve these chicken breasts with a Cajun rémoulade sauce. This rémoulade sauce includes mayonnaise, anchovies, capers, mustard, herbs, and pickles.

Highland Haggis at Duneagle

When the Crawleys visit "Shrimpy," his wife, and his rebellious daughter, Rose, it's anyone's guess if they have the stomach for "classic" Scottish fare, such as Scotland's national dish, haggis, a savory pudding that traditionally contains a sheep's pluck, or "liver and lights" (liver, heart, and lungs), minced with spices, encased in an animal's stomach, and simmered for around three hours. Note that this recipe substitutes tongue for lungs.

YIELDS 4 SERVINGS

1 sheep stomach

1 sheep liver

1 sheep heart

1 sheep tongue

½ pound suet, minced

3 medium red onions, quartered

¾ pound old-fashioned oats, toasted

2 teaspoons kosher salt

1 teaspoon freshly ground black pepper

1 teaspoon paprika

1 teaspoon Jamaican allspice

½ teaspoon mace

Highland Haggis at Duneagle
(continued)

1. Thoroughly rinse the sheep stomach. Let soak overnight in cold, heavily salted water.
2. Rinse the sheep liver, heart, and tongue, then cook in a large pot of boiling water over medium-low heat for at least 2 hours, no more than 3.
3. Remove sheep offal (the liver, heart, and tongue), then mince. Discard any skin or gristle.
4. In a large ceramic or glass bowl, combine the minced liver, heart, tongue, suet, onions, and toasted oats. Mix in salt, pepper, paprika, allspice, and mace. Slowly moisten with drops of water so the mixture binds together.
5. Remove stomach from its saltwater bath and fill ⅔ of it with the sheep mixture. Make sure you leave room for the mixture to expand. Sew or tie the stomach shut, then pierce the stomach several times to prevent haggis from bursting.
6. Gently place stomach in a large pot of water over high heat. Be careful not to splash or break the stomach. Bring water to a boil, then immediately reduce heat and let simmer for 3 hours. Avoid heavy boil, as this will cause the skin to burst.

TIMES GONE BY

Haggis is the *pièce de résistance* at a traditional Scottish "Burns Night," held every January 25th in honor of Scotland's national poet Robert Burns (January 25, 1759–July 21, 1796), on the anniversary of his birth. Burns's closest friends originally started the celebration, but it is now celebrated across the country. Burns Night comes complete with songs, tributes, and a feast where Robert Burns's poem "Address to a Haggis" is read, bagpipes are played, and speeches (the more enthralling and humorous the better) are made.

Lord Grantham's American Italian: Risotto alla Milanese

Thanks to Prohibition, an onslaught of new Italian dishes reached American kitchens in the 1920s, as restaurants run by the (very often Italian) mob were one of the few places Americans could sneak a drink. It's likely that Cora's mother, Martha, would have offered this dish to her son-in-law, Lord Grantham, when he was in town supporting her son in the Teapot Dome Scandal. Hopefully the use of the expensive and unique saffron spice would cause Lord Grantham to see this risotto as more than just a "plain" dish!

YIELDS 4 ENTRÉE-SIZED SERVINGS

6–8 cups low-sodium chicken stock

6 tablespoons unsalted butter, divided

1 medium yellow onion, finely chopped

1 teaspoon saffron threads

2 cups Arborio rice

½ cup dry white wine

2 teaspoons sea salt

½ teaspoon pepper

1 cup finely grated Parmigiano-Reggiano cheese

Lord Grantham's American Italian: Risotto alla Milanese

(continued)

1. Heat stock in a large pot over medium-high heat. Keep hot throughout this process.
2. In a large, heavy saucepan, melt 3 tablespoons butter over medium heat. Add chopped onion and cook until translucent, no more then 7 minutes.
3. Add saffron to stock. Stock should turn bright yellow.
4. Add rice to onion mixture and stir constantly for 3 minutes. Make sure rice and onion are thoroughly covered with butter.
5. Over medium-high heat add wine to rice mixture, followed by salt and pepper. Let wine be almost completely absorbed by rice.
6. Add enough saffron-chicken stock to cover rice, about 1 cup. Once fully absorbed, ladle in another cup of stock. Once absorbed, repeat the process until rice is creamy and no longer crunchy. (This should take at least 6 cups of stock.) Rice should still hold its own shape. Remove rice from heat. Stir in cheese and rest of butter. Serve hot.

TIMES GONE BY

The history of this dish dates back to the mid-sixteenth century. Legend has it that artist Valerio di Fiandra, while painting Milan's Duomo Cathedral, would mix saffron into his glaze to achieve its golden color. Fellow artists teased Valerio that he loved the plant so much he would one day eat it. When it came time for his daughter to be wed, a saffron risotto like this one appeared at the wedding banquet as a practical joke.

Chapter 4

FOURTH AND FIFTH COURSES: JUICY JOINTS AND SUCCULENT STEAKS

The joint—a large piece of meat cooked in one piece—often offered with vegetables (see Chapter 6), would be cut on a heating rack called a *réchaud* and then served, followed by sorbets and cigars for the men. The sorbets were meant to cleanse the palate, though with the addition of cigars the men's mouths wouldn't be cleansed for long. Regardless, with the advent of *Service à la Russe*, the joint would lose its impressiveness. Writer James Edward Austen-Leigh lamented how dinners were suddenly "carved and handed round by the servants, instead of smoking before our eyes and noses on the table." That said, these joints and steaks pack quite a powerful punch and would be impressive to the inhabitants of Downton Abbey in their own way!

Seven-Hour Leg of Lamb

This is a classic recipe that every experienced cook would have in her repertoire. It's fun to imagine Mrs. Patmore trying to teach patience to an already flustered and somewhat ditzy Daisy. And yet, it is important to note that, whereas this recipe might be traditionally known as "seven-hour leg of lamb," the long cook time reflects a time past when animals were tougher and older than the ones we eat today. Nowadays, cooking this leg of lamb for 5 hours is more than enough cooking time.

YIELDS 10–12 SERVINGS

1 (5- to 6-pound) lamb leg, bone in

¼ cup extra-virgin olive oil

Kosher salt and freshly ground black pepper to taste

4 large onions, quartered

4 large carrots, quartered

1 head garlic, cloves halved

4 bay leaves

4 teaspoons dried thyme

4 teaspoons rosemary

2 (750-ml) bottles dry white wine

5 pounds large red potatoes, peeled and quartered

4 tomatoes, peeled and chopped

Seven-Hour Leg of Lamb

(continued)

1. Preheat the oven to 400°F. Rub lamb with olive oil, and season with salt and pepper.
2. Layer onions, carrots, garlic, bay leaves, thyme, and rosemary in an ovenproof dutch oven large enough to hold lamb. Place lamb on top of onions and carrots.
3. Roast lamb uncovered in oven for 45 minutes.
4. Remove dutch oven with lamb from oven, leaving the oven on. Place dutch oven on top of stove, then slowly pour the white wine over the lamb. Cover and bring mixture to a boil. Return dutch oven with lamb, now covered, to the oven. Roast for an additional 4 hours or until lamb is fork tender but still not falling off its bone. (Please note that the timing will vary depending on the size and age of the lamb, not to mention the pan used.) Be sure to check on lamb every half-hour; if lamb begins to burn, reduce heat.
5. When lamb is tender, add potatoes and tomatoes. Cover dutch oven and roast until potatoes are cooked through, about 45 minutes–1 hour. By now the lamb should be very tender and juicy, literally falling off the bone.

TIMES GONE BY

This recipe has indeed been modernized a bit, as few households during the Edwardian era had gas stoves. In fact, most large country estates used a range in lieu of a "gas cooker" well into and even after World War I. Mrs. Patmore would have been thankful for a basic refrigerator, which back then consisted of two compartments—one for food and the other for ice to keep the food cold. A freezer-refrigerator (especially one with an icemaker) would have given Mrs. Patmore a heart attack!

Stuffed Leg of Lamb with Almond Fig Sauce

The Sunday roast was a traditional meal served at all middle-class homes, offered as proof to both the families themselves and to anyone visiting that they could afford such a feast. This dish, however, is rather fancy for a Sunday roast, and would likely be enjoyed as the roast course at Downton Abbey.

YIELDS 6 SERVINGS

½ cup coarsely chopped prunes

¼ cup dried cranberries

1 tablespoon crème de cassis liqueur

1 tablespoon red currant jelly

1 tablespoon minced fresh thyme

2 tablespoons minced fresh rosemary

2 teaspoons kosher salt

1 teaspoon freshly ground black pepper

½ teaspoon ground coriander

1 (4-pound) boneless leg of lamb, rolled and tied

1 cup roasted almonds, chopped

2 tablespoons chopped mint

4 cloves garlic, chopped

2 tablespoons extra-virgin olive oil

½ cup balsamic vinegar

4 tablespoons honey

⅓ cup thinly sliced figs

¼ cup unsalted butter

1 tablespoon chopped fresh basil

Stuffed Leg of Lamb with Almond Fig Sauce
(continued)

1. Preheat oven to 400°F.
2. Combine prunes, cranberries, crème de cassis, and red currant jelly in a small bowl; set aside. In another small bowl, combine thyme, rosemary, salt, pepper, and coriander and set aside. There is no need to refrigerate.
3. Roll lamb out on a flat, clean counter or cutting board. Trim off any thick parts so that meat is evenly thick. Cover lamb with ½–¾ of the herb mixture.
4. Add almonds and mint to prune mixture, stirring until thoroughly combined, then evenly spread mixture all over the lamb. Roll up the meat and tie with twine at 1-inch intervals. Cut 10–15 slits about 1 inch deep into the top of lamb, inserting chopped garlic into each depression. Rub meat all over with olive oil, and sprinkle with remaining herbs.
5. Place lamb in a large roasting pan. Make sure the lamb is seam-side up. Place in preheated oven. For a medium-rare doneness, roast until thermometer inserted in the center reads 140°F. Remove lamb from oven and cover with foil for 15 minutes.
6. Meanwhile, in a small saucepan, bring balsamic vinegar to a boil. Boil until vinegar is reduced by half, about 4–6 minutes. Once reduced, stir in honey, sliced figs, and butter. Stir until butter has completely melted. Stir in chopped basil then remove from heat and set aside.
7. To serve, remove twine from lamb and cut into ½-inch-thick slices. Serve with fig sauce.

TIMES GONE BY

Sunday roast came about as a way for the housewife to kill two birds with one stone. She could spend all day cooking this fancy roast on the "day of rest," then serve the leftovers on Monday while doing the weekly wash.

Guard of Honor Lamb with Mint Sauce

Lamb chops were a particularly popular dish during the Edwardian era. A variation on a crown roast, the lamb chops in a Guard of Honor are trimmed and criss-crossed like swords at a military wedding. Mint sauce, served on the side or spooned into the central cavity of the dish, would be a standard and expected side. It's likely that the Countess of Grantham, when daydreaming about Lady Mary's nuptials, would imagine this regal dish at the wedding.

YIELDS 12 LAMB CHOPS

For Lamb

4 tablespoons extra-virgin olive oil

4 cloves garlic, minced

2 tablespoons finely chopped shallots

1 tablespoon balsamic vinegar

2 teaspoons Worcestershire sauce

1 tablespoon plus 1 teaspoon freshly chopped rosemary

1 tablespoon plus 1 teaspoon freshly chopped thyme

1 cup Italian seasoned bread crumbs

2 racks of lamb (about 6 chops each), trimmed and frenched

2 teaspoons kosher salt

2 teaspoons freshly ground black pepper

2 tablespoons Dijon mustard

For Mint Sauce

1 cup fresh mint, chopped very fine

3 tablespoons boiling water

3 tablespoons white sugar

4 tablespoons white wine vinegar

Guard of Honor Lamb with Mint Sauce

(continued)

1. **For lamb:** Preheat oven to 450°F. Make sure rack is in center of oven.
2. In a medium-sized skillet, heat 2 tablespoons of the olive oil over medium-high heat. Add garlic and shallots, and sauté for 5 minutes. Then lower to a simmer and add balsamic vinegar and Worcestershire sauce. Stir, then sprinkle in rosemary and thyme. Sauté for an additional 3–5 minutes, then pour garlic mixture into a medium-sized bowl. Toss in bread crumbs, thoroughly mix ingredients, and set aside.
3. Season the racks of lamb all over with salt and pepper. Heat remaining 2 tablespoons olive oil in a large ovenproof skillet over high heat. Sear racks of lamb for 3–5 minutes on all sides. Let cool for another 3–5 minutes.
4. Stand cooled chops on their ends and push them together so that the exposed bones cross each other alternately. Skewer the meat together at either end across the bottom. Brush racks of lamb with the mustard, then smear with the bread-crumb mixture until evenly coated. To prevent charring, cover the ends of the bones with foil.
5. Roast the lamb in preheated oven for 18–25 minutes, depending on the degree of doneness you desire. With a meat thermometer, take a reading in the center of each rack of lamb meat after 12–15 minutes and cook to taste. Once removed from heat, allow lamb to rest for 8–10 minutes, loosely covered, before carving between the ribs.
6. **For mint sauce:** Place the mint in a small pitcher or bowl, and cover with boiling water. Wait 25–30 minutes to allow the water to become infused. Stir in sugar and wine vinegar. Mix well and serve.

Etiquette Lessons

In the early twentieth century it was expected that no female guest would enter the dining room alone. According to tradition, a woman needed a man to "guide" her. Thus, after the butler formally announced "Dinner is served" to the waiting guests, each male guest—having already been informed of his partner—would offer his arm to a woman and guide her to her chair. The host would enter first, himself being partnered with the most esteemed and senior woman guest. Then the other paired guests would follow, according to the woman's rank, with the hostess entering and sitting last, the senior male guest on her arm.

Filet Mignon with Foie Gras and Truffle Sauce

This dish is a perfect example of the height of Edwardian excess in dining. Here, a choice cut of steak is covered with *foie gras* and topped with an expensive and elegant truffle sauce. It's likely that Mrs. Patmore would have saved this dish for days when fewer courses would be served, as she wouldn't want guests to be *too* full when this comes around!

YIELDS 6 SERVINGS

For Sauce

½ cup unsalted butter, room temperature

¼ cup white truffle oil

1 cup dry white wine

2 teaspoons minced garlic

2 teaspoons sea salt

1 teaspoon freshly ground white pepper

⅔ cup heavy cream

1 or 2 small black truffles, shaved

For Steaks

1 tablespoon unsalted butter

1 tablespoon extra-virgin olive oil

6 filet mignons (2–2½ pounds total)

Kosher salt and freshly ground black pepper to taste

6 ounces *foie gras*, cut into 6 slices

1. **For sauce:** In a large mixing bowl, mix together butter and truffle oil. Form a log of truffle butter on plastic wrap, then wrap tightly and refrigerate until firm.
2. In a medium-sized saucepan, combine white wine and garlic. Season with salt and white pepper. Bring liquid to a boil and cook for 5 minutes.
3. Stir in cream and cook for another 1–2 minutes. Cut the truffle butter log into 1-inch pieces, then reduce heat and gently whisk in butter, a piece at a time. Reduce heat to a low simmer and keep sauce warm. Garnish with shaved truffles.
4. **For steaks:** Heat butter and olive oil in a large sauté pan over medium-high heat. Season the steaks with salt and pepper, then gently sauté in oil and butter for 10–12 minutes, turning once, so sides are brown but middles are still pink.
5. Keep steaks warm in oven while preparing the *foie gras*. Treating *foie gras* incredibly gently and using a sharp knife, score a diamond pattern into *foie gras* slices. Season with salt and pepper to taste, then gently sauté *foie gras* in a small nonstick pan over low to medium heat until the *foie gras* develops some color. Lay slices of *foie gras* over steaks, then dribble with truffle sauce. Serve immediately.

TIMES GONE BY

Truffles have always been rare. Back during the Edwardian period, white truffles were only available a few months out of the year in a particular area of Italy, where they had to be foraged for by special pigs.

Creamless Steak au Poivre

Rich yet popular, this French dish is one that Mrs. Patmore would feel confident to serve to any of Downton Abbey's respected guests. While the sauce normally contains cream, this recipe takes out that thick ingredient and allows the other flavors to shine through.

YIELDS 4 SERVINGS

4 (1-inch-thick) beef tenderloin steaks

2½ teaspoons kosher salt

1 tablespoon coarsely ground black pepper

4 tablespoons unsalted butter, chopped

1 tablespoon extra-virgin olive oil

½ cup chopped shallots

½ cup sliced mushrooms

1 cup low-sodium beef broth

⅔ cup good brandy

1. Preheat oven to 400°F. Remove steaks from the refrigerator and let sit at room temperature for 30 minutes before cooking.
2. Sprinkle 2 teaspoons of the salt all over steaks. Then press black pepper evenly on all sides of meat until it coats the steaks' surface, and set aside.
3. Heat 2 tablespoons of the butter and the oil in a large, oven-proof sauté pan over medium-high heat until the butter is close to smoking. Lower the heat to medium, then place steaks on the pan and sear for 3 minutes per side. Then place entire pan in preheated oven for 10 minutes for medium to medium-well-done steaks.
4. Remove pan from oven, place steaks on a platter, and keep warm. Remove all but 2 tablespoons of steak fat from pan. Add shallots and mushrooms to fat in pan, and cook over medium heat for 5 minutes. Add beef broth and increase heat, cooking on high heat for 6 minutes until sauce is reduced by half. Be sure to scrape the brown bits from the bottom. Add brandy and cook for another 3 minutes. Turn off heat and stir in remaining butter and the extra ½ teaspoon salt. Serve steaks hot with the sauce poured on top.

Etiquette Lessons

When eating in the classic "English" manner, the fork, having just impaled its food, enters the mouth with the tines facing down. The impaled food must then be balanced on the *back* of the fork tines. As it is extremely difficult to eat like this, it is of course considered the height of good manners.

Steak Chasseur

This classic French dish would be served with much aplomb to Downton Abbey regulars and guests alike. Its simplistic nature is certain to appeal to the Earl of Grantham, who seems like a more "meat and potatoes" kind of eater than, say, his nitpicky mother. Mrs. Patmore might offer this dish accompanied by the delicious Daisy's Noisette Potoatoes (see Chapter 6). With or without them, however, the thick chasseur sauce on these steaks guarantees a hit.

YIELDS 4 SERVINGS

For Steak

4 (6- to 8-ounce) filet mignon steaks

1 teaspoon kosher salt

½ teaspoon cayenne pepper

1 tablespoon extra-virgin olive oil

For Chasseur Sauce

2 tablespoons extra-virgin olive oil

1 tablespoon minced shallot

3 teaspoons minced garlic

1 pound button mushrooms, thinly sliced

2 tomatoes, diced

¼ cup dry white wine

1 cup veal stock

¼ cup unsalted butter

½ teaspoon freshly ground white pepper

1 teaspoon chopped thyme

1 teaspoon chopped parsley

Steak Chasseur

(continued)

1. Season the filets equally with salt and cayenne pepper.
2. In a large saucepan, heat olive oil over medium-high heat. Sear steaks for about 7–9 minutes per side.
3. **You can prepare the sauce while the steaks cook:** Heat olive oil in another large saucepan. Add shallot and garlic, and sauté over medium heat for 2–3 minutes. Then add the button mushrooms and sauté, constantly stirring, for an additional 3–5 minutes. Toss in the diced tomatoes. Finally, add the wine and veal stock, and bring entire mixture to a boil. Then lower heat and let simmer for 5 minutes. Stir in butter and white pepper until thoroughly incorporated, then add thyme and parsley. Spoon sauce over steaks on their respective plates.

TIMES GONE BY

Chasseur sauce, often known as "hunter's sauce," is used in French cuisine. As the name suggests, this brown sauce is often paired with game meats such as venison or rabbit. While the sauce was invented by Duke Philippe de Mornay (also the inventor of Mornay sauce, béchamel sauce, and sauce Lyonnaise), it was the famed chef Escoffier, the "father of modern French cuisine," who really helped to make it popular in England.

Classic Beef Wellington

Depending on who you want to impress, you could call this dish by its French name, *Filet de Boeuf en Croûte,* **or by its British name, Beef Wellington. Some claim that a rather patriotic British chef named this dish Beef Wellington out of British pride; others claim it is named after a seventeenth-century duke. Either way, this favorite—consisting of a solid filet of beef covered by pâté and surrounded by a pastry crust—would be a staple for many a dinner at Downton Abbey.**

YIELDS 6 SERVINGS

2½ pounds beef tenderloin

4 tablespoons unsalted butter, softened

2 tablespoons extra-virgin olive oil

1 large onion, chopped

1 pound white button mushrooms

2 cloves garlic, chopped

2 ounces liver pâté

Kosher salt and freshly ground black pepper to taste

1 (17.5-ounce) frozen puff pastry, thawed

2 egg yolks, beaten

1½ cups beef broth

¼ cup red wine

Classic Beef Wellington
(continued)

1. Preheat oven to 425°F.
2. Place beef tenderloin in a medium-sized baking dish and cover with 2 tablespoons of the softened unsalted butter. Bake for 15–20 minutes or until thoroughly browned. Remove beef from pan and allow to cool completely. Reserve juices.
3. Heat the extra-virgin olive oil in a medium-sized skillet over medium-high heat. Sauté onion, mushrooms, and garlic in olive oil for 5 minutes, then remove from heat and set aside.
4. In a small bowl, mix together pâté and remaining 2 tablespoons of the softened butter, then season with salt and pepper. Spread pâté mixture evenly over cooled beef, then top with onion and mushroom mixture.
5. Using a rolling pin, roll out pastry dough on a lightly floured surface. Place beef in center of dough, then fold dough up and seal all the edges, making sure the seams are not too thick and unseemly.
6. Place beef pastry in a 9×13-inch baking dish. Cut a few slits at top of beef pastry; then wash pastry with egg yolks.
7. Cook beef pastry in oven for 30–35 minutes or until pastry is a rich, golden brown. Set aside, keeping warm.
8. In a small saucepan over high heat, mix together all reserved juices, plus the beef broth and red wine for 10–15 minutes or until slightly reduced. Strain, then serve with beef.

Etiquette Lessons

Although nowadays no one would look twice if you cut your meat into bite-sized pieces before eating, back in the nineteenth century and early twentieth century it was considered rude to do so. Rather, you were supposed to cut yourself one bite-sized piece of your meal, put down your knife, take a bite, then repeat. No wonder dinners took so long to finish!

Succulent Pork Shoulder

Made from few ingredients, the small amount of spice in this recipe brings out a surprising amount of flavor in this succulent pork shoulder. After a full day of hunting at Downton Abbey, the guests and their hosts would happily chow down on this juicy dish.

YIELDS 4–6 SERVINGS

4 tablespoons extra-virgin olive oil
3 tablespoons chopped garlic
Kosher salt and freshly ground black pepper to taste
1 (4-pound) pork shoulder

1. Preheat oven to 400°F.
2. In a small bowl, mix together olive oil, garlic, salt, and pepper. Using a pastry brush, slather mixture all over the pork shoulder.
3. Set the meat on a rack in a roasting pan. Roast for 25–30 minutes, and then reduce heat to 350°F. Continue to cook until meat thermometer inserted into middle of shoulder reaches 185°F, about 4–4½ hours. Remove pork from oven and cool until easy enough to handle, about 30–45 minutes.

TIMES GONE BY

With *Service à la Russe*, each dish was presented one at a time. However, an impressive dish such as this would be shown to the guests for the appropriate kudos, then taken to the sideboard or back to the kitchen for carving.

Mrs. Patmore's Perfect Pork Roast

Considering the healthy appetites attached to the unhealthy soldiers entering Downton Abbey, Mrs. Patmore couldn't go wrong serving this large, delicious roast! This large, filling dish requires sparse ingredients and, more importantly, little time to concoct, thus making it perfect for when Mrs. Patmore was trying to find the time to feed the wounded, the family, and her staff.

YIELDS 8–10 SERVINGS

2 cloves garlic, minced

2 teaspoons marjoram

1 teaspoon kosher salt

1 teaspoon rubbed sage

2 tablespoons extra-virgin olive oil

1 (4-pound) boneless pork loin

1. Preheat oven to 350°F.

2. In a small bowl, combine minced garlic, marjoram, salt, sage, and olive oil.

3. Rub spice mixture all over roast, then place roast in a shallow roasting pan.

4. Bake roast uncovered in preheated oven for 1 hour or until the meat thermometer reads 150°F. Let stand for 10 minutes before slicing.

Etiquette Lessons

While modern parties might suggest serving this pork roast with pine-apple and oranges (à la Hawaiian luau), such would not be the case during Victorian and Edwardian times. In fact, one Victorian etiquette guide advised, "Never embark on an orange," as it was considered rude to use your fingers to peel fruit and there wasn't another way to get to an orange's juicy interior.

The Criterion's Swanky Steak Tartare

This classic dish was invented and popularized by the great French chef Escoffier, who was famous for popularizing and updating classic French cooking methods. However, it wouldn't just be served at the London Ritz; fancy restaurants like The Criterion (where Lady Edith and her beloved Michael Gregson meet) would offer this dish for their more sophisticated—not to mention adventurous—clientele.

YIELDS 4–6 SERVINGS

3 oil-packed anchovy fillets, rinsed and minced

2 teaspoons capers, drained and rinsed

2 cloves garlic, crushed

1 large egg yolk

2 tablespoons Dijon mustard

1 teaspoon Worcestershire sauce

2 teaspoons fresh lime juice

Kosher salt and freshly ground black pepper

¼ cup extra-virgin olive oil

1 pound freshly ground beef tenderloin (Note: As you will be serving this dish raw, it is important that you get your meat from a reputable source. Be sure to let your butcher know that this will be used for steak tartare so he gives you the best cut.)

1. In a small bowl, combine the anchovies, capers, and garlic, crushing them together until they form a paste. Stir in egg yolk, mustard, Worcestershire sauce, and lime juice, followed by salt and pepper, and, finally, the olive oil to form an emulsion.
2. Set ground beef in a chilled mixing bowl. Using a rubber spatula, slowly fold in the mustard emulsion, mixing well.
3. Form the tartare into 4-ounce rounds, about 1–1½ inches thick. Place tartare in the center of chilled plates. Serve with toast points or French fries.

TIMES GONE BY

What is generally celebrated as "steak tartare" was originally called "steak à l'Americaine." Steak tartare is a variation of the dish without the egg yolk. However, as the years went on the distinction vanished, and steak tartare can be served with or without egg yolk mixed in.

Sixth Course: Resplendent Roasts, Gorgeous Game, and Accompanying Salads

In case the preceding barrage of meat courses weren't enough to satisfy your appetite, the following roasts—an appetizing mixture of veal, goose, and other game meats—would be ready and waiting for you. All roasts and game would be served with a suggested side salad or vegetable (see Chapter 6) and an elegant glass of champagne, which was the drink of choice by the end of the nineteenth century. It's important to note that while there was a great deal of meat served at Downton Abbey, the guests were not required to eat large portions, thus giving their stomachs room to at least have a taste of each offered course.

Regal Veal Prince Orloff

During this time period when French cuisine was quite *de rigueur*, this popular Franco-Russian dish was quite fashionable to serve at a dinner party. This dish is created by slicing veal and layering it with onion and mushroom stuffings, then covering with more stuffing and Mornay sauce. Perhaps in an attempt to woo Matthew Crawley, the Countess of Grantham would request that this indulgent dish be made to illustrate her family's wealth and generosity. But outsiders beware: The Countess of Grantham—and all the daughters of Downton—are just as layered as this meal.

YIELDS 6–8 SERVINGS

For Veal Roast
½ cup all-purpose flour

1 teaspoon garlic powder

1 (4-pound) tied boneless loin of veal, tenderized

½ teaspoon freshly ground black pepper

1 teaspoon kosher salt

2 tablespoons vegetable oil

½ cup chopped white onion

1 clove garlic, minced

2 celery hearts, finely chopped

1 large carrot, finely chopped

4 sprigs fresh parsley

5 sprigs fresh thyme

1 bay leaf

1 cup dry white wine

For Onion Stuffing
⅓ cup long-grain basmati rice

2 tablespoons unsalted butter

3 cups thinly-sliced white or yellow onions

1 teaspoon kosher salt

½ teaspoon sugar

⅓ cup chicken broth

For Mushroom Stuffing
1 pound mushrooms, finely chopped or minced

4 tablespoons unsalted butter

¼ cup heavy cream

½ teaspoon kosher salt

¼ teaspoon freshly ground black pepper

½ teaspoon sugar

Regal Veal Prince Orloff

(continued)

For Mornay Sauce

1½ cups whole milk

4 tablespoons unsalted butter

6 tablespoons all-purpose flour

⅓ cup grated Gruyère cheese

1 teaspoon kosher salt

¼ teaspoon freshly ground black pepper

¼ teaspoon freshly ground nutmeg

1. Preheat oven to 350°F.
2. **First, prepare the veal:** In a small or medium-sized bowl, mix together the flour and garlic powder. Dredge veal in flour mixture, then season with black pepper and salt.
3. Heat oil in a 5- or 6-quart dutch oven (or other ovensafe pot) over medium heat. Add onion and minced garlic, and sauté until brown. Place veal in dish and brown, turning on all sides, about 10 minutes.
4. Remove veal from dutch oven. Add celery and carrots, stirring frequently to prevent brown bits. Cook until vegetables soften, about 5 minutes.
5. Wrap parsley, fresh thyme, and bay leaf in a cheesecloth square, and tie into a bundle with a string to make a bouquet garni. Add

to vegetables, then add wine. Finally, place veal on top and bring to a simmer.

6. Cover dutch oven or pot with lid, then transfer to lower third of oven and braise until veal registers 145°F, about 1–1½ hours.
7. Transfer veal to a wooden cutting board. Let stand for at least 30 minutes. Pour cooking juices through a fine-mesh sieve into a medium-sized glass bowl. Discard solids. Skim off fat and reserve for Mornay sauce. Be sure to add any juices that leak from veal to plate.
8. **While veal braises, make the onion stuffing:** Cook basmati rice in a large saucepan of boiling salted water for 5 minutes, then drain and rinse and drain again.

Regal Veal Prince Orloff

(continued)

9. In a large, ovenproof skillet, heat butter over low heat until foam subsides. Stir in onions, salt, and sugar. Cover with a lid or foil and cook over low heat, stirring occasionally for about 7 minutes. Mix in rice and broth, then bring to a simmer.

10. Cover skillet tightly, then transfer to the upper third of the oven and bake until onions and rice are very soft, about 45 minutes–1 hour.

11. Leaving oven on, transfer onion stuffing to a food processor and coarsely purée. Transfer to a medium-sized bowl to cool.

12. **While the veal and onion stuffing cook, make the mushroom stuffing:** Place a handful of mushrooms in a kitchen towel that is not terrycloth. Gather towel around mushrooms and wring out in kitchen sink, removing as much liquid as possible. Wring out remaining mushrooms a handful at a time following the same process.

13. In a large skillet, heat butter over medium-high heat until foam subsides. Then add mushrooms and sauté until lightly brown and any liquid from the mushrooms has evaporated. This should take 6–8 minutes.

Mix in cream, salt, pepper, and sugar. Cook, constantly stirring, until cream is absorbed by mushrooms. Transfer to a bowl and let cool.

14. **As veal stands, make the Mornay sauce:** Add enough milk to reserved veal juices in glass bowl to total 3 cups.

15. Using a medium-sized saucepan, melt butter over low heat. Add flour and continue to cook over low heat, whisking constantly for 3 minutes. Add milk mixture in a steady stream, whisking vigorously, and bring mixture to a boil. Reduce heat to a gentle simmer, whisking less frequently, for 10 minutes. Remove saucepan from heat and add Gruyère, stirring until melted, then whisk in salt, pepper, and nutmeg.

16. **Now prepare the Veal Prince Orloff:** Move the top rack of the oven to the middle of oven and raise heat to 375°F.

17. Mix a ½ cup of the onion stuffing into all of the mushroom stuffing. Place remaining onion stuffing in a zip-top bag. Then transfer the onion and mushroom stuffing mixture into a different zip-top bag. Make sure to squeeze out excess air from both bags.

Regal Veal Prince Orloff

(continued)

Then snip off ¾ of an inch to 1 inch from the corner of each bag.

18. Remove string from veal loin, and trim off and discard the ends of veal and any excess fat. Cut roast crosswise into 16–20 slices, about ¼-inch thick, taking care to keep slices together.

19. Transfer 1 slice of veal to the end of an ovenproof platter. Squeeze from zip-top bag about 2 tablespoons of the onion and mushroom stuffing onto half of the slice, starting at the bottom of the slice and working toward the top of the slice. Then pipe 2 tablespoons of the mushroom stuffing onto the other half of the slice in the same manner. Overlap with another slice of meat, leaving ½ inch of stuffing exposed. Repeat with remaining veal slices and remaining stuffings, keeping slices aligned.

20. Reheat Mornay sauce over low heat until hot, stirring occasionally. If desired, thin with a little milk. Transfer to a gravy boat and serve on the side.

Etiquette Lessons

At a formal dinner party, or at any dinner party, you may not eat until your host picks up his fork to eat. Do not start before then unless your host insists that you begin eating; only then is it polite to eat. Similarly, your host will signal the end of the meal by placing his napkin on the table. Once the dinner is over, you should follow suit and place your napkin cleanly on the table to the left of your dinner plate. However, you should not refold your napkin, nor should you crumple it up.

Roasted Veal Chops with Rosemary-Basil Butter

A delicious and majestic dish, these veal chops make a perfect base for Mrs. Patmore's light rosemary-basil butter. As Thomas and William serve these juicy treats, it would likely be hard for them to keep their mouths from salivating—especially when they compare this dish to their heartier—yet much less delicate—food downstairs.

YIELDS 4 SERVINGS

½ cup unsalted butter, room temperature

3 teaspoons chopped fresh rosemary, divided

1 teaspoon chopped fresh basil

2 teaspoons chopped fresh thyme, divided

1½ teaspoons kosher salt, divided

4 (10- to 12-ounce) veal chops, each about 1–1½ inches thick

¼ cup extra-virgin olive oil

½ teaspoon freshly ground black pepper

1 tablespoon sugar

2 sprigs rosemary

2 cloves garlic, minced

4 tablespoons dry white wine

4 tablespoons low-sodium chicken broth

1. In a small bowl, blend together butter, 2 teaspoons of the rosemary, basil, 1 teaspoon of the thyme, and ½ teaspoon of the salt. Wrap butter in plastic wrap, forming a 1½-inch log. Chill for at least 2 hours, preferably 3–4.

2. Arrange veal chops in a single layer on a large baking dish. Drizzle with 2 tablespoons of the olive oil, then cover with remaining rosemary and thyme. Sprinkle with remaining 1 teaspoon salt, the black pepper, and sugar. Thoroughly rub oil and spices into chops.

3. In a large skillet, heat remaining 2 tablespoons olive oil over medium-high heat. Add rosemary sprigs and garlic, sautéing until fragrant but not brown. Increase heat to high, then add veal, cooking chops until they are brown and a meat thermometer inserted into the center reads 130°F. Add wine and cook until reduced by about half, about 30 seconds, then add chicken broth until reduced again by half. Drizzle sauce over chops.

4. Serve chops with rosemary butter sauce atop each one.

TIMES GONE BY

We know from Victorian paintings that children often stood to eat their food while at the same table with adults. This was not only due to basic necessity—not all families possessed enough chairs—but as a way to denote a lower status. It was also believed that eating while standing or sitting upright promoted digestion. Luckily, rules like this had relaxed by the Edwardian era.

Traditional Apple Cider Veal

A tender dish enjoyed by many of the English elite, this veal would be served with much aplomb by great houses such as Downton Abbey. For an extra kick, perhaps the daughters of Downton Abbey would pick the apples for the cider themselves, though this seems to be more like something Daisy would enjoy.

YIELDS 4–6 SERVINGS

2 tablespoons Crisco or fat

1 pound veal, cut into 4 equal pieces

4 tablespoons brandy

4 shallots, finely chopped

2 tablespoons all-purpose flour

1½ cups apple cider

1 clove

1 bay leaf

2 sprigs thyme

3 sprigs parsley

1 clove garlic, crushed

Kosher salt and freshly ground black pepper to taste

2 teaspoons sugar

1. In a large, flame-proof skillet, heat Crisco over medium heat. Once melted, add veal and fry until browned.
2. With the skillet still over medium heat, pour brandy over veal and let flame. Once flames have died down, add the shallots and brown around the veal for 3–5 minutes.
3. Still simmering the veal, sprinkle flour over top of the meat, then stir into the fat mixture to form a roux. Cook for 2–3 minutes, stirring constantly, then pour in cider a few tablespoons at a time until completely incorporated.
4. Add clove, bay leaf, thyme, parsley, and garlic to the veal, seasoning to taste with salt, pepper, and sugar. Still simmering, cover the pan and cook gently for 35–40 minutes.

Suggested Pairings

Sweet potatoes and apple sauce are traditional sides to serve with this type of veal dish, providing a filling—but sweet—accompaniment.

Squab with Fig Foie Gras

Squab, also known as a young domestic pigeon, will soon be a popular dish at Downton Abbey once the *second* world war erupts. During that war, while other meat is rationed, pigeon meat will be left alone. Until that happens, delicate and delicious (not to mention sumptuous) dishes like this would impress any visiting dignitaries, as squab is considered a delicacy.

YIELDS 4 SERVINGS

For Squabs

4 whole squabs

8 cloves garlic

4 bay leaves

2 cups sea salt

4 cups duck fat

½ cup brewed Darjeeling tea, room temperature

4 tablespoons unsalted butter, room temperature

For Fig Foie Gras

1½ pounds slightly chilled *foie gras*, veins removed

Coarse sea salt, to taste

Freshly ground black pepper, to taste

6 slices white bread, cut into rounds

2 tablespoons extra-virgin olive oil

4 black mission figs, halved

2 medium onions, finely chopped

½ cup port

Juice of ½ orange

2 tablespoons balsamic vinegar

2 tablespoons butter

1 tablespoon plus 1 teaspoon granulated sugar

1 tablespoon brown sugar

½ teaspoon orange zest

Squab with Fig Foie Gras

(continued)

1. **For squabs:** Remove the breasts and legs from each squab. Crush together the garlic and bay leaves, and mix together in a large bowl with the sea salt. Pack the squab legs in the salt mixture and cure for 45 minutes–1 hour, then lightly rinse under cold water. Place the legs and duck fat in a large saucepan, bring to a simmer, and cook until the legs are tender. Remove from fat and allow to cool.

2. Pour brewed tea and butter in a food processor and blend; then place butter mixture in a medium-sized zip-top bag with the duck breasts.

3. Bring a large saucepan of water to no less than 135°F and no more than 140°F (do not cook above 140°F). Put the zip-top bag with the squab breasts in the warmed water, and poach until medium rare. Remove breasts from bag, then roast them skin-side down until crispy, about 5–10 minutes.

4. **For fig *foie gras*:** Line a warmed platter with paper towels. Pull apart the 2 lobes of *foie gras*. Cut each lobe into 1-inch sections, then score the top of each section. Season with sea salt and pepper. Sear the sections in a dry pan for 25–30 seconds per side. Remove sections to platter.

5. Lower heat to medium-low and remove a small amount of the duck fat. Place duck fat in a small skillet and fry the bread in fat until brown, about 2–3 minutes per side. Remove fat from pan, then coat with olive oil. Briefly brown the figs, then add onions and cook together for 3–5 minutes. Mix together port, orange juice, and balsamic vinegar. Use mixture to deglaze the pan, cooking mixture down for 2–3 minutes. Add butter, white sugar, brown sugar, orange zest, salt, and pepper to complete the sauce.

6. Gently place one piece of *foie gras* on each individual toast. Top with figs, then drizzle with port sauce. Serve with squab.

Etiquette Lessons

The *Baronne Staffe*, the be-all and end-all of French etiquette, warns hosts to never invite people richer than themselves. After all, it would be the host's duty to serve food and wines on the level to which the guests are accustomed, which would be more difficult for some (not the Crawleys) than others. Fortunately, this dish is worthy of even the greatest of dignitaries.

Roasted Rosemary Cornish Game Hen

Don't let the name fool you—this hen is not actually a game bird, but a type of domestic chicken. Originating from the county of Cornwall, one of the poorest areas of the United Kingdom, the Cornish game hen would be a familiar sight to both the aristocrats and the staff of Downton Abbey. (Whether the staff ever had the chance to try this dish is another story.) Nonetheless, this incredibly small bird was considered a delicacy, and would be eaten with great aplomb at a formal dinner.

YIELDS 4 SERVINGS

4 Cornish game hens

¼ cup extra-virgin olive oil

Kosher salt and freshly ground black pepper to taste

2 lemons, quartered

2 tablespoons chopped fresh rosemary

20 cloves garlic

⅓ cup apple juice

1 cup low-sodium chicken broth

⅔ cup dry white wine

4 sprigs fresh rosemary, for garnish

Roasted Rosemary Cornish Game Hen

(continued)

1. Preheat oven to 400°F.
2. Rub hens with 2 tablespoons of the olive oil, then thoroughly season hens with salt and pepper. Place 2 lemon wedges and 2 teaspoons of chopped fresh rosemary in cavity of each hen.
3. Lightly pour a tablespoon of olive oil in a large roasting pan, spreading evenly. Place hens in pan, and carefully arrange garlic cloves around each hen. Roast in oven for 30 minutes, then reduce temperature to 350°F.
4. In a medium-sized mixing bowl, stir together apple juice, chicken broth, wine, and remaining olive oil. Pour juice over hens, then roast hens for 30–35 minutes or until they are golden and juices run clear. Hens should be basted with pan juices every 10–15 minutes.
5. Place hens on a serving platter. Do not discard pan juices. Lightly cover hens with aluminum foil to trap heat as you transfer pan juices and garlic cloves to a small saucepan. Boil juices and garlic cloves until liquid reduces by half and reaches a saucelike consistency, about 7–10 minutes. To serve, cut hens in half lengthwise and arrange on plate. Spoon sauce over and place garlic around hens. Garnish with rosemary sprigs and serve.

Etiquette Lessons

In both Victorian and Edwardian England, it was considered impolite to leave a single piece of uneaten food on the table. Once *Service à la Russe* was introduced, this was easier to avoid. However, if a piece of food was left behind on a serving plate, it was the host's job to beg a chosen guest to eat it. Not doing so would give the host bad luck, while following through was said to grant the guest good luck. Some particularly superstitious guests would save a choice morsel on their plate for last as a treat, hence the phrase "saving the best for last."

Roast Quail with Fig Sauce

As Downton Abbey is the perfect estate for hunting game, it's likely that Lady Mary and her guests would hunt their fair share of quail. Mrs. Patmore would take that quail and make a delicious dish to serve as the fourth or fifth course of the dinner party following the hunt.

YIELDS 4–6 SERVINGS

For Quail

4 cups dry white wine

¼ cup plus 1 teaspoon kosher salt

12 bay leaves

12 semi-boneless quail

½ cup unsalted butter, melted

½ teaspoon freshly ground black pepper

2 tablespoons unsalted butter

2 tablespoons vegetable oil

For Fig Sauce

½ cup plus 2 tablespoons unsalted butter

2 cups fresh figs, halved lengthwise, stems discarded

¼ cup finely chopped shallots

½ cup chopped celery

1 cup dry red wine

1½ cups veal demi-glace

3 tablespoons fig balsamic vinegar

1 tablespoon chopped fresh tarragon

1 teaspoon kosher salt

½ teaspoon freshly ground black pepper

Roast Quail with Fig Sauce

(continued)

1. In a medium-sized pot, boil white wine, ¼ cup of the salt, and bay leaves. Once boiled, set aside and let cool. Submerge quail in this brine and refrigerate for 4–6 hours.

2. While brining, make the sauce: Heat ½ cup of the butter in a medium-sized skillet over medium-high heat. Brown figs for 3–5 minutes. Transfer figs to a medium-sized bowl. Place shallots and celery into skillet and brown for 3–5 minutes. Add wine and 10–12 browned fig halves (reserving the rest) and boil, stirring repeatedly while mashing figs, until wine is reduced to a syrup, about 5 minutes. Mix in demi-glace and bring mixture to a boil. Whisk in balsamic vinegar. Heat to a rolling boil for 3 minutes, then pour through a fine-mesh sieve into a heavy saucepan, discarding solids. Stir in tarragon, salt, and pepper.

3. Preheat oven to 350°F. While the oven preheats, free quail from fridge and pat dry. Cover quail with melted butter, and season generously with salt and pepper.

4. Heat 1 tablespoon of the butter and 1 tablespoon of the oil in a medium-sized skillet over medium-high heat for 45 seconds. One by one, brown half the quail for 10–15 minutes, transferring browned quail to a large baking pan, placing them breast-side up. Add remaining butter and oil to skillet, and continue to brown the remaining six quail.

5. Roast quail in preheated oven until just cooked through, about 10–15 minutes. Add reserved browned figs to pan for the last 2–3 minutes of roasting.

6. Bring sauce back to a low bubble, stirring in remaining 2 tablespoons of butter until butter is fully incorporated with the sauce. Arrange quail and figs on a large serving platter. Pour leftover pan juices into sauce. Serve sauce on the side in an elegant sauce container.

Etiquette Lessons

By the 1920s, it was proper etiquette for the guests to arrive for a function no later than 8 P.M., and for the dinner to be finished no later than 10:30 P.M. With the advent of *Service à la Russe,* the time for 6-hour dinners of the Victorian era had passed. Of course, it helped that, after World War I, many of the courses were cut.

Crispy Roast Duck with Blackberry Sauce

While entertaining guests, the Earl of Grantham might perhaps offer a bit of hunting—should the weather permit. Although foul such as pheasants or wild game like hare might be preferred, should a guest kill a mallard or some other duck, it would not go to waste. Mrs. Patmore could certainly use the duck in a fine recipe such as this one to offer the guests a taste of their own hunting prowess.

YIELDS 2–3 SERVINGS

½ cup plus 1 tablespoon unsalted butter

¼ cup white sugar

⅓ cup dry white wine: Chenin Blanc or Sauvignon Blanc

¼ cup orange juice

¼ cup lemon juice

2 tablespoons red wine vinegar

1½ cups frozen blackberries, thawed

1¾ cups chicken broth

2 tablespoons Cognac

1 tablespoon Vermont maple syrup

4 (5- to 6-ounce) duck breast halves with skin

Kosher salt to taste

Black pepper to taste

Additional blackberries, for presentation

Crispy Roast Duck with Blackberry Sauce

(continued)

1. Melt ½ cup butter in a large skillet over medium-high heat.
2. Slowly stir in sugar, stirring until sugar thoroughly dissolves and sauce turns a deep amber color, about 5–8 minutes. Pour in wine, orange juice, lemon juice, and red wine vinegar. Still stirring, bring entire mixture to a boil.
3. Add berries and chicken broth to sauce; continue to boil until sauce thickens and is reduced to about 1½ cups, stirring occasionally. This will take about 20–30 minutes.
4. Add Cognac and maple syrup. Using the back of a spoon, mash the berries into the mixture. Set aside.
5. Preheat oven to 400°F. After trimming any excess fat from the duck breasts, cut small slits in the skin (but not in the meat) of the duck. Thoroughly season breasts with salt and pepper.
6. Heat a heavy, ovenproof skillet over high heat. Add duck—skin-side down—and sear until lightly brown, about 5 minutes. Turn over and cook for an additional 2–3 minutes. Transfer skillet to oven and cook until duck reaches desired doneness (about 5 minutes for medium).

7. As duck bakes, reheat blackberry sauce over low heat. Add last tablespoon of butter and whisk until just barely melted. Season to taste with salt and pepper.
8. Spoon sauce onto plates, then place duck atop sauce. Garnish with additional sauce and blackberries if so desired.

Etiquette Lessons

It is out of respect for your guests that you serve their duck already carved into breasts. When served a half duck or a half chicken, a guest is expected to seamlessly use his knife and fork to cut the wing and leg away from the breast before he begins to eat any of the meal.

Daisy's Downton Rib Roast

While this recipe requires few ingredients and little attention, Daisy with her curious nature would likely find this recipe quite difficult, as it involves not opening your oven for several hours to peek at the rib roast's progress!

YIELDS 6 SERVINGS

1 (5-pound) standing beef
   rib roast
¼ cup extra-virgin olive oil
1 teaspoon garlic powder
1 teaspoon fresh rosemary
2 teaspoons kosher salt
1 teaspoon freshly ground
   black pepper

1. Allow roast to stand at room temperature for 1 hour, then thoroughly coat roast with olive oil.
2. Preheat oven to 375°F. Whisk together garlic powder, rosemary, salt, and pepper in a small bowl. Rub seasoning all over roast. Place roast, fatty-side up, in roasting pan.
3. Place roast in oven and cook for 1¼ hours. Turn oven off, leaving roast inside. Whatever you do, do not open the oven. Leave roast in turned-off oven for 3 hours. About 40–45 minutes before serving, turn oven temperature up to 375°F, roasting for 30 minutes. Remove from oven and let rest for 10 minutes in a warm place before carving.

Suggested Pairings

Mrs. Patmore would know that one should never carve a roast immediately after cooking, or it will be tough. Instead, as directed in this recipe, a roast should be allowed to rest in a warm place for at least 10 minutes prior to carving. An aged Merlot or Cabernet would be excellent choices to accompany this dish, as the fat in the rib roast provides the meat with great flavor, thus necessitating a wine that is not overpowering but still holds its own against the dish.

Mrs. Patmore's Dropped Roasted Chicken

Before her disastrous salted raspberry meringues, Mrs. Patmore dropped a delicious-looking roasted chicken on the floor due to her failing eyesight. Yet, as both the staff and the chef see clearly, what the aristocrats upstairs don't know won't hurt them—and so they serve the chicken anyway. Luckily, you'll notice that dropping the chicken isn't a required step for this particular recipe.

YIELDS 4–6 SERVINGS

1 (3-pound) whole chicken, giblets removed

Kosher salt and freshly ground black pepper to taste

1 tablespoon onion powder

⅔ cup unsalted butter, divided by tablespoons

1 stalk celery, leaves removed

½ fresh lemon, sliced

4 sprigs fresh rosemary

1. Preheat oven to 350°F.
2. Place chicken in a large roasting pan, and season generously, inside and out, with salt, pepper, and onion powder. Carefully place 3 tablespoons butter in the chicken cavity, then smother remaining butter all over chicken exterior. Cut celery into four pieces, and place in the chicken cavity, along with lemon slices. Sprinkle exterior of chicken with rosemary sprigs.
3. Bake chicken uncovered in preheated oven for 1 hour and 15 minutes so chicken reaches a minimum internal temperature of 180°F. Remove chicken from oven and baste with melted butter and other drippings. Tent with aluminum foil, and allow to rest for 30 minutes before serving.

Etiquette Lessons

After dinner, the women would head to the drawing room. The men would stay in the dining room. Only when everyone had left the dining room would the maids be allowed to come upstairs and help clear the table. Like children, the maids were to be seen and not heard.

Spinach Salad with Goat Cheese, Toasted Walnuts, and Pears

This is a classic salad with a combination of both sweet and tart flavors, much like the Crawley sisters themselves! Yet, like this salad, while the girls themselves possess hints of sharpness, underneath it all they are well-meaning and quite delightful.

YIELDS 4 SERVINGS

For Dressing

1 tablespoon red wine
  vinegar
1 tablespoon balsamic
  vinegar
1 tablespoon minced shallot
½ cup extra-virgin olive oil
1 teaspoon fresh lemon juice
2 teaspoons Dijon mustard
1 teaspoon sugar
1 teaspoon sea salt
½ teaspoon freshly ground
  black pepper

For Salad

½ cup dried cranberries
8 cups lightly packed fresh
  spinach leaves
3 firm but ripe pears, not
  peeled, but quartered,
  cored, and cut into long
  slices
1½ cups toasted walnuts
½ cup goat cheese,
  crumbled

1. In a small bowl, thoroughly whisk together red wine vinegar, balsamic vinegar, shallot, olive oil, lemon juice, Dijon mustard, sugar, sea salt, and pepper. Set aside.
2. Soak dried cranberries in 2 tablespoons of the dressing. Let soak for 20 minutes.
3. Place 6 cups of the spinach in a large bowl. Add pears. Toss with most of the remaining dressing, then add last 2 cups of spinach and toss again until well coated. Add cranberries and toasted walnuts, and toss again. Pour into bowls and sprinkle with goat cheese.

TIMES GONE BY

Part of Daisy's daily duties would be to inspect each and every individual piece of lettuce in every salad served, as even one lightly brown or wilted leaf or piece of fruit could be grounds for immediate dismissal . . . not to mention Mrs. Patmore's utter horror.

Creamy Crab and Celery Salad

This traditional British salad might look rather lumpy and unappealing, but all at Downton Abbey would be aware that—despite its less-than-appetizing appearance—it's a surprisingly delicious addition to the table.

YIELDS 6–8 SERVINGS

2 cups seashell pasta

1 cup mayonnaise

1 tablespoon rice vinegar

1 teaspoon fresh lemon juice

¼ teaspoon sugar

½ teaspoon garlic powder

½ teaspoon basil

1 teaspoon oregano

1½ cups crabmeat

½ cup diced carrots

¼ cup diced green onions

1 cup sliced celery

½ cup shredded Parmesan cheese

1. Bring a large pot of water to a boil. Add pasta and cook for 10 minutes or until pasta is al dente. Rinse with cold water and drain.
2. In a large bowl, whisk together mayonnaise, rice vinegar, lemon juice, sugar, garlic powder, basil, and oregano. Adjust seasonings to suit your own personal taste.
3. Add pasta to dressing and toss to coat. Add crabmeat, carrots, green onions, and celery, gently folding into the salad mixture. Finally, mix in Parmesan cheese. Cover and refrigerate for at least 3 hours (preferably overnight) before serving.

TIMES GONE BY

Creamy Crab and Celery Salad is *not* to be mistaken for Crab Louie, which is distinctly American. This Creamy Crab and Celery Salad contains a great deal more mayonnaise than Crab Louie, and is built from a pasta base rather than one of lettuce.

Spinach and Feta Salad with Fresh Beetroot

The unique addition of fresh beets—known as beetroot in London—mixed with these ingredients makes for a surprising, but delicious salad that everyone at Downton Abbey would enjoy. The festive mix of sweet flavors (such as maple syrup and orange juice) would provide guests at any garden party or luncheon with an extra excuse to smile.

YIELDS 4–6 SERVINGS

4 medium beets, scrubbed, trimmed, and cut in half
½ cup walnuts, chopped
3 tablespoons maple syrup
1 tablespoon unsalted butter
½ cup frozen orange juice concentrate
¼ cup balsamic vinegar
½ cup extra-virgin olive oil
10 ounces fresh spinach, washed and dried
4 ounces feta cheese, crumbled
2 oranges, sliced

1. Place beets in saucepan and cover with water. Bring to a boil, then cook for 30 minutes or until tender. Drain and cool, then cut beets into cubes.
2. Place walnuts in a skillet and briefly heat over medium-low heat. Add maple syrup and butter. Cook and stir until walnuts are evenly coated, then remove from heat and let cool.
3. In a small bowl whisk together orange juice concentrate, balsamic vinegar, and olive oil, and set aside.
4. Place a large helping of spinach leaves on plates, then divide candied walnuts among plates over greens. Place equal amount of beets over greens, then top with feta cheese. Drizzle each plate with some of the dressing, followed by orange slices.

Suggested Pairings

This salad would be an excellent dish to serve before Creamless Steak *au Poivre* (see Chapter 4), Daisy's Downton Rib Roast (see recipe in this chapter), or the Seven-Hour Leg of Lamb (see Chapter 4).

A Waldorf Salad for the British Tourist

"You Americans never understand the importance of tradition," the Dowager Countess chides Martha Levinson. "Yes we do—we just don't give it power over us," Cora's willful mother replies. And yet even Americans have traditional dishes—and few possess the fame and power of the Waldorf Salad. Created in the 1890s by maître d'hôtel Oscar Tschirky for the Waldorf Hotel (soon to be the famous Waldorf Astoria), this salad would only grow in popularity and fame. While Martha might find dining at the ritzy Waldorf "gauche," no doubt her visitors from "across the pond" would want to try this mayonnaise-laden dish when visiting her in New York!

YIELDS 4–6 SERVINGS

⅓ cup mayonnaise

½ teaspoon fresh lemon juice

¼ teaspoon salt

1 cup thinly sliced celery

½ cup thinly chopped walnuts

½ cup raisins

4 medium-sized crisp apples

1. In a medium-sized bowl, mix together the mayonnaise, lemon juice, and salt. Set aside in fridge.
2. Mix together the celery, walnuts, and raisins. Finally, chop the apples to ½-inch pieces, then quickly add to celery mixture to prevent browning. Stir in mayonnaise mixture. Serve immediately or cover and refrigerate for up to 48 hours.

TIMES GONE BY

The Waldorf Salad would rise to even more prominence in 1934 thanks to Cole Porter's hit song "You're the Top" from his musical *Anything Goes*, where the Waldorf Salad is specifically mentioned.

Chapter 6

SEVENTH COURSE: THE NECESSARY VEGETABLE

In Edwardian-era society, vegetables weren't high on the list of important culinary necessities for a meal, as Edwardian socialites—and more importantly, their chefs—had little fundamental knowledge of basic nutrition. Thus, the following vegetable recipes are quite heavy on the butter—and subsequent tastiness. Nonetheless, these dishes would serve as a nice buffer between meat courses and the following decadent desserts (see Chapters 7 and 12).

Potatoes Lyonnaise

A delicious side that goes especially well with the meat dishes favored at Downton Abbey, including Crispy Roast Duck with Blackberry Sauce (see Chapter 5) and Guard of Honor Lamb with Mint Sauce (Chapter 4), this dish was created in the French city of Lyon (hence the name Lyonnaise), which is one of the capitals of French gastronomy. Lyon has also produced delicious dishes such as *Coq au Vin* (see Chapter 10).

YIELDS 6–8 SERVINGS

3 pounds Yukon Gold potatoes, brushed and washed

Kosher salt to taste

4 tablespoons extra-virgin olive oil

4 yellow onions, sliced

2 tablespoons minced garlic

½ cup unsalted butter, chopped

White pepper, to taste

2 tablespoons chopped curly parsley

Potatoes Lyonnaise

(continued)

1. Preheat oven to 400°F.
2. Place potatoes in a large pot and fill with cold water until potatoes are just covered. Bring water to a boil, adding 1 teaspoon of the salt. Reduce heat to medium-high and cook potatoes for 12–15 minutes. Potatoes are ready when they are only slightly tender. Remove potatoes from pot and drain thoroughly; do not rinse. Once potatoes are cool enough to touch and have dried thoroughly, remove skin. Cut them into ½-inch slices.
3. Heat olive oil in a large, ovenproof skillet over medium-high heat. Lower heat, then add onions and cook for 10–12 minutes, stirring frequently, until onions are golden brown and tender. Season to taste with salt and add garlic. Cook garlic for 3–5 minutes until also golden. Transfer to a platter and set aside.
4. Place the same ovenproof skillet over low heat. Melt butter, then cover bottom of pan with a third of the potatoes. Season with more salt and white pepper. Cover with half of onion mixture, and season again with salt and white pepper. Cover with half of remaining potatoes, and season with rest of salt and white pepper. Spread the rest of onion mixture over potatoes, then top with remaining potatoes and season with white pepper. Cover with foil.
5. Bake potatoes in preheated oven for 12–15 minutes or until potatoes are tender and browning on top. Remove skillet from oven and use a spatula to carefully transfer potatoes to a serving platter. Sprinkle with curly parsley and serve hot.

Etiquette Lessons

No matter how large a slice of potato, in the Edwardian era you were never to use a knife on a dish to cut the food if it could be done with simply a fork. As the 1886 manners guide *Etiquette: Rules & Usages of the Best Society* explains: "Everything that can be cut without using a knife should be eaten with the fork alone." That said, do not toy with your knife or any of your cutlery. One was not to fidget at a dinner party.

British Brussels Sprouts with Chestnuts

Just like the British aristocracy, Brussels sprouts are seen as rather snooty and hard to like. However, Mrs. Patmore would know that even the Dowager Countess would enjoy this dish when a hint of half-and-half (or even heavy cream) is added! Even the Earl of Grantham would be tempted to lose his manners in an attempt to acquire a second serving of this side dish.

YIELDS 6–8 SERVINGS

2 tablespoons unsalted butter
1 teaspoon kosher salt
½ teaspoon freshly ground black pepper
½ teaspoon sugar
1 cup water
8 cups Brussels sprouts, trimmed and halved lengthwise
1½ cups half-and-half
1 cup crumbled roasted chestnuts

1. Using a large, heavy skillet, bring butter, salt, pepper, sugar, and water to a boil over high heat. Lower heat and slowly stir in Brussels sprouts and let simmer, partially covered and stirring occasionally, for 8–10 minutes.
2. Remove lid and turn up heat. Boil over medium-high heat for 4–5 minutes, or until water evaporates and Brussels sprouts are lightly browned.
3. Stir in half-and-half and turn up heat. Bring mixture to a boil, stirring frequently. Reduce heat and add in chestnuts, letting simmer while stirring occasionally, about 3–5 minutes or until chestnuts are heated through.

Suggested Pairings

The simple yet pleasing taste of these Brussels sprouts would go well with the regal Steak Chasseur (see Chapter 4) or incredibly sweet and fancy Filet Mignon with *Foie Gras* and Truffle Sauce (see Chapter 4).

Asparagus with Hollandaise Sauce

Mrs. Patmore would likely serve more than asparagus with this creamy hollandaise sauce, but this dish would be a particularly popular offering. Mrs. Patmore would also be quite proud of herself for making this dish, as good hollandaise sauce is difficult to make.

YIELDS 4 SERVINGS

For Asparagus

1 pound medium-sized
  asparagus
1 tablespoon extra-virgin
  olive oil
½ teaspoon kosher salt
¼ teaspoon freshly ground
  white pepper

For Sauce

1 large egg yolk
2 teaspoons lemon juice
1 teaspoon cayenne pepper
¼ cup unsalted butter,
  melted
1 teaspoon kosher salt

1. Preheat oven to 400°F.
2. **To make the asparagus:** Trim asparagus. On a well-greased shallow roasting dish, spread asparagus spears in a single layer. Drizzle asparagus with olive oil, then sprinkle with salt and white pepper.
3. Roast the asparagus until lightly browned and incredibly tender, about 15–20 minutes.
4. **To make the sauce:** Blend together the egg yolk, lemon juice, and cayenne pepper. Gradually add the melted butter to the egg mixture to make a frothy sauce. Season with kosher salt and serve immediately.
5. Spread the roasted asparagus on a serving platter. For a spicier option, grind a fair amount of black or white pepper on top.

TIMES GONE BY

The word *menu* is derived from the Latin word "minor" or "minutus," a.k.a. the "minutes" of a meeting. Menus are a gift to the guests of a feast or dinner party, as menus lay out the plan for the evening and allow guests to judge just how much of everything they want to eat.

Daisy's Noisette Potatoes

This is a very basic yet scrumptious side that novice cook Daisy could make while Mrs. Patmore does the more heavy lifting. Later, of course, Daisy would prove herself to be quite the competent chef and even asks for a promotion, much to the consternation of Mrs. Patmore, who would prefer that Daisy continue making this potato dish for quite a bit more time.

YIELDS 4 SERVINGS

6 Russet potatoes
¼ cup clarified butter
Kosher salt
Freshly ground black
  pepper

1. Preheat oven to 375°F.
2. Scrub and peel the potatoes under cold water. Use the smaller end of a melon-baller to scoop out at least 25 small balls of potato flesh. Keep round balls of potatoes in cold water until ready to cook.
3. Heat butter in an ovenproof pan over medium heat. Sauté the potato balls in butter over medium heat for 5 minutes, stirring often.
4. Transfer pan to preheated oven and bake for 25–30 minutes, stirring occasionally, until potato balls are tender and golden. Season with salt and pepper, and serve.

TIMES GONE BY

These potatoes are called noisette potatoes because their size, once balled, is similar to that of a hazelnut, or *noisette*, in French. Because most refined ladies would know what *noisette* means in English, they would smile at this dish and understand its name.

Red Wine–Braised Red Cabbage with Apples

A German-inspired recipe, this sweet dish with a spice of sour red cabbage would add a bit of flair to the most formal of occasions. This would be especially popular during the winter months at Downton Abbey when the Crawleys are feeling a bit Christmas-y and in need of extra warmth. For an additional bit of sweetness, add a few teaspoons of honey.

YIELDS 4–6 SERVINGS

- 4 tablespoons unsalted butter
- 1 medium head red cabbage, shredded
- 2 large tart apples, thinly sliced
- 1 medium to large red onion, thinly sliced
- 1 cup good red wine
- ¼ cup red wine vinegar
- ½ cup apple juice
- 1 teaspoon ground cinnamon
- ½ teaspoon nutmeg
- 1 teaspoon kosher salt
- ¼ teaspoon freshly ground black pepper
- 1 tablespoon plus 1 teaspoon packed light brown sugar

Heat butter over medium-high heat in a large saucepan. Lower to medium heat and add cabbage, apples, and onion. Cook for 5 minutes, stirring to fully coat. Reduce heat to low; then stir in red wine, wine vinegar, and apple juice, followed by spices and brown sugar. Cover and simmer for 40–45 minutes, then uncover and cook for an additional 10 minutes until excess juices have evaporated.

TIMES GONE BY

During the late 1800s and early 1900s, the men liked to be left alone after the meal not only to over-drink and to tell coarse jokes but to smoke . . . a habit originally considered unacceptable for respectable women. However, by World War I, Emily Post and other leaders of etiquette claimed it was okay and even acceptable for women to smoke—though not to get drunk, of course! Still, both men and women liked their alone time after a meal, as the dinner party with its somewhat risqué seating (men and women sitting next to one another) could be an exhausting performance for both sexes, and it was believed that the women could only be at ease with other women, and the same for men.

Decadent Duchess Potatoes

These bites of potato are little works of art. Daisy would have to spend a great deal of time with Mrs. Patmore to perfect these so they were acceptable for the Granthams's table.

YIELDS 4–6 SERVINGS

2 pounds Yukon Gold potatoes, peeled and cut into chunks

¼ cup heavy cream

½ cup unsalted butter, divided

⅓ cup grated Parmesan cheese

¼ teaspoon nutmeg

1 teaspoon kosher salt

1 teaspoon white pepper

3 large egg yolks

2 tablespoons melted butter

1. Place potatoes in a large pot and cover with salted cold water. Bring to a simmer and cook until the potatoes are tender, about 30 minutes.
2. While the potatoes are cooking, melt 2 tablespoons of butter in a small bowl and set aside. Preheat oven to 350°F.
3. When the potatoes are cooked, drain and place potatoes back in the pot over low heat. Allow them to release steam, then add the remaining butter and mash until the butter is incorporated. Thoroughly mix in cheese, nutmeg, salt, and white pepper. Finally, mix in egg yolks. Mash until the mixture is smooth, but do not mash too much.
4. Using a piping bag with a large star point, pipe the potatoes onto a cookie sheet. Drizzle the rosettes with the melted butter. Bake the potatoes for 15–30 minutes or until heated through. Then place the baking sheet under a preheated broiler, about 6–8 inches from the heat, and broil until the tops are golden brown.

TIMES GONE BY

The influential French chef Georges Auguste Escoffier (1846–1935) included a recipe for this dish in his pivotal book on "haute cuisine" titled *Le Guide Culinaire*, which was published in France in 1903. Although the English translation of this cookbook wasn't printed until 1907, Escoffier's reputation preceded him and many chefs by then already knew his recipes.

Creamed Carrots

Thanks to the amount of butter in this recipe, these carrots are a delicious addition to any meal, such as Steak Chasseur (see Chapter 4) or Daisy's Downton Rib Roast (see Chapter 5). Thanks to the low amount of effort needed to cook this vegetable dish, Mrs. Patmore could focus on the other courses while Daisy kept an eye on the carrots.

YIELDS 6–8 SERVINGS

1 cup low-sodium vegetable broth

3 pounds fresh carrots, cut into ¼- to ½-inch slices

¼ cup unsalted butter

1 tablespoon sugar

2 tablespoons all-purpose flour

1 teaspoon kosher salt

½ teaspoon freshly ground white pepper

1 cup heavy cream

1. In a large saucepan, bring broth to a boil. Add carrots, then reduce heat to a simmer. Cover and let simmer for 15 minutes or until the carrots are tender.
2. Meanwhile, melt butter in a small saucepan. Stir in sugar, flour, salt, and white pepper until smooth. Gradually add cream. Bring mixture to a boil, then cook, stirring often, until thickened.
3. Drain carrots. Coat with cream sauce and then toss to thoroughly coat.

Etiquette Lessons

The place setting for each guest is a matter of strict propriety. From the right of the plate, going from outside in, should be the oyster fork in the bowl of the soup spoon, the fish knife, and the meat knife, followed by the fruit or salad knife. On the left, again from the outside in, should be the fish fork, the meat fork, and the salad or fruit fork. This is because silverware is placed in the order in which it is used, thus cutlery used for first courses would be found on the outer edge of the setting. As this is a *British* table setting, where salad is typically eaten *last*, the salad fork will be found on the inside of the setting. In America, where salad is eaten *first*, the salad fork would be found on the outside of the setting.

Pommes de Terre Sarladaise
(Potatoes Cooked in Duck Fat)

While it's not a familiar delicacy for Americans, duck fat is a well-known ingredient in France and for the culinary elite of England. Mrs. Patmore would know that the duck fat enhances the agreeable rustic flavor of the fried potatoes.

YIELDS 4–6 SERVINGS

2 pounds Yukon Gold
   potatoes
4 tablespoons duck fat
1 bunch fresh parsley
4 cloves garlic
1 teaspoon kosher salt
½ teaspoon freshly ground
   black pepper

1. Peel, rinse, and dry potatoes. Cut them into ¼-inch-thick slices.
2. Heat duck fat in a medium-sized heavy pot over medium-high heat until fat is fully melted. When the fat is nice and hot, put in potatoes and cover them. Reduce the heat to low and let potatoes cook for ½ hour.
3. While potatoes cook, chop parsley and garlic together.
4. After the potatoes have cooked for ½ hour, turn them over gently with a wooden spoon, moving the crispy bottom to the top. Keep potatoes covered in duck fat. Add salt, chopped parsley–garlic mix, and pepper. Cover and cook for an additional 15 minutes.

Etiquette Lessons

To help dinner guests prepare themselves for the meal ahead of them, they would find at their place settings a menu listing the courses awaiting them. Menus would also be used as a means of "showing off" the many exotic ingredients and/or methods of cooking the chef used. Restaurants would later copy this idea by giving fancy names to rather mundane dishes as a means of suggesting that the diners could not find or make the same dishes at home. Translating the dish's name into French was a sure-fire way of impressing customers without any additional work.

Cucumbers à la Poulette

Want to know one way to make cucumbers delicious? Cover them with butter and sugar. Any guest visiting Downton with a sweet tooth would eat these vegetables with gusto while the silent staff would look eagerly on, hoping for leftovers.

YIELDS 4 SERVINGS

4 large cucumbers, sliced

4 tablespoons unsalted butter

1 tablespoon all-purpose flour

1½ cups low-sodium chicken broth

2 teaspoons kosher salt

½ teaspoon freshly ground black pepper

1 teaspoon sugar

2 large egg yolks, beaten

1 tablespoon chopped fresh parsley

1. Place cucumbers in a large pot and cover with water. Let soak for 1 hour, then drain and let dry on cloth.
2. Heat butter in a large saucepan over medium-high heat. Add cucumbers and fry over moderate heat, without browning, for 5 minutes. Lower heat, then add flour, stirring. When thoroughly mixed, add broth and simmer gently for 25 minutes. Stir in salt, pepper, and sugar.
3. Drawing the pan to one side, add beaten egg yolks and parsley, beating thoroughly. Remove from heat.

Suggested Pairings

This would be an excellent accompaniment to Mrs. Patmore's Dropped Roasted Chicken (see Chapter 5), Classic Beef Wellington (see Chapter 4), or even Roasted Veal Chops with Rosemary-Basil Butter (see Chapter 5).

Baked and Buttery Balsamic Asparagus with Sea Salt

Likely served at Downton Abbey as part of the vegetable course, a version of this dish was served in the first-class cabins of the *Titanic*, whose sinking changed the lives of everyone at Downton Abbey. It's likely that the sea salt used in this recipe would have had everyone thinking of their loved ones lost at sea.

YIELDS 4 SERVINGS

1 bunch fresh asparagus, trimmed
Extra-virgin olive oil
Sea salt and freshly ground black pepper to taste
¼ cup unsalted butter
1 tablespoon balsamic vinegar
1½ teaspoons soy sauce

1. Preheat oven to 400°F.
2. Lightly oil a baking sheet with olive oil. Place asparagus on greased baking sheet, then season heavily with salt and pepper.
3. Bake asparagus for 10–15 minutes or until tender.
4. Melt and brown butter in a small saucepan over medium-high heat. Remove from heat, then stir in balsamic vinegar and soy sauce. Pour over baked asparagus and serve.

Etiquette Lessons

While it is common for the host to take the first bite of food, a tradition likely passed on from medieval times to prove that the food is not poisoned, many leaders of etiquette—especially those frequenting Downton Abbey—would be horrified at such an act of rudeness. Instead, the guest of honor should be served—and should eat—first.

Mrs. Patmore's Easy Roasted Parsnips

If Mrs. Patmore wanted to take a day off, or at least give herself an easier evening, she could simply whip up these relatively effortless roasted parsnips as one of the vegetable offerings. They're so delicious that no one would know that she needed an easy dinner service.

YIELDS 4 SERVINGS

5 teaspoons extra-virgin olive oil

1 tablespoon lemon juice

Kosher salt and freshly ground black pepper to taste

2 pounds parsnips, peeled and cut into 2-inch slices

⅓ cup vegetable stock

½ cup unsalted butter, softened

4 teaspoons drained horseradish

1 tablespoon light brown sugar

2 teaspoons maple syrup

1 tablespoon finely chopped flat-leaf parsley

1 teaspoon chopped fresh rosemary

1 teaspoon chopped fresh thyme

1. Preheat oven to 400°F. Whisk together olive oil, lemon juice, salt, and pepper in a medium bowl. In a large yet shallow roasting pan, toss the parsnips with lemon and olive oil mixture. Add the broth, cover with aluminum foil, and roast, stirring once or twice, until the parsnips are tender and the stock has evaporated or been absorbed, about 20–45 minutes. Check often to avoid mushiness.

2. Combine the softened butter with the horseradish, brown sugar, maple syrup, parsley, rosemary, and thyme. Toss the warm parsnips with the herb butter and serve.

Suggested Pairings

Parsnips are a root vegetable closely related to the carrot. Though sweeter in taste, they can be cooked and used much like carrots. Thus, you could pair this dish with any entrée in need of a carrot-like side, whether it be the Classic Beef Wellington (see Chapter 4), Mrs. Patmore's Dropped Roasted Chicken (see Chapter 5), or any of the dishes enjoyed by the servants (see Part 2).

Ivy's Asparagus Feuillettés

Though Jimmy asks—with marked disdain—of Ivy's pastry, "Do they really like that stuff? Or do they just order it to show off?" just one bite of her amazing asparagus *feuillettés*, asparagus in a puff pastry shell, would show him how delicious her pastry dishes really are! And don't let the name of this dish name fool you—this is a very British dish. *Feuilletté* is simply "puff pastry" in French!

YIELDS 8 SERVINGS

1 puff pastry sheet, thawed
Flour, for dusting
8 fresh asparagus spears, trimmed to 3-inch lengths (just the tips, you may discard the bottoms)
1 large egg, beaten
4 ounces high-quality Brie, cut into 8 thick slices

1. Unfold the thawed pastry sheet and cut in half. Discard one half of the pastry. Lightly flour a clean working surface and roll out the remaining half with a floured rolling pin until it is about ¼ inch thick. Cut into 8 squares, 2–3 inches square (depending on your preference). Place 8 squares on a lightly dampened baking sheet and chill in refrigerator for 30 minutes.

2. Preheat oven to 400°F.

3. Bring a heavy pan of salted water to a boil. Add asparagus spears and cook for 3–5 minutes, or until tender. Drain asparagus, then bathe in an ice-water bath for 5–7 minutes, drain again, and let cool on a chilled plate.

4. Remove pastry squares from fridge. Brush top of surfaces with egg, being careful not to brush the sides. Lightly score the top of the pastry squares with a fork or knife in a crisscross pattern.

5. Place pastry on a medium-sized baking sheet and bake for 15 minutes or until crisp and golden brown. Cut each square in half and scrape out any excess soft dough. On one half of each of the squares, place a chunk of Brie topped with the asparagus spear. Asparagus will stick out. Use the other half of the square as the top, or as a box lid, to make a pastry case. Keep warm until ready to serve.

Suggested Pairings

Brits are quick to pronounce that they grow the best asparagus in the world. In fact, Ivy's Asparagus Feuillettés go especially well with the hollandaise sauce in the recipe for Asparagus with Hollandaise Sauce (see recipe in this chapter).

Chapter 7

THE FINISHING TOUCH: SWEETS AND DESSERTS

Nowadays, dessert brings connotations of decadent chocolate cakes, opulent ice-cream sundaes, and tangy tarts. But during the era of Downton Abbey, what we would consider dessert was most commonly called "pudding" or "afters." In fact, in England the "afters" would not be called "dessert" by the upper-middle and upper classes unless fruit was involved. Yet nothing unites the classes like a love for sugar—unless you sprinkle salt all over the Raspberry Meringue Pie like poor blind Mrs. Patmore! The dishes in this chapter, from Sir Anthony's beloved Apple Charlotte to the Vanilla Wafers with Double Chocolate Ice Cream to the ever-impressive Grand Gougères, will be admired and enjoyed by all, regardless of sex or salary.

Grand Gougères

A French, and according to Edwardian society thus fancy, dessert, this is a savory choux pastry (also known as French cheese puff) filled with upscale cheeses such as Gruyère or Comté that is an aristocratic response to more plebeian puff pastries such as Yorkshire Pudding (see Chapter 10). The Countess of Grantham would gladly offer this pastry at any cocktail or garden party.

ABOUT 30 GOUGÈRES (FRENCH CHEESE PUFFS)

¾ cup whole milk

1 stick unsalted butter, cut into tablespoons

1 pinch white sugar

1 teaspoon kosher salt

1 cup all-purpose flour

4 large eggs

¾ cup grated Gruyère cheese, plus some for topping

¼ cup grated Parmigiano-Reggiano cheese

1 pinch white pepper

1 pinch nutmeg

1. Preheat oven to 400°F. Line two large baking sheets with parchment paper.
2. Combine milk, butter, sugar, and salt in a medium-sized saucepan. Bring mixture to a boil, then add flour. Stir with a wooden spoon until dough forms, then lower heat and stir dough until it dries and pulls away from the pan, about 3–5 minutes.
3. Scrape dough into a medium-sized bowl and allow it to cool for 2 minutes. Beat eggs into dough one at a time, being careful to beat thoroughly after each addition. Add cheeses, a pinch of white pepper, and a pinch of nutmeg.
4. Transfer dough to a pastry bag with a ½-inch round tip and pipe tablespoon-sized mounds onto the baking sheet. Keep mounds at least 2 inches apart. Sprinkle with extra Gruyère and bake for 25 minutes or until puffy and golden brown. Serve hot.

TIMES GONE BY

While this dish might appear perfect for a tea party—it is, after all, a finger food—savory dishes were considered improper for a tea, where the food is required to be sweet unless it's a sandwich.

Vanilla Wafers with Double Chocolate Ice Cream

With the advent of *Service à la Russe*, ice cream and wafers became the standard nonfruit dessert, while a "hot sweet" dessert, otherwise known as a dessert served warm, was offered beforehand. Mrs. Patmore may have served this decadent dessert on those warmer nights, when tempers at dinner were really steaming up and in need of a good cooling down.

YIELDS 4–6 SERVINGS

For Wafers

½ cup unsalted butter, softened

1 cup white sugar

1 large egg

2 tablespoons bourbon vanilla extract

1⅓ cups all-purpose flour

¾ teaspoon baking powder

½ teaspoon kosher salt

For Ice Cream

3 egg yolks

⅔ cup white sugar

½ cup high-quality unsweetened cocoa powder

1 teaspoon kosher salt

1 teaspoon bourbon vanilla extract

2 cups heavy cream

⅔ cup half-and-half

⅓ cup high-quality semisweet chocolate chips

1. **For wafers:** Preheat oven to 350°F.
2. In a medium-sized mixing bowl, cream together butter and sugar. Gradually beat in egg and bourbon vanilla extract.
3. In another medium-sized bowl, combine flour, baking powder, and salt. Add to wet ingredients in small batches and mix well.
4. Drop by teaspoonfuls 2–3 inches apart on a greased baking sheet. Flatten cookie drops with the back of a spoon, then bake in preheated oven for 10–12 minutes until edges are golden brown. Remove to wire rack to cool.
5. **For ice cream:** In a small bowl, beat egg yolks for 2–3 minutes until they are light and fluffy. Set aside.
6. In a large bowl, mix together sugar, cocoa powder, salt, and bourbon vanilla extract. Pour in beaten egg yolks and thoroughly blend using an electric mixer. Add cream and half-and-half a little at a time, beating after each addition. Chill mixture in refrigerator for 2–3 hours.
7. While cream mixture chills in refrigerator, grate chocolate chips using a blender or food processor. Stir into cream mixture, then freeze mixture in the canister of an ice-cream maker according to manufacturer's instructions.

Etiquette Lessons

After dinner, the women at Downton Abbey and their guests would excuse themselves after the fruit course (or the last dessert course) and head to the drawing room. The men would stay in the dining room and have their coffee, Cognac, or liquor of choice.

Dark Desires Chocolate Cake

It's a well-known stereotype that women love to eat chocolate when under stress—and this cake fits the bill. Perhaps Lady Mary would indulge in this delicious chocolate cake while considering Matthew's first marriage proposal.

YIELDS 6–8 SERVINGS

For Cake

2 cups all-purpose flour

1½ cups white sugar

½ cup light brown sugar

1 cup fine-quality unsweetened cocoa powder, such as Scharffen Berger

2 teaspoons baking soda

1 teaspoon baking powder

½ teaspoon sea salt

2 eggs, room temperature

1 teaspoon Bourbon vanilla extract

1 cup cold-brewed coffee

1 cup buttermilk

½ cup vegetable oil

For Icing

2 cups (1-pound) butter (no substitutes), softened

9 cups confectioners' sugar

2½ cups fine-quality unsweetened cocoa powder

1 teaspoon Bourbon vanilla extract

1 cup whole milk

1. Preheat oven to 350°F. Grease and flour a 9×13-inch pan.
2. In a large bowl, sift together the flour, sugars, cocoa powder, baking soda, baking powder, and salt. Make a well in the center and pour in the eggs, vanilla, coffee, buttermilk, and oil. Mix with a wooden spoon until smooth; batter will be thin. Pour into prepared pan.
3. Bake for 35–40 minutes or until a toothpick inserted into the center of the cake comes out clean. Allow to cool in the pan for 45 minutes.
4. As cake cools, prepare the icing. In a stand mixer with a paddle attachment on medium speed, beat butter until smooth and creamy. Reduce speed to low and add confectioners' sugar, cocoa powder, and vanilla, scraping down sides of the bowl with a spatula as you go. Add milk as needed until frosting reaches preferred spreading consistency. (For thicker frosting, add less than a cup of milk. To thin out your frosting, add more milk.)
5. Once cake has thoroughly cooled, spread icing over the top.

TIMES GONE BY

When people think of chocolate and England, they often think of Cadbury chocolates. In 1905, Cadbury introduced its Dairy Milk bars to the world, which became its bestselling product by 1913. Many of the workers in the Cadbury factory would go on to join Matthew Crawley in fighting for their country during World War I.

The Dowager Countess's Dark Chocolate Truffles

If anyone really wanted to win the approval of the ever-opinionated Dowager Countess, they would simply have to bring her these chocolates—which only became readily available in Europe in 1902—as a peace offering. Perhaps the Countess of Grantham would bring these to the Dowager Countess in an attempt to sweeten her up to the idea of breaking the entail. Luckily for the Countess of Grantham, no sweets were needed!

YIELDS 60 TRUFFLES

1 (8-ounce) package cream cheese, softened
2 tablespoons heavy cream
2 cups confectioners' sugar
10 ounces dark chocolate, melted
10 ounces milk chocolate, melted
2 teaspoons vanilla

1. In a large bowl, beat cream cheese until smooth. Slowly beat in cream, followed by confectioners' sugar, until well-blended, then stir in dark and milk chocolates and vanilla until no streaks remain. Refrigerate mixture for 1 hour.
2. Line a large baking sheet with parchment paper. Using a melon-baller or your hands, shape chocolate into 1-inch balls. Refrigerate for another hour, then serve.

TIMES GONE BY

While the Dowager Countess might appreciate these truffles, she'd be even more impressed with truffles from Prestat, one of London's oldest and most prestigious chocolate retailers. Prestat was founded in 1902 by Frenchman Antoine Dufour, whose family, in 1895, created the chocolate truffle we all know and love.

Sir Anthony's Apple Charlotte

The Countess of Grantham requested that Mrs. Patmore bake this "new" dessert for Sir Anthony, but Mrs. Patmore, who was not fond of the recipe, requested that they stick to the original dessert, Raspberry Meringue Pie (see Chapter 7). Nonetheless, if Mrs. Patmore had given up her tart, raspberry-esque attitude and been more willing to try new recipes she'd have found this to be one fantastically sweet "ice-box cake."

YIELDS 5 SERVINGS

2 cups light brown sugar

2 tablespoons cinnamon

2 teaspoons nutmeg

1 teaspoon ground ginger

1 teaspoon allspice

5 large, tart apples, peeled, cored, sliced thin

1 tablespoon fresh lemon juice

1 tablespoon fresh orange juice

1 loaf French bread, shredded into crumbs, 1 cup reserved

½ cup cold butter, chopped

½ cup butter, melted

Butter, for topping

1. Preheat oven to 350°F.
2. In a medium-sized bowl, mix together brown sugar, cinnamon, nutmeg, ground ginger, and allspice. Reserve 1 cup of the mixture to be used for topping.
3. In a separate bowl, mix together apple slices, lemon juice, and orange juice.
4. Cover the bottom of a medium-sized dutch oven with bread crumbs and bits of the cold butter. Layer with sliced apples and brown-sugar mix, then with another few tabs of butter. Repeat until dutch oven is filled.
5. For the top layer, combine reserved bread crumbs and ½ cup melted butter. Top with more butter. Bake for 30 minutes or until golden brown.

TIMES GONE BY

Legend has it that this dessert, Apple Charlotte, was named for Queen Charlotte, wife of King George III. Others say this dessert is named for Tsar Nicholas I's wife, Charlotte of Prussia.

Traditional Bakewell Tart

This traditional tart would be made available not just to the aristocrats of Downton Abbey but to their servants as well, thanks to its nature as a traditional dessert served in many bakeries. It's possible that Mrs. Patmore would whip this up for Daisy to thank her for agreeing to marry poor William.

YIELDS 1 PIE, OR 6–8 SERVINGS

For Pastry
1 cup flour

⅓ cup ground almonds

¾ cup unsalted butter, diced

¼ cup sugar

1 large egg yolk

1 teaspoon almond extract

2 teaspoons cold water

1 large egg white

For Filling
4 tablespoons cherry, raspberry, or strawberry jam

1 cup unsalted butter, softened

1 cup sugar

3 large eggs, beaten, room temperature

1 large egg yolk

1 cup ground almonds

Zest of 1 clementine (small mandarin orange)

Zest of 1 lemon

2 tablespoons almond flakes

Confectioners' sugar, for garnish

Traditional Bakewell Tart

(continued)

1. In a large bowl, mix together flour, ground almonds, butter, and sugar. Blend until mixture resembles coarse bread crumbs. Mix in egg yolk, almond extract, and cold water, and blend until mixture just begins to come together.

2. Flatten dough into a large disc and cover with plastic wrap. Chill for no more than 1 hour. Remove from refrigerator and roll out pastry on a clean, lightly floured surface so it reaches about ⅛-inch thickness. Press down into a medium tart tin, and prick the base with a fork. Chill crust for 15 minutes.

3. Preheat oven to 350°F.

4. Cover chilled tart crust with parchment paper, then weigh down with pastry weights. Bake in preheated oven for 20 minutes or until the pastry reaches a pale, golden color. Remove pastry weights, lightly brush tart crust with egg white, then cook for another 3 minutes. Let cool slightly.

5. Spread jam in an even layer over tart crust.

6. Cream together butter and sugar, then gradually add the 3 beaten eggs and 1 egg yolk. Fold in ground almonds and zests of clementine and lemon. Carefully and evenly spoon mixture over the jam, creating an even layer.

Bake tart for another 15–20 minutes, then sprinkle with almond flakes and bake for an additional 20 minutes until the tart is both set and golden. Let cool to room temperature, then sprinkle with confectioners' sugar and serve.

TIMES GONE BY

Mrs. Patmore would appreciate the accident that brought about this tart. Legend has it that in the early 1800s the proprietress of an inn in the Derbyshire town of Bakewell left instructions for her cook to make a jam tart. The cook misunderstood the instructions, and voilà—the Bakewell Tart was created!

Decadent Chocolate Almond Cake with Sour Cream Icing

The rich dark chocolate and creamy, one-of-a-kind icing in this recipe are worthy of the lords and ladies of Downton Abbey. While later made famous by chef Julia Child, this cake was enjoyed in Europe—and made by chefs like Mrs. Patmore—for years before Mrs. Child came around.

YIELDS 6–8 SERVINGS

For Cake

4 ounces high-quality semisweet chocolate, melted

2 tablespoons ground coffee granules

1 stick unsalted butter, softened, cut into ½-inch cubes

1 cup granulated sugar

3 egg yolks

1 teaspoon bourbon vanilla extract

3 egg whites

1 teaspoon kosher salt

½ cup crushed almonds

½ teaspoon almond extract

½ cup cake flour, sifted

For Icing

8 ounces high-quality semisweet chocolate, chopped

1 teaspoon instant espresso powder

1¼ cups sour cream, room temperature

½ cup corn syrup

1 teaspoon kosher salt

1 teaspoon vanilla extract

Chopped almonds, as desired

Decadent Chocolate Almond Cake with Sour Cream Icing

(continued)

1. Preheat oven to 350°F. Butter and flour one 8-inch round baking pan.
2. Place chocolate and ground coffee in the top of a double boiler over low heat. Stir until chocolate is thoroughly melted, then remove from heat.
3. Cream together the butter and sugar for several minutes until they form a pale, fluffy mixture.
4. In a small bowl, beat together egg yolks with vanilla extract, then add to butter-sugar mixture and thoroughly combine.
5. In another small bowl, beat the egg whites and salt together until soft peaks are formed.
6. Pour the melted chocolate into the butter-sugar mixture and thoroughly mix. Then mix in almonds and almond extract. Immediately stir in a quarter of the egg-white mixture so as to lighten the cake. Then mix in the cake flour in small amounts, alternating with the rest of the egg whites.
7. Pour the batter into the cake pan, then bake in preheated oven for 25–30 minutes. Cake is done when it has puffed and a toothpick inserted around the circumference comes out clean while another stuck in the middle comes out slightly oily.
8. Allow cake to cool for 15 minutes. Loosen cake rim with a knife, then reverse onto a cooling rack. Allow to thoroughly cool for 1–2 hours, then ice with icing.
9. **To make icing:** Mix together the chocolate and espresso powder in the top of a double-boiler. Stir until chocolate is melted. Remove from heat and let chocolate cool until tepid.
10. In a medium-sized bowl, mix together the sour cream, corn syrup, salt, and vanilla extract. Slowly add chocolate and stir quickly until the mixture is uniform. Let cool in refrigerator until the frosting is a spreadable consistency, no more than 25 minutes. Spread over cake with a spatula, then decorate with a design of chopped almonds.

Etiquette Lessons

While nowadays a child can leave the dinner table by politely asking to be excused, during the era of *Downton Abbey* it was unacceptable that anyone would dare leave the table during a dinner. Until the meal was finished, it was required by etiquette that everyone stay seated, which meant that any bathroom runs would have to be taken care of before or after the meal.

Fancy French Meringues

These delicate delights would be offered before or with the fresh fruits served near the completion of a meal at Downton Abbey. Even those guests claiming to be full would find room for this fluffy treat.

YIELDS 3 DOZEN COOKIES

4 egg whites, room
   temperature
1 teaspoon vanilla extract
2½ cups confectioners'
   sugar

1. Preheat oven to 185°F. Cover a baking sheet with greased parchment paper.
2. In a metal bowl, whisk egg whites until foamy. Add vanilla extract and sprinkle in confectioners' sugar a little at a time, while continuing to whisk at medium speed. When the mixture becomes stiff and shiny (this may take up to 17 minutes depending on the temperature of your egg whites), stop mixing and transfer the mixture to a large pastry bag. Using a large star tip, pipe the meringue out of the pastry bag and onto the greased parchment paper.
3. Place meringues in oven and bake for 2½–3 hours, or until the meringues are dry and can be easily removed from the pan. Allow cookies to cool completely before storing in an airtight container.

TIMES GONE BY

While originally a Swiss dessert, these treats were quickly co-opted by French and English haute cuisine chefs. Celebrated French chef Marie-Antoine Carême introduced the idea of piping meringues through a pastry bag. Previously, they had been shaped with spoons.

Crêpes Française

This is the basic crêpe recipe that all other crêpes, such as Ethel's Crêpes Suzette found in this chapter), are based on. Before Mrs. Patmore would teach Daisy how to make fancier crêpe dishes, she would likely introduce Daisy to this one.

YIELDS 10–12 SERVINGS

1 cup all-purpose flour, sifted

3 tablespoons white sugar

1 teaspoon kosher salt

3 eggs, room temperature

2 cups whole milk

1½ teaspoons vanilla extract

2 tablespoons butter, melted

1. In a large bowl, stir together sifted flour, sugar, and salt.
2. In another bowl, whisk together eggs, milk, and vanilla extract until combined. Slowly add wet mixture to dry ingredients, beating until smooth. Stir in melted butter. Cover and chill mixture for 20–30 minutes.
3. Heat a 10- to 12-inch pan over high heat. Pour or scoop about 2–3 tablespoons of the batter onto the pan, swirling or tipping pan so batter completely covers the bottom. Brown for 2–3 minutes on one side, then 1–2 minutes on the other. Stack crêpes on top of one another on a serving plate; serve hot.

TIMES GONE BY

The well-educated Crawley sisters would know the translation for the two types of crêpes—*crêpes sucrées*, or sweet crêpes, and *crêpes salées*, or savory crepes. Most of what we consider dessert crêpes would be *crêpes sucrées*. Perhaps, if the sisters felt particularly foreigner-friendly, they would know that crêpes are traditionally served in France on Candlemas (February 2), also known as the Virgin Mary's Blessing Day or more recently as "Avec Crêpe Day." Tradition had it that if you could catch a crêpe with a frying pan after tossing it in the air, holding the pan with your left hand and a gold coin with your right hand, you would become wealthy sometime that year.

Mrs. Patmore's Extravagant Parisian Éclairs

The residents of Downton Abbey wouldn't have to travel to Paris for a taste of these delicious French pastries! Since French cuisine was en vogue, Mrs. Patmore would be sure to have a recipe ready in case any of the family developed a longing for a taste of France.

YIELDS 9 ÉCLAIRS

For Éclairs
½ cup unsalted butter

1 cup water

1 cup all-purpose flour

1 teaspoon kosher salt

4 eggs, room temperature

For Filling
1 (5-ounce) package instant vanilla pudding mix

2½ cups whole milk, cold

1 cup heavy cream

¼ cup confectioners' sugar

1 teaspoon bourbon vanilla extract

For Icing
4 ounces high-quality semisweet chocolate

2 tablespoons plus 2 teaspoons butter

1¼ cups confectioners' sugar

1 teaspoon bourbon vanilla extract

2 tablespoons whole milk

3 tablespoons hot water

Mrs. Patmore's Extravagant Parisian Éclairs

(continued)

1. Preheat oven to 425°F. Thoroughly grease a medium-sized cookie sheet.

2. In a medium-sized saucepan, combine butter and water. Stirring until butter melts completely, bring mixture to a boil. As mixture heats, whisk together flour and salt in a medium-sized bowl. Once boiling, reduce heat to low, then slowly pour in flour-salt mixture. Stir mixture vigorously until it begins to form a stiff ball. Remove mixture from heat. Add eggs one at a time, beating until thoroughly incorporated. Spoon dough onto a cookie sheet in 1½×4-inch strips.

3. After baking for 20 minutes in the preheated oven, reduce heat to 325°F and bake for an additional 20 minutes, or until a hollow sound is emitted when pastry is lightly tapped on bottom. Cool completely on a wire rack.

4. **While éclairs bake, make éclair filling:** Whisk together pudding mix and whole milk in a medium bowl. Using an electric mixer, beat cream in a separate bowl until soft peaks form. Stir in ¼ cup confectioners' sugar and 1 teaspoon vanilla, mixing until thoroughly incorporated. Finally, fold whipped cream and vanilla mixture into pudding.

5. Using a sharp knife, gently cut off tops of cooled pastry shells. Do not discard tops! Fill shells with pudding mix, then replace tops.

6. **For icing:** In a medium saucepan over low heat, melt chocolate and butter. Stir in 1¼ cups confectioners' sugar and 1 teaspoon vanilla extract. Stir in whole milk, then stir in hot water 1 tablespoon at a time until icing is smooth. Remove from heat and let cool a fair amount. Drizzle over filled éclairs, then refrigerate before serving.

TIMES GONE BY

While the Edwardian era was known for its extravagance, there was a noticeable reduction of such lavishness when King George V took the throne in 1911. His Coronation Banquet of fourteen courses was actually the last great traditional banquet to be offered in Buckingham Palace. After World War I, even President Wilson's visit garnered only ten courses.

Ethel's Crêpes Suzette

It's no wonder why impertinent maid Ethel requested that Mrs. Patmore save her one of these delicious French desserts: These crêpes, with a sauce of caramelized sugar with Grand Marnier or another orange liqueur, would tempt even the most humble of servants. Nonetheless, righteous Mrs. Patmore would rather feed these sweet crêpes to a dog than let Ethel think she warranted one of these treats.

YIELDS 4 SERVINGS

For Crêpes

1½ cups all-purpose flour

1 teaspoon kosher salt

3 eggs, room temperature

½ cup granulated white sugar

2 cups whole milk

1 tablespoon Grand Marnier (or other orange liqueur)

1½ teaspoons bourbon vanilla extract

1 tablespoon orange zest

½ cup clarified butter

For Sauce

1 cup fresh orange juice

½ cup unsalted butter, chopped into tablespoons

2 tablespoons granulated white sugar

2 tablespoons dark brown sugar

2½ teaspoons orange zest

2 tablespoons plus 1 teaspoon Grand Marnier (or other orange liqueur)

3 clementines or mandarin oranges, peeled and quartered

Vanilla ice cream, for garnish

Ethel's Crêpes Suzette

(continued)

1. **For crêpes:** In a medium-sized bowl, whisk together flour and kosher salt. In a large bowl, whisk together eggs and granulated sugar until pale, then whisk in 1½ cups of the whole milk, Grand Marnier, vanilla extract, and orange zest. Add to dry flour mixture, whisking constantly. If mixture feels too thick, add remaining ½ cup milk. Cover and refrigerate batter for 1 hour.

2. Heat an 8-inch skillet over medium heat, then cover the surface with clarified butter so the surface sizzles. Ladle some of the crêpe batter onto the pan and immediately swirl the pan to evenly distribute batter over the surface. Cook for no more than 60 seconds or until the batter is a light golden brown, then flip crêpe over and cook for an additional 20 seconds. Remove to a room-temperature plate and continue with rest of batter.

3. **For sauce:** In a large skillet over medium-high heat, bring the orange juice to a boil. Reduce to a simmer, then add butter, white sugar, brown sugar, and orange zest. Cook until the sugar mixture has slightly reduced, about 7–10 minutes. Remove from heat and add Grand Marnier and orange quarters. Set aside.

4. One at a time, gently place crêpe in the skillet holding orange sauce. Leave crêpe resting on orange sauce for 1 minute so it can absorb some of the juices. Using a narrow wooden or rubber spatula, remove crêpe to a warm serving plate. Repeat with other crêpes, then roll each crêpe into a cylinder and cover with orange sauce and orange sections. Serve with vanilla ice cream.

TIMES GONE BY

The ladies of Downton Abbey would have a great time disputing the origins of this dessert. Some claim this treat was created by accident by a fourteen-year-old assistant waiter at Monte-Carlo Café de Paris, which, in order to please the Prince of Wales, named the dish for the prince's companion, Princess Suzette. Others suggest that Crêpes Suzette were named for the respected French actress Suzanne Reichenberg, who worked under the name Suzette, and who served these crêpes, designed for her, on stage in her role as a maid performing in the Comédie-Française. Regardless of the Crêpe Suzette's true namesake, the Earl of Grantham's daughters will all agree that this is one superb dessert.

The English Trifle

Some would say that the characters in *Downton Abbey* have as many hidden layers as this dessert! A nonalcoholic version of the most famous of English desserts, this is a filling yet airy summer treat. While some may claim otherwise, Mrs. Patmore would know that true trifles, such as this one, do not contain jelly.

YIELDS 12–14 SERVINGS

4 cups fresh strawberries, sliced, plus more for garnish

1 cup sugar

1 (3.5-ounce) package cheesecake pudding mix

2 cups whole milk

2 (8- or 9-inch) white or vanilla cake layers, baked and cooled

2 cups fresh blueberries

2 cups fresh blackberries

1 cup heavy whipping cream

1 teaspoon vanilla extract

1. In a medium-sized bowl, mix sliced strawberries with sugar. Set aside.
2. In another bowl, combine cheesecake pudding mix with milk, stirring until smooth.
3. Cut baked cake layers into 1-inch cubes. Line the bottom of a large glass bowl with half of the cake cubes, followed by half of the sugared strawberries. Then top with half of the blueberries, followed by half of the blackberries. Spread half of the pudding over the fruit, then repeat layers in the same order: cake, strawberries, blueberries, blackberries, pudding. Refrigerate overnight.
4. Whip cream and vanilla extract together in a medium-sized bowl using a hand blender until cream forms stiff peaks. Spread over the trifle. Garnish with sliced strawberries.

Etiquette of Lessons

With the advent of *Service à la Russe*, table settings and table décor became all the more important as the cutlery was set out throughout the entire meal and not brought dish by dish. Maids would be trained and tested repeatedly on the placement of flatware, and they would be lectured heavily if a knife, for example, was not a proper ½ inch from the edge of the table. In fact, it was due to this new style of service that etiquette books—which explained the purpose of each utensil—first became popular, as did the idea of a different wine with each course.

Raspberry Meringue Pie

A twist on Mrs. Patmore's ill-fated raspberry meringues, this is a light and fluffy dessert with a nearly shortbread-like crust, sure to engage even the pickiest of eaters . . . just be sure to leave off the salt topping!

YIELDS 4–6 SERVINGS

For Crust

1 cup all-purpose flour
½ cup sugar
1 teaspoon baking powder
½ teaspoon kosher salt
3 tablespoons cold butter
1 egg, beaten
1 teaspoon vanilla extract
2 tablespoons whole milk

For Topping

2 egg whites, room
  temperature
½ cup sugar
2½ cups raspberries
Confectioners' sugar (if
  desired)

1. In a medium-sized bowl, combine flour, sugar, baking powder, and salt. Cut in butter, until it resembles bread crumbs.
2. In a small bowl, whisk together egg, vanilla extract, and whole milk. Stir into flour mixture (mixture will be sticky). Press dough into the bottom and sides of a greased 9-inch pie tin and set aside.
3. Preheat oven to 350°F.
4. For topping: In another medium-sized bowl, beat egg whites until soft peaks form. Depending on the temperature of the egg whites, this may take a while. Gradually beat in sugar, a tablespoon at a time, until stiff peaks form. Gently fold in raspberries, then spoon mixture over the crust. Place in preheated oven and bake for 30–35 minutes or until lightly browned. Cool before serving and dust with confectioners' sugar if desired.

TIMES GONE BY

Although *Downton Abbey* portrays the servants as all sleeping "downstairs," in real stately houses—such as Highclere Castle, where *Downton Abbey* is filmed—the maids would sleep in the high floors above everyone else. In the event of a fire, it was the maids who faced the most peril, as there weren't any fire escapes.

Sussex Pond Pudding

While perhaps too fattening for modern diets, this was once a traditional and popular dish during the 1700s and 1800s. This supremely succulent dessert was known as "pond pudding" for the pool of caramelized sauce that leaks out when it is cut. Mrs. Patmore would be a pro at baking this dish, as it would be a recipe passed down to her from her own parents and grandparents. No resident of Downton Abbey would turn down the opportunity to (ever-so-eloquently) dig into this syrupy sweet!

YIELDS 4–6 SERVINGS

2 cups all-purpose flour

2 teaspoons baking powder

½ cup shredded beef suet

¾ cup whole milk

¼ cup water

1½ cups unsalted butter, diced

2 cups dark brown sugar

3 small lemons

Confectioners' sugar, for garnish

Sussex Pond Pudding

(continued)

1. In a large bowl, whisk together flour and baking powder until thoroughly incorporated and there are no lumps. Mix in suet, milk, and water, stirring until the dough holds together without crumbling. Using ⅓ of the dough, shape into a small ball. Then shape the rest of the dough (⅔ of dough) into another, larger ball. Wrap both balls in plastic wrap. Refrigerate for at least 1 hour, preferably 2 hours.

2. Grease a large, ovenproof bowl with vegetable oil. On a clean, lightly floured surface, roll out the larger ball until it is no more than 12 inches in diameter and no less than 10 inches. Place dough in greased bowl, pressing against sides so dough fits snugly and forms a bowl. Place ¾ cup of the butter and 1 cup of the dark brown sugar in the dough-bowl.

3. Prick lemons all over with a fork. Be sure to prick lemons deep enough so juices can escape. Place pricked lemons on top of the butter and sugar, topping lemons with the rest of the butter and sugar.

4. On a floured surface, roll out smaller ball into a 6- or 7-inch circle. Place smaller circle on top of filling. Dampen the edges of two dough forms with water, then pinch the crust together to seal. Cover pastry with aluminum foil, being careful to leave room for pudding to expand. Hold in place with a kitchen string.

5. Place ovenproof bowl in an even larger pot. Add just enough water to come halfway up the side of the bowl, then cover and simmer over medium-low heat for 3–3½ hours. Carefully lift bowl from pot and allow to cool for 10–15 minutes, only then removing foil. Invert pudding onto a medium-sized platter lightly dusted with confectioners' sugar. To serve, spoon pudding into nice bowls—don't worry, lemons will be soft enough to pierce, and eat.

TIMES GONE BY

To make this dish into a Kentish Well Pudding, simply add ½ cup raisins or currants with the suet!

Dark Chocolate Bread Pudding with Salted Caramel Sauce

This exceptionally sugary chocolate dessert might not look fancy, but it's one of the most delicious Edwardian treats available. From the Earl of Grantham all the way down to Daisy, everyone at Downton Abbey would enjoy this dish. As it's not as beautiful as many of the desserts in Mrs. Patmore's canon, it is likely that this would be reserved for just the family when they have no guests.

YIELDS 8–10 SERVINGS

For Sauce
½ cup white sugar

½ cup brown sugar

¼ cup water

1 cup heavy cream

3½ tablespoons unsalted butter

1 teaspoon kosher salt

For Bread Pudding

1 pound French baguette bread, cubed

2¾ cups whole milk

½ cup heavy cream

½ cup coffee liqueur such as amaretto

1 cup white sugar

½ cup packed light brown sugar

¼ cup high-quality cocoa powder

1 teaspoon kosher salt

1 tablespoon vanilla extract

2 teaspoons almond extract

2 teaspoons cinnamon

6 eggs, lightly beaten

8 ounces high-quality semisweet chocolate, grated

2 ounces high-quality milk chocolate, grated

Dark Chocolate Bread Pudding with Salted Caramel Sauce

(continued)

1. **For sauce:** In a heavy-bottom saucepan over medium-low heat, combine white sugar, brown sugar, and water until sugar dissolves, stirring frequently. Then increase heat but stop stirring. Brush sides of pan to wash down any crystals. Boil until syrup reaches a dark amber color, about 5 minutes.

2. Remove sugar from heat, then whisk in heavy cream. Allow mixture to bubble. Stir in butter and salt. Transfer caramel to dish to cool.

3. **For pudding:** Preheat oven to 325°F.

4. Lightly grease a 9×13-inch baking dish, then place bread cubes in dish.

5. In a large bowl, mix together milk, cream, and coffee liqueur.

6. In another bowl, thoroughly whisk together white sugar, brown sugar, cocoa powder, and salt. Add wet mixture to dry mixture, mixing well.

7. In a small bowl, whisk together vanilla extract, almond extract, and cinnamon and add to the lightly beaten eggs. Combine the egg mixture and the milk and coffee liqueur mixture and mix well.

8. Add grated semisweet and milk chocolates into mixture, then pour over bread in the pan. Let mixture stand, stirring occasionally, for 30 minutes or until bread absorbs most of the milk mixture.

9. Place baking pan in preheated oven and bake for 1 hour or until a knife inserted in middle of pudding comes out clean. Serve warm with caramel sauce.

Times Gone By

Bread pudding was originally invented as a way to use up excess stale bread found in English pantries; after all, in the past it was inconceivable for most people to simply throw away food. If you want to make this bread pudding a little fancier, swap out those baguettes for some upscale Italian Panettone bread instead.

Nothing Makes You Hungrier Than Grief Apple Tart

After the funeral of the Earl of Grantham's original heir, Mrs. Patmore remarks to Daisy, "Nothing makes you hungrier than grief." While Daisy might doubt it, this sweet apple tart would lift anyone's spirits, even sour Lady Mary's.

YIELDS 8–10 SERVINGS

For Crust
1 cup all-purpose flour

1 teaspoon kosher salt

½ cup sugar

½ cup cold unsalted butter, cut into pieces

For Filling
1 (8-ounce) package cream cheese, room temperature

½ cup sugar

1 large egg, room temperature

1 tablespoon apple brandy

1 teaspoon bourbon vanilla extract

½ teaspoon almond extract

For Topping
¼ cup granulated white sugar

¼ cup brown sugar

1 teaspoon pumpkin pie spice

1 teaspoon ground cinnamon

4 large, tart apples, peeled and cut into ¼-inch slices

⅔ cup sliced almonds

¼ cup apricot jelly

Vanilla ice cream, for garnish

Nothing Makes You Hungrier Than Grief Apple Tart

(continued)

1. Preheat oven to 400°F. Make sure rack is in the middle of the oven. Grease a 9-inch springform pan.
2. **For crust:** In a large bowl, thoroughly blend together flour, salt, and sugar. Knead in butter until it resembles coarse bread crumbs. Pat the dough onto the bottom of the springform pan and up an inch on the sides. Cover with plastic wrap and chill in refrigerator for at least 30 minutes.
3. **For filling:** Beat cream cheese until it reaches a smooth consistency, then add sugar and mix thoroughly. Mix in the egg, apple brandy, vanilla extract, and almond extract. Fill chilled crust with filling, then return to refrigerator.
4. **For topping:** In a large bowl, blend together white and brown sugars, pumpkin pie spice, and cinnamon. Toss the sliced apples into the mixture and coat slices. Spoon the apple mixture over the cream-cheese filling, then sprinkle with almonds. Place the springform pan on a medium-sized baking sheet to catch drips.
5. Place apple pastry in preheated oven and bake for 30–35 minutes or until the crust is brown, the filling is close to being set, and the apples are tender when pierced with a knife. Remove from oven and cool on a wire rack. A short time before serving tart, warm apricot jelly, adding water if necessary for jelly to reach a liquid consistency. Brush apricot jelly onto the tart for a glistening shine, and serve with vanilla ice cream if desired.

Etiquette Lessons

Just as there was a strict ritual for dining etiquette, there was also a set of rules that all Edwardians had to follow to properly express their grief in the event of a death. After someone in the family died, it was expected that the family should send a death notice to all friends and relatives on nice paper bordered in black. Other than perhaps visiting some close relatives, the family would not be seen in public so as to properly respect their grief. In fact, the family would not organize the funeral themselves; a trusted male friend would organize it instead.

Mrs. Patmore's Christmas Pudding

This pudding didn't become a traditional Christmas dish until the Victorian era, when Prince Albert introduced it. The only difference between this traditional Christmas pudding and a Christmas cake is that this pudding contains a suet and is steamed rather than baked. During the *Downton Abbey* Christmas Special, note how much the upper crust enjoyed this treat, especially when it was flamed (another tradition, meant to represent the passion of Christ).

YIELDS 8–10 SERVINGS

1 pound mixed dried fruit (golden raisins, regular raisins, and currants)

1 ounce mixed candied peel, finely chopped

1 small apple, peeled and finely chopped

1 large orange, juiced and peel used for zest

½ lemon, juiced and peel used for zest

¼ cup brandy, plus extra for topping

2 ounces self-rising flour, sifted

2 teaspoons pumpkin pie spice

1 teaspoon cinnamon

4 ounces shredded suet

⅔ cup dark brown sugar

½ cup fresh bread crumbs

¼ cup ground almonds

½ cup chopped walnuts

2 large eggs

Mrs. Patmore's Christmas Pudding

(continued)

1. Lightly grease a 1.4-liter (1½-quart) pudding pan. Place the dried fruits, candied peel, apple, orange zest, and lemon zest in a large mixing bowl. Add the brandy and stir well. Cover the bowl with a clean tea towel and marinate overnight.

2. In another large mixing bowl, stir together the self-rising flour, pumpkin pie spice, and cinnamon. Add the suet, brown sugar, bread crumbs, almonds, and walnuts one ingredient at a time, mixing thoroughly after each addition. Add the marinated dried fruits and stir well.

3. In a small bowl, beat together the large eggs. Then stir into the dry ingredients. The mixture by now should have a fairly soft consistency.

4. Now each member of your family should drop in coins and take a turn stirring the pudding. (See following "Times Gone By.")

5. Using a wooden spoon, spoon the pudding into the pudding pan, pressing the mixture down with the back of the spoon. Cover with two layers of parchment paper, followed by a layer of aluminum foil. Tie with a string.

6. Place the pudding in a steamer over simmering water and steam the pudding for at least 7 hours. Make sure you check the water frequently so that it doesn't boil dry. The pudding should become a dark brown. This is a recipe for a dark, sticky, and dense pudding.

7. Remove the pudding from the steamer and let it cool completely. This may take a while. Remove aluminum foil and parchment paper, then prick the pudding with a skewer and pour in a little extra brandy. Cover with another set of parchment paper and tie again with string. Store until Christmas, then reheat. Note: The pudding should not be served immediately after baking. It needs to be stored to rest for at least 48 hours. Eating the pudding immediately will not only cause it to collapse but will stop the flavors from officially ripening.

TIMES GONE BY

Another tradition is to make this cake on the Sunday before Advent, also known as "Stir Up Sunday." Each member of the family is expected to take a turn stirring the pudding mixture and adding good-luck coins to the batter to be found on Christmas Day.

Upstairs Downstairs Christmas Plum Pudding

Plum pudding is a well-regarded Christmas tradition, one that both the downstairs and upstairs inhabitants of Downton Abbey would enjoy during the holiday season. Granted, the aristocrats upstairs would get to enjoy theirs first.

YIELDS 8 SERVINGS, OR 2 PUDDINGS

2 cups assorted raisins

3 cups brandy

1 cup assorted candied fruits

5 tablespoons cold unsalted butter, diced

2 cups day-old bread crumbs

1 cup blanched almond meal

½ cup dark brown sugar

3 tablespoons all-purpose flour

½ teaspoon lemon zest

1 teaspoon orange zest

2 teaspoons ground cinnamon

1 teaspoon allspice

½ teaspoon freshly ground nutmeg

1 large egg

2 teaspoons molasses

⅓ cup Guinness stout

¼ cup orange juice

1 teaspoon fresh lemon juice

Upstairs Downstairs Christmas Plum Pudding

(continued)

1. Soak raisins in brandy for at least 1 hour. Drain, reserving ½ cup brandy. Preheat oven to 450°F.

2. In a large bowl, mix together raisins, candied fruit, butter, bread crumbs, almond meal, brown sugar, flour, lemon zest, orange zest, cinnamon, allspice, and nutmeg.

3. In a separate bowl, mix together egg and molasses, then add reserved brandy, beer, orange juice, and lemon juice. Add combination to fruit mixture and mix until thoroughly moist. Split batter between two greased 3-inch-deep, ovenproof bowls, then cover with two sheets of waxed paper, then foil. Secure with twine, then put bowls on a rack in a deep pot. Add enough boiling water to pot to reach 2 inches up the sides of bowls. Cover pot and steam puddings in oven, replenishing water as necessary, for 4 hours.

4. Remove bowls from pot and let cool. Store puddings in a cool, dry spot for at least 1 week and for as long as 2 years. If storing for longer than 1 day, replace covers. Reheat puddings by steaming them, still covered, for 1 hour. Unmold onto plates.

TIMES GONE BY

Back in medieval times, the Roman Catholic Church decreed that "the pudding should be made on the twenty-fifth Sunday after Trinity, that it be prepared with thirteen ingredients to represent Christ and the twelve apostles, and that every family member stir it in turn from East to West to honor the Magi and their supposed journey in that direction." While this pudding recipe isn't quite as specific as that, it's likely that many of Downton Abbey's staff have family who would still follow these directions come Christmastime.

Bûche de Noël

Another holiday dessert, Bûche de Noël is a cake covered in frosting shaped to resemble a "yule log," a log burned as part of a traditional Christmas celebration. Whether French or British, rich or poor, all would enjoy this dessert come Christmastime—including both the staff and aristocrats at Downton Abbey. Though it is traditionally made with yellow cake, this recipe uses chocolate to give the cake an added richness.

YIELDS 10–12 SERVINGS, OR 1 LOG

For Cake

5 eggs, separated

1½ cups white sugar

½ cup cake flour

½ cup high-quality baking cocoa

½ teaspoon kosher salt

½ teaspoon cream of tartar

For Filling

1 cup whipping cream

1 teaspoon vanilla extract

½ cup confectioners' sugar

For Chocolate Buttercream Frosting

½ cup butter, softened

½ cup high-quality baking cocoa

2 cups confectioners' sugar, plus extra for garnish

2 teaspoons vanilla extract

2 tablespoons whole milk

Bûche de Noël

(continued)

1. Preheat oven to 350°F. Line a 10×15×1-inch baking pan with parchment paper, then grease the paper.
2. Place egg whites in a small bowl, then let stand at room temperature for ½ hour. Then in a large mixing bowl, beat egg yolks until they are light and fluffy. Mix in ½ cup of the white sugar, beating until thick and lemon-colored.
3. In a separate bowl, combine flour, cocoa, and salt. Gradually add to egg-yolk mixture until well blended.
4. Beat egg whites until foamy, add cream of tartar, and beat until soft peaks form. Gradually add remaining sugar, beating on high until stiff peaks form. Fold egg-white mixture into cocoa mixture until no streaks remain.
5. Pour mixture into the baking pan, then spread evenly. Bake in preheated oven for 15 minutes or until cake springs back when pressed. Cool for 5 minutes, then invert onto a linen towel dusted with confectioners' sugar. Peel off the parchment paper, then roll the cake in the towel, starting with the end. Cool on a wire rack.
6. In a medium mixing bowl, pour in cream and vanilla. Beat cream mixture until it begins to thicken, then add confectioners' sugar. Beat until stiff peaks form and chill.
7. Unroll cooled cake, and spread filling to within a ½ inch of the edges. Roll up again, then place on a serving platter and chill in refrigerator.
8. In a mixing bowl, beat together the frosting ingredients until smooth. Frost cake. Using a fork or knife, make lines resembling tree bark, and sprinkle with confectioners' sugar to resemble snow if desired.

TIMES GONE BY

While America had the fat and jolly Santa Claus to help celebrate Christmas, before the 1950s (and the influx of American influence) the celebrated Christmas icon in England was Father Christmas. Although Father Christmas was originally a religious figure, by the Victorian and Edwardian eras he was thought of as more of a jovial figure (like Santa), as a symbol of the goodwill of Christmas.

Festive Fruitcake

A traditional British holiday fruitcake is covered in marzipan and then royal icing. Oddly enough, in Yorkshire the fruitcake is served with cheese. Fruitcake is also used as the base of traditional English wedding cake, with the top layer called the "christening cake," which is meant to be saved for the christening of the couple's first child. Marriage or no marriage, this highly alcoholic dessert would be enjoyed by all at Downton Abbey.

YIELDS 6–8 SERVINGS

1 cup golden raisins
⅛ cup chopped dried cherries
¼ cup dried cranberries
½ cup dried blueberries
¼ cup chopped candied ginger
⅔ cup dark rum
1 cup butter
½ cup packed light brown sugar
¼ cup white sugar
1 egg, room temperature
1 teaspoon vanilla extract
½ cup all-purpose flour
⅛ teaspoon baking soda
1 teaspoon kosher salt
½ teaspoon ground cinnamon
¼ cup molasses
2 tablespoons whole milk
½ cup toasted pecans, broken

1. In a large bowl, soak raisins and other dried fruit with candied ginger in ½ cup of the dark rum for at least 24 hours, preferably longer. Cover tightly and store at room temperature.
2. Preheat oven to 350°F. Line a 6-inch round pan that is 3 inches deep with greased parchment paper.
3. In a large bowl, cream together butter, brown sugar, and white sugar until fluffy. Beat in egg and vanilla extract.
4. In a separate bowl, whisk together flour, baking soda, salt, and cinnamon. Mix into butter mixture in 3–4 batches, alternating with molasses and whole milk. Stir in soaked fruit and nuts. Pour batter into prepared pan.
5. Cook in preheated oven for 30–35 minutes or until a toothpick inserted comes out relatively clean. Cool in pan for 15 minutes, then sprinkle with 3–4 tablespoons of the rum.
6. Cut out 1 piece parchment paper and 1 piece cheesecloth, each large enough to wrap around top and bottom sides of cake. Arrange cheesecloth on top of parchment paper, and place cake on it. Spritz cake top and sides with remaining rum. Wrap cheesecloth close to the surface of the cake, then wrap with paper. Place in an airtight tin and age for at least 2½ months. If storing longer, spritz with additional rum every 6 weeks.

TIMES GONE BY

For a period of time in Victorian England, it was the custom for single wedding guests to put a slice of the wedding fruitcake under their pillows at night and then they would dream of the person they'd marry.

Upper-Class Fruit Salad

No Edwardian meal could end without a proper selection of sweets, especially fresh fruit. The fact that a house could serve fruit such as oranges would show great wealth, as citrus fruits were still a rarity in England during Edwardian times. It's likely that the Earl and Countess of Grantham would treat their esteemed guests to this fruit salad before retiring to their respective sitting rooms for coffee and conversation.

YIELDS 4 SERVINGS

4 fresh pears, cut into bite-sized pieces

4 peaches, cut into bite-sized pieces

4 oranges, peeled and cut into bite-sized pieces

½ cup raspberries

2 tablespoons lemon juice

¾ cup simple syrup (1 part sugar, 1 part water)

¼ cup lightly packed mint leaves

4 tablespoons rum

1 cup slivered almonds

1. Preheat oven to 350°F.
2. Stir together the diced fruit, raspberries, and lemon juice.
3. Purée together the simple syrup and mint until fully liquefied. Pour over fruit. Add rum, then stir to combine. Let stand at room temperature for 2 hours, stirring occasionally.
4. Spread slivered almonds on a rimmed baking sheet. Place in preheated oven for 5 minutes or until almonds are lightly toasted. Sprinkle almonds over fruit mixture before serving.

TIMES GONE BY

While French etiquette would insist that no salad, regardless of its ingredients, should be cut with a knife, the British felt themselves above such nitpickiness and would use knives freely to cut their fruit.

Mrs. Patmore's Fruit and Nut Gelatin Salad

Advances in refrigeration in the 1920s spurred the popularity of gelatin desserts, which could be kept cold until they needed to be served. This means that, while Mrs. Patmore spends a great deal of time fighting Lady Crawley on the issue of purchasing a refrigerator, there's no fighting progress, and whether she wants a fridge or not, Mrs. Patmore is going to end up with one!

YIELDS 6–8 SERVINGS

2½ cups crushed
   pineapple, with juice
1 (3-ounce) package orange
   Jell-O
1 (3-ounce) package cream
   cheese, softened
½ cup chopped pimiento
1 cup heavy cream,
   whipped
1 (11-ounce) can mandarin
   oranges, drained
1 cup diced celery
¾ cup chopped walnuts

1. In a medium-sized saucepan, heat pineapple and pineapple juice over medium heat until boiling. Stir in Jell-O until it dissolves. Remove from heat, and refrigerate for 30 minutes or until it starts to set.
2. In a medium bowl, mix together the softened cream cheese with the pimientos. Then stir in gelatin mixture until cream cheese and gelatin are thoroughly combined. Fold in whipped cream, mandarin orange slices, celery, and walnuts.
3. Pour mixture into a 1½-quart gelatin mold. Chill for 2 hours or until firm.

Etiquette Lessons

Various etiquette pamphlets from the 1920s warn men to never, ever, offer their arm to a lady who is not their immediate relative or wife. Hopefully Lady Mary remembers these guidelines when working with Charles Blake over the pigpen! Then again, these same guidelines claim men and women should never whisper together in public—a lesson *all* the Crawleys blatantly disregard!

Daisy's Mousse au Chocolat

Before the invention of the electric mixer—which made foaming egg whites much, much easier—mousse often held a more pudding-like consistency. As whipping egg whites by hand is not nearly as easy or efficient for most cooks, it makes sense that Daisy—and eventually the reluctant Mrs. Patmore—will quickly see the usefulness of this new tool.

YIELDS 6–8 SERVINGS

6 ounces high-quality bittersweet chocolate

¾ cup unsalted butter, cut into cubes

3 ounces espresso or dark coffee

4 large eggs, separated

⅔ cup plus 1 tablespoon sugar

1½ tablespoons dark rum

1 tablespoon water

1 teaspoon fine salt

1 teaspoon bourbon vanilla extract

Daisy's Mousse au Chocolat

(continued)

1. Fill a large metal bowl with ice water and set aside in fridge.
2. Fill a medium saucepan ¼ to ⅓ full of hot water, and place a bowl on top, creating a double boiler. Set heat to low, then melt together chocolate, butter, and espresso over barely simmering water. Stir until smooth. Remove chocolate from heat, but keep saucepan simmering.
3. In another large bowl that can both fit in the bowl of ice and rest comfortably on top of the saucepan used for double boiling, whisk egg yolks with ⅔ cup sugar, rum, and water using an electric mixer above the simmering water. Whisk for 3 minutes or until the mixture is thick and resembles mayonnaise.
4. Immediately remove whipped egg yolks from heat and place the bowl within the bowl of ice water. Beat until cool and thick, then fold in chocolate mixture.
5. In a separate bowl, beat egg whites and salt until frothy. Continue to beat, adding 1 tablespoon of sugar once they start to hold their shape. Once they are thick, but not stiff, add vanilla. Fold ⅓ of the egg whites into the chocolate mixture, followed by the rest until just incorporated. Do not overfold.
6. Transfer mousse to a serving bowl, then chill for 4–6 hours, or at least until firm. Do not skimp on chill time.

Etiquette Lessons

Prior to World War I, the idea that a man would wear a tux in place of tails was unspeakable. However, thanks to the rising popularity of jazz clubs and other venues with less stringent rules, tuxes increased in popularity. Indeed, manners guru Emily Post herself would concede in the mid-1920s that were a man only able to purchase either a tux or tails, he should go with the tux. Tails became increasingly "old-fashioned," and no one wanted to appear out-of-date!

Nellie Melba's Peach Melba

The Crawleys complete quite the coup when they tempt world-famous opera singer Nellie Melba to sing at Downton Abbey. The only thing sweeter—and more tempting!—than the Crawleys's triumph is this dessert that Chef Escoffier named after Melba! Maybe the Crawleys served this dish while Nellie sang for their guests?

YIELDS 6–8 SERVINGS

3 cups water

3½ cups sugar

Seeds of 1 vanilla bean

2 tablespoons fresh lemon juice

6–8 ripe peaches

3 cups fresh raspberries

½ cup confectioners' sugar

1 tablespoon freshly squeezed lemon juice

1 (half-gallon) tub high-quality vanilla ice cream

6 mint sprigs, for garnish

1. Place water, sugar, vanilla seeds, and fresh lemon juice in a large saucepan over low heat. Gently dissolve the sugar, bring mixture to a boil, let reduce for 5 minutes, then turn heat down to a simmer.
2. Cut the peaches in half and remove their stones. Poach peach halves in the vanilla sugar syrup for 3 minutes on each side. Once soft, move peach halves to a plate using a slotted spoon.
3. Peel the skins from poached peaches, then allow them to cool thoroughly. Once cool, pour remaining syrup over peaches and set aside.
4. Using a blender or food processor, thoroughly liquify raspberries, confectioners' sugar, and lemon juice. Pour sauce through a sieve until all seeds have been removed. Place sauce in small dish.
5. Place 2 peach halves on each plate, one plate per person. Place high-quality vanilla ice cream next to peaches on plate. Drizzle raspberry sauce over each. Garnish with mint sprigs.

TIMES GONE BY

According to legend, Nellie Melba sent Escoffier tickets to her performance in the opera *Lohengrin*. The opera featured a boat in the shape of a swan. After attending the opera, Escoffier presented Nellie with a dessert of fresh peaches over ice cream with ice carved into the shape of a swan atop it. This dish was called "Pecheau Cygne," a.k.a. "peach with a swan." When Escoffier opened The Ritz in London, he added the raspberry sauce component and renamed the dish "Pêche Melba," or Peach Melba.

Chapter 8

TEA AT DOWNTON ABBEY

Served between 3 and 5 P.M., "afternoon tea" was more of an elegant snack than an actual meal. Nonetheless, afternoon tea was not nearly as low-key as it sounds—at least not for the cook! The menu usually consisted of several kinds of tea, finger sandwiches, scones, pastries, fruitcakes, and perhaps a more elaborate layer cake served as the grand finale. If you were invited to a "high tea," you'd find more of a working-class meal, part of a homey, sit-down meal that included meat dishes and lots of bread and cheese.

Serving from a low side table with good china and silver, the Victorian and Edwardian hostess would offer tea in the drawing room, living room, or library, careful to pour the right tea for each guest. In addition, while the Dowager Countess of Grantham is known to just "show up" at the Crawley's or at Downton Abbey expecting tea, it is proper to give two weeks' notice so the host can prepare—and to show up for tea only when invited. While Henry James claims, "There are few hours in life more agreeable than the hours dedicated to the ceremony known as afternoon tea," those scheming over the tea service might find the tea anything but agreeable. After all, it was over tea that the Countess of Grantham and the Dowager Countess schemed to return the entail to Mary, and it's over tea when many a marriage is proposed—and denied.

Mrs. Isobel Crawley's Smoked Salmon Tea Sandwiches

This is a tea sandwich that even Mrs. Isobel Crawley's cook would be able to prepare for last-minute tea visits from the nosey Dowager Countess. Whether or not their conversation would be as enjoyable as these sandwiches is another question.

YIELDS 3 DOZEN SANDWICHES

1 pound unsalted butter, room temperature

1½ tablespoons minced chives

1½ tablespoons finely chopped fresh dill

1 teaspoon minced garlic

2 teaspoons fresh lemon juice

2 teaspoons sea salt

½ teaspoon freshly ground black pepper

1½ loaves grain bread, sliced ¼-inch thick

1½ pounds smoked salmon, thinly sliced

1. In a medium-sized bowl, combine butter, chives, dill, garlic, lemon juice, sea salt, and pepper. Beat until mixed, but do not whip.
2. Lay out bread slices, then spread with butter mixture. Top half of bread slices with smoked salmon. Lay remaining bread slices buttered-side down on top of the salmon slices. Place sandwiches on a large baking sheet, then cover with plastic wrap, and place in refrigerator until butter is cold, about 35 minutes.
3. Transfer sandwiches to a cutting board. Remove crusts, then cut diagonally, twice, to make small triangle sandwiches. Serve chilled.

Etiquette Lessons

Just as there is an etiquette to serving tea, there's even an etiquette for making the food served at said tea! For instance, a true tea sandwich has the crusts removed only after the sandwich has been prepared and not before.

Classic Cucumber Sandwich

No tea party is complete without this classic finger food. If the Countess of Grantham had tea without this delicacy, she would likely raise many an eyebrow—especially one belonging to her mother-in-law. However, if the Crawleys realized just how common the ingredients were, they might not feel so pleased with these treats.

**YIELDS 10–12
SANDWICHES**

1 (8-ounce) package cream
  cheese, softened
⅓ cup mayonnaise
1 medium cucumber,
  peeled, seeded, and finely
  chopped
¼ teaspoon garlic salt
½ teaspoon white pepper
1 tablespoon chopped
  fresh dill
24 slices white bread
12 sprigs dill, for garnish

1. Blend cream cheese and mayonnaise in a blender until smooth, scraping down sides and blending thoroughly.
2. Combine cream cheese mixture with cucumber, garlic salt, white pepper, and chopped dill. Spread mixture on top of 12 white bread slices, and garnish with dill sprigs. Cover with other bread slices to form sandwiches. Cut and discard crusts from bread, then cut sandwiches into quarters.

TIMES GONE BY

Legend has it that one of Queen Victoria's ladies-in-waiting is the creator of afternoon tea. Knowing the Queen felt hungry around 4 P.M. and perhaps fretted before dinner, her lady-in-waiting started the trend of serving tea with a few breadstuffs. Soon, tea time had taken hold of England.

Classic Egg Salad Tea Sandwiches

No tea at Downton Abbey would be complete without these delicious tea sandwiches. One can just imagine the Dowager Countess nibbling on these sandwiches while plotting with Lady Grantham.

YIELDS 10–12
FINGER SANDWICHES

6 large eggs
4 tablespoons mayonnaise
1 tablespoon mustard
⅛ teaspoon cayenne
   pepper
1 teaspoon kosher salt
20 slices soft white bread

1. For bright yellow egg yolks, place eggs in a large saucepan and cover with water. Bring to a rolling boil over high heat, then reduce heat to a medium boil for an additional 10 minutes. Immediately place eggs in ice water and chill for 10 minutes.
2. Once chilled, remove eggshells and cut eggs into cubes.
3. In a medium-sized bowl, mix together cubed eggs, mayonnaise, mustard, cayenne pepper, and salt.
4. Spread egg salad over 10 slices white bread. Cover with bread. Remove crusts. Place sandwiches on a large baking sheet and cover in plastic wrap. Chill in refrigerator for 35 minutes. Use a cookie cutter to cut out shapes, or use a knife to quarter sandwiches diagonally.

Etiquette Lessons

A courteous hostess would never ask her guests if they wanted another cup of tea. Instead, she would refill the guests' cups until they told her they had had enough. Leaving a cup empty without being told that the guest had finished was the height of poor taste.

Sweet Cream Scones

While scones were originally oat-based, round, and flat—and about the size of a plate—the scones we have come to know and love became available with the advent of baking powder. This is exactly the type of scone the ladies of Downton Abbey would enjoy, as it is not too sweet and has the right texture for nibbling—perhaps with some Clotted Cream (see recipe in this chapter).

YIELDS 1 DOZEN SCONES

1 cup sour cream

1 teaspoon vanilla extract

1 teaspoon baking soda

4 cups all-purpose flour

1½ cups sugar

2 teaspoons baking powder

¼ teaspoon cream of tartar

1 teaspoon kosher salt

1 cup unsalted butter, room temperature, cut into pieces

1 egg, at room temperature

Heavy cream, for brushing

Granulated sugar, for sprinkling

1. Blend sour cream, vanilla extract, and baking soda together in a small bowl. Set aside.
2. Preheat oven to 350°F. Grease a large baking sheet.
3. In a large bowl, blend together flour, sugar, baking powder, cream of tartar, and salt. Cut in butter until mixture resembles coarse bread crumbs. Stir in sour-cream mixture and egg until just barely moistened.
4. Turn dough out onto a lightly floured surface, kneading briefly. Pat dough out into a ¾-inch-thick round. Cut into 12 wedges and place them 2–3 inches apart on the greased baking sheet. Lightly brush with cream, then sprinkle with granulated sugar.
5. Bake 12–15 minutes or until golden brown on the bottom.

TIMES GONE BY

There's a bit of debate about the origins of the word *scone*. Some historians say it hails from the Dutch word *schoonbrot*, which roughly translates to "beautiful bread," while others argue its origins can be found in the Stone of Destiny, where the Kings of Scotland were crowned. All we know for sure is that scones were invented in the early 1500s, with the first printed mention of the word being found in 1513; most sources also believe scones were invented in Scotland. Hundreds of years later, the scone is still a much-requested treat.

Mixed Berry Scones

Another take on the Sweet Cream Scones (see recipe in this chapter), this dish would be a favorite of Countess Cora's to offer to her younger guests with their tea. While visitors such as the Dowager Countess might prefer less flavorful options, these scones would give a needed variety—not to mention flavor—to a meal that most of Cora's guests would have experienced on a daily basis.

MAKES 10–12 SCONES

3 cups all-purpose flour

½ cup white sugar

¼ cup turbinado sugar

½ teaspoon baking soda

2½ teaspoons baking powder

1 teaspoon kosher salt

¾ cup (1½ sticks) unsalted butter, cut into ¼- to ½-inch pieces

½ cup fresh blueberries

½ cup fresh blackberries

½ cup fresh raspberries

½ cup hulled and quartered fresh strawberries

1¼ cups buttermilk

1½ teaspoons vanilla extract

½ cup heavy cream, for brushing

½ cup sugar, for sprinkling

Mixed Berry Scones

(continued)

1. Preheat oven to 375°F. Lightly oil a baking sheet.
2. In a large bowl and using a wooden spoon, mix together the flour, both sugars, baking soda, baking powder, and salt.
3. Using your bare hands, work the butter into the flour mixture until it has the consistency of bread crumbs. Add berries, mixing well, so that the berries are evenly distributed.
4. In a small bowl, mix together the buttermilk and vanilla extract with a fork.
5. Once again using your hands, dig a well in the center of the dry mixture and pour the buttermilk mixture into the well. Still using your hands, combine the ingredients until the entire mixture appears wet. Do not overknead.
6. Turn the mixture out onto a lightly floured surface. Gently pat down the dough to make a disc about 1½–2 inches thick. Using a biscuit cutter (or a knife if you don't have a biscuit cutter), cut out as many scones as possible and lay them on the baking sheet. Gather together the remaining dough to cut out more scones . . . but once again, don't knead the dough too much.
7. Liberally brush heavy cream over the top of each scone, then sprinkle them with sugar. Bake the scones for 10–12 minutes or until they are lightly browned.

Etiquette Lessons

Contrary to popular belief, a lady should *never* hold her teacup with her pinkie finger extended. Instead, a woman should place her index finger into the handle of the cup up to the knuckle while placing her thumb on the top of the handle to secure the cup. The bottom of the handle should then rest on her middle finger. The third and fourth fingers should curve back toward the wrist.

Clotted Cream

All British chefs worth their salt know how to make this classic accompaniment for scones, crêpes, and even toast. Clotted cream is an integral part of cream tea, where tea is served with clotted cream, jam, and scones. Most teas offered by the ladies of Downton Abbey are cream teas, and thus Mrs. Patmore would be quite skilled at making—and storing— clotted cream.

YIELDS 4 CUPS

4 cups heavy whipping
   cream

1. Preheat oven to 180°F.
2. Pour the cream into an ovensafe pot or dutch oven. The cream should come up to about 3 inches. Cover the pot, then place in the oven for at least 6 hours. The cream will be done when there is a thick, yellowish skin on top.
3. Let the cream cool to room temperature, then put the pot in the refrigerator for 8–12 hours. Remove clotted cream from the top of the pot and serve cold.

TIMES GONE BY

Even though menus were extravagant at Downton Abbey, Mrs. Patmore still wouldn't want to waste a thing. She'd likely save the cream that remained in the pot once the clotted cream was scooped out and use it in another recipe for either the aristocrats or the staff.

Mrs. Patmore's Madeira Pound Cake

This British cake would be served with great aplomb by Mrs. Patmore, on an elegant platter, perhaps with sliced strawberries and confectioners' sugar. Moist yet firm, this Madeira pound cake would be quickly gobbled up by even the most delicate of ladies.

YIELDS 10–12 SERVINGS

3 cups sifted cake flour, plus more for dusting

1 teaspoon kosher salt

1 teaspoon cardamom

1 cup unsalted butter, softened

2¾ cups sugar

7 large eggs, room temperature

3 teaspoons vanilla paste (bourbon vanilla extract acceptable)

1½ teaspoons fresh lemon juice

1 cup heavy cream

1. Thoroughly grease a 10-inch bundt pan and lightly dust with flour.
2. In a medium-sized bowl, sift together flour, salt, and cardamom.
3. In a large bowl, beat together butter and sugar until pale and fluffy, about 5–10 minutes. Add eggs one at a time, thoroughly beating between each addition, then mix in vanilla paste and lemon juice.
4. Still stirring/beating the mixture, mix in 1½ cups of the cake flour, followed by all of the cream, then the rest of the cake flour. Scrape down sides of bowl and continue beating until batter becomes creamy and smooth.
5. Slowly spoon batter into greased pan, rapping on edges to eliminate air bubbles. Place pan in cold oven and only then turn oven temperature up to 350°F. Bake until golden brown and a toothpick inserted in the middle of the cake comes out with only a few crumbs, about 1–1¼ hours. Cool cake in pan on a rack for 25–30 minutes, then run a knife around outer edges of cake. Then invert rack over pan and invert cake onto rack to cool completely.

TIMES GONE BY

Madeira pound cake originated in the eighteenth century and was named for the Madeira wine that was popular at the time. We all know the Crawleys don't need an excuse to open up a bottle of wine! Perhaps they'd ask for this cake for a late-night drinking snack.

British Battenberg Cake

Created in honor of the marriage of Queen Victoria's granddaughter to Prince Louis of Battenberg, Battenberg Cake is a classic dish to serve at tea time. Perhaps the Countess of Grantham would mention this when serving her tea guests, who would undoubtedly love this light, yet luscious sponge cake.

YIELDS 10–12 SERVINGS, OR 2 CAKES

For Cake

1 cup unsalted butter, softened

1½ cups sugar

3 eggs, room temperature

1 teaspoon vanilla extract

½ teaspoon almond extract

2 cups all-purpose flour

1 teaspoon baking powder

1 teaspoon kosher salt

⅛ cup whole milk

4 drops red food coloring

1 cup apricot jam

For Almond Paste

2 cups ground almonds

3 cups confectioners' sugar

1 egg, room temperature

1 teaspoon fresh lemon juice

1½ teaspoons almond extract

British Battenberg Cake

(continued)

1. Preheat oven to 350°F. Grease two 8-inch square baking pans.
2. In a large bowl, cream together butter and sugar. In a small bowl, whisk together eggs, vanilla extract, and almond extract, then slowly add to butter mixture followed by flour, baking powder, and salt. Finally, stir in milk.
3. Divide batter in half. Add red food coloring to one batch, turning dough to a dark pink or even red if desired. Evenly spread red batter into one greased pan and spread pale batter into the other greased pan.
4. Place pans in a preheated oven and bake for 25–30 minutes or until a toothpick inserted into cakes comes out clean. Let cool in pans for 10 minutes, then fully cool on cooling racks.
5. Trim off edges from both cakes, then cut cakes into four long strips about 2 inches wide. Trim cake strips so they all are of equal length.
6. In a small saucepan, heat jam slightly. Spread on sides of cake strips to glue two pink and two white strips together to form a checkerboard effect. Spread all four sides of completed cake with jam, then repeat with remaining pink and white strips for the second cake.
7. Meanwhile, for almond paste: mix together ground almonds, sugar, egg, lemon juice, and almond extract. Knead until smooth. If paste feels too dry to roll, add a little bit more lemon juice. But do not be surprised if it is stiff—this *should* be stiff. Divide into two equal parts.
8. On a clean surface lightly dusted with confectioners' sugar, roll half of the almond paste to ⅙- to ⅛-inch thick. Cut almond paste to fit around first cake, making sure it's long enough to cover all four sides. Lay cake on one end of paste, wrapping to completely enclose all four sides. Wet fingertips and pinch paste to seal. Serve or store in airtight container. Repeat for second cake.

Etiquette Lessons

As with most things in Edwardian England, there was an etiquette that informed the order in which to eat the delicacies put out for afternoon tea. First, one enjoyed the savory items, followed by the scones, and then the sweets. When it came to tea, one first poured in sugar, followed by lemon, and then milk. One never put in milk before the sugar, or put the lemon and milk in together.

O'Brien's Crumpets

Even spiteful O'Brien wouldn't turn down a chance to taste these delicious crumpets, a staple of the English diet. Most would cover these crumpets with jam, butter, or even Sweet Lemon Curd (see recipe in this chapter) for a more decadent bite.

YIELDS 8–10 CRUMPETS

3 teaspoons active dry yeast

½ cup warm water (between 105°F and 115°F)

2½ teaspoons sugar

⅔ cup warm whole milk

1 teaspoon honey

¼ cup unsalted butter, melted, divided

2 eggs

2 cups all-purpose flour

1 teaspoon kosher salt

1. In a medium mixing bowl, dissolve yeast in warm water. Add sugar and let mixture stand for 5 minutes. Add milk, honey, 2 tablespoons of the butter, and the eggs, mixing well. Add flour and salt, kneading with hands until smooth. Cover with a warm, moist towel and let rise in a warm place until doubled, about 45 minutes–1 hour.

2. After an additional hour, knead gently and let rise for another hour.

3. Thoroughly grease a cast-iron skillet and 3-inch metal rings (such as cookie or pastry cutters) with remaining butter. Heat over very low heat. Pour 3 tablespoons of batter into each ring. Cook for 10–15 minutes or until bubbles begin to pop and top appears dry. Remove rings, then turn over crumpets and cook for an additional 3–4 minutes or until the second side is brown (this will take less time if you aren't using extremely low heat). Serve warm.

TIMES GONE BY

While not all of the working class could afford Mixed Berry Scones or Sweet Cream Scones (see recipes in this chapter), these crumpets would be an affordable and excellent side for any tea, especially if they were topped with honey. The popular British food spread Vegemite would be another spread option as well, although Vegemite wasn't invented until World War I when Marmite production was interrupted and Vegemite took its place.

Sweet Brown Sugar Shortbread

While this delicious snack hails from Scotland, it became a popular and traditional tea treat in Britain that all of the Crawley sisters would agree is delicious. Perhaps they'd agree to go down to tea simply to taste this fabulous dessert!

MAKES 24 SQUARES

½ cup unsalted butter, softened

2 cups firmly packed dark brown sugar

3 eggs, room temperature

1½ cups all-purpose flour

1 teaspoon baking powder

¼ teaspoon kosher salt

2 teaspoons vanilla extract

1 teaspoon orange juice

1. Preheat the oven to 350°F. Lightly grease a 9×13-inch baking pan with vegetable oil and set aside.
2. Using an electric mixer, cream butter and brown sugar together in a large bowl until fully combined, at least 5 minutes. Add one egg at a time and continue to mix until light and fluffy.
3. Sift together flour, baking powder, and salt. Add dry mixture to the creamed mixture and, using the electric mixer, mix until smooth. Blend in the vanilla and orange juice, mixing thoroughly.
4. Slowly pour batter into greased pan, spreading mixture evenly. Bake in preheated oven for 30 minutes or until golden brown.
5. Let shortbread cool for at least 15 minutes, then cut into squares.

TIMES GONE BY

While shortbread was around as early as the twelfth century, Mary, Queen of Scots, is thought to be responsible for the refinement and subsequent popularity of this tea-time favorite.

Classic Custard Creams

This is a classic biscuit that all of the Earl of Grantham's daughters would enjoy, with or without a cup of tea or their usual bickering. It's easy to imagine Lady Sybil nibbling on these while Lady Mary and Lady Edith squabble after Lady Mary ruins her possible engagement out of spite. Not even this sweet dish could sweeten up those girls and stop the bickering!

YIELDS 1 DOZEN COOKIES

For Cookies
1 cup unsalted butter, softened

1 teaspoon almond extract

½ cup sugar

1 cup plus 3 tablespoons all-purpose flour

½ cup custard powder*

For Cream Filling
½ cup unsalted butter, softened

2 teaspoons vanilla extract

1 tablespoon whipping cream

2½ cups confectioners' sugar

*Custard powder is popular in Britain, but it's likely that American cooks will have to special-order custard powder; it is not found in the average American supermarket.

Classic Custard Creams

(continued)

1. Preheat oven to 350°F. Grease a medium-sized baking sheet and set aside.
2. Cream together butter, almond extract, and sugar until light and fluffy.
3. In a medium-sized bowl, sift together flour and custard powder, then slowly mix into butter-sugar mixture to form a malleable dough. Roll dough into small balls and place on greased baking sheet about 1 inch apart. With a fork, press down lightly on balls to make an impression.
4. Bake balls for 10–12 minutes until set, but do not let brown. Let cool for 7–10 minutes on cookie sheet, then move to rack to cool completely while you make cream filling.
5. **For cream filling:** Cream butter until smooth. Mix together vanilla extract and whipping cream, then add to creamed butter. Slowly mix in confectioners' sugar, being careful to avoid lumps. Beat with a mixer until smooth.
6. Form sandwiches with cookies, putting cream in the middle. Let cookies set for 2 hours before serving.

Etiquette Lessons

In Edwardian times, the drinking and enjoying of tea and its accoutrements—such as this biscuit—was a noiseless affair. Stirring a cup of tea was to be done quietly by moving the teaspoon in a small arc back and forth. To let the teaspoon touch the side or rim of the cup was considered rude, as was drinking from a teacup with the spoon inside it. Instead, the spoon should be placed on its saucer with the end pointing in the same direction as the handle of its cup. Remember that the saucer shouldn't be left behind on the table. Rather, when you take a sip of tea, the saucer comes with you. Do not, by any means, cradle the teacup if there is a handle.

Chocolate Digestive Biscuits

In the United Kingdom, as well as in Greece and Ireland, digestive biscuits were thought to aid in digestion. It was believed that the sodium bicarbonate (baking soda) in these cookies —known as "digestives"—helped the digestive system. It is likely that many of the family members in *Downton Abbey* would have digestive biscuits, both with and without chocolate, lying around their room for times when they were feeling queasy. Considering the heaviness of their meals, the need for such biscuits would be quite great!

**YIELDS 1
DOZEN COOKIES**

¾ cup whole-wheat flour
¼ cup all-purpose flour
1 teaspoon kosher salt
½ teaspoon baking powder
1 tablespoon rolled oats
4 tablespoons unsalted
  butter
6 tablespoons brown sugar
4 tablespoons whole milk
6 ounces high-quality
  bittersweet chocolate,
  melted

1. Preheat oven to 350°F. Grease medium to large baking sheets.
2. Sift together whole-wheat flour, all-purpose flour, salt, and baking powder in a large bowl, then mix in oats. Set aside.
3. In a medium-sized bowl, cream together butter and brown sugar. Add to dry mixture, then stir in milk until mixture forms a thick (and quite sticky) paste. Cover and chill in refrigerator for 1 hour.
4. Knead dough on a lightly floured surface until smooth. Dough will be sticky; wet your hands to combat stickiness. Roll out dough to approximately ⅛-inch thickness. Using a biscuit or cookie cutter, cut into 2- to 2½-inch rounds. Transfer to cookie sheets, impressing patterns on biscuits with a fork.
5. Bake cookies for 20–25 minutes or until golden brown. Let cool on a wire rack before coating with melted chocolate, then let cool again. Store in an airtight container.

TIMES GONE BY

The British enjoy their digestives with coffee or tea, often dunking their cookies directly into their beverages. It is said that Alexander Grant, an employee of McVitie's Biscuits in Scotland, developed the digestive biscuit in the nineteenth century, with the first advertisement for this particular type of biscuits run by the British company Huntley & Palmers in 1876.

Sybil's Ginger Biscuits

With or without prompting, it's no wonder Daisy takes up the chance to nibble on some of these sweet biscuits—much to the consternation of Mr. Carson. The sweet scent of ginger and golden syrup (a popular sweetener in the United Kingdom) would lure even the most well-behaved of ladies.

YIELDS 4
DOZEN COOKIES

1 cup unsalted butter,
    room temperature
1½ cups sugar
½ teaspoon vanilla extract
1 cup golden syrup
3 cups all-purpose flour
½ teaspoon kosher salt
1 heaping tablespoon
    ground ginger
1 teaspoon baking soda

1. Preheat oven to 350°F. Thoroughly grease a baking sheet.
2. In a large bowl, cream together the butter and sugar. Slowly mix in vanilla extract and golden syrup.
3. In another bowl, whisk together the flour, salt, ground ginger, and baking soda. Slowly add to wet ingredients and thoroughly mix together. Roll dough into small balls, then place balls on greased baking sheet. With the back of a spoon, gently press balls down.
4. Bake biscuits in preheated oven for 15 minutes. Cool on a wire rack to room temperature, then store in an airtight container.

TIMES GONE BY

What the British call biscuits Americans know as cookies or crackers. Other than Sybil's Ginger Biscuits, other famous biscuits that date back to the Victorian and Edwardian eras include the Chocolate Digestive Biscuits and Classic Custard Creams (see recipes in this chapter). All of these were invented as a means to have delicious snacks that could last during long voyages or for long periods of time.

Dainty Petits Fours with Buttercream Fondant

Also known as Fondant Fancies or French Fancies, these fancy confections would be served at the end of dinner or with coffee and tea. All the women of *Downton Abbey* would want to offer this rather beautiful treat with their tea service.

YIELDS 30 PETITS FOURS

For Cake
¼ cup unsalted butter
¼ cup shortening
1½ cups sugar
2 teaspoons vanilla extract
1⅓ cups all-purpose flour
2 teaspoons baking powder
1 teaspoon kosher salt
⅔ cup whole milk
3 large egg whites, room temperature

For Glaze
2 pounds confectioners' sugar
⅔ cup plus 2 tablespoons water
2 teaspoons orange extract
1 teaspoon almond extract

For Fondant
1 cup light corn syrup
1 cup shortening
1 teaspoon kosher salt
2 teaspoons clear vanilla extract
2 pounds confectioners' sugar

Dainty Petits Fours with Buttercream Fondant

(continued)

1. Preheat oven to 350°F.
2. **For cake:** In a large bowl, cream together the butter, shortening, and sugar until light and fluffy. Then beat in vanilla extract.
3. In a separate bowl, mix together flour, baking powder, and salt. Add to creamed mixture alternately with milk. Be sure to beat well after each addition.
4. In a small bowl, beat egg whites until soft peaks form, then add to batter.
5. Pour mixture into a well-greased and lightly floured 9-inch baking pan. Bake in preheated oven for 20 minutes or until toothpick inserted in center comes out clean. Cool for 10 minutes before moving cake to wire rack to cool completely.
6. Cut a thin slice off each side of the cake, then cut cake into 1-inch squares. Place squares ½ inch apart on a large baking sheet.
7. **For glaze:** In a large bowl, combine 2 pounds confectioners' sugar, water, and orange and almond extracts. Beat until well blended, then apply glaze evenly over tops and sides of cake squares. Let dry. Repeat if necessarily to thoroughly coat squares. Make sure glaze dries completely.

8. **For fondant:** In another large bowl, mix together corn syrup and shortening. Mix in salt and vanilla, then gradually mix in confectioners' sugar and knead by hand until it forms a stiff dough. If dough is sticky, add more confectioners' sugar until smooth.
9. Roll out dough on a clean surface that has been dusted with confectioners' sugar. Roll dough until it is no thicker than ⅛ inch. Cut fondant to fit over cakes, and smooth fondant down over the sides of the cakes.

Etiquette Lessons

There is a certain etiquette for eating a petit four depending on its size. Large petits fours that take more than two bites to eat should be eaten with a fork. Small petits fours of one or two bites are eaten with the fingers. Either way, it is polite to serve your petits fours in a paper wrapper to protect your guests' fingers from the delicate frosting.

Sweet Lemon Curd

A popular spread or topping for bread and scones served at afternoon tea, lemon curd was also used as a filling for cakes, pastries, and tarts. Mrs. Patmore would be sure to have plenty of this on hand for the Crawleys and any last-minute tea cravings.

YIELDS 10–12 SERVINGS

¾ cup fresh lemon juice

2 teaspoons lemon zest

3 eggs

¾ cup sugar

½ cup unsalted butter,
  cubed

1. Heat lemon juice and lemon zest in a double boiler until hot but not boiling.
2. Whisk eggs in a medium-sized bowl, followed by sugar when juice is heated. Place a towel under bowl holding egg-sugar mixture to prevent the bowl from moving when subsequent ingredients are added.
3. Slowly add a little of the heated juice mixture to eggs, stirring constantly. Pour just enough juice to temper the eggs so they are about the same temperature as the juice.
4. Holding a strainer over the heated juice mixture, pour the egg mixture that has been tempered with juice back into the juice mixture. Cook curd over low heat until thick enough to show whisk marks and the first bubbles appear. This could take up to 15 minutes.
5. Once whisk marks are showing, add butter a cube at a time, stirring to help melt. Chill curd for 2–3 hours (or overnight), covered.

TIMES GONE BY

While it was still more common for cooks or hostesses to whip up lemon curd on their own, due to the advent of new technology in the mid- to late 1800s (not to mention the refrigerator), more branded goods became available at the market, including pudding mixes and, yes, lemon curd. So if Mrs. Patmore was feeling particularly lazy—and if she trusted that the Countess of Grantham wouldn't notice the difference—she could run out to the store and simply purchase some lemon curd—at least before war rationing made these store-bought goods hard to come by.

Anna Bates's Chocolate Crumpets

When Anna loses her composure over the unfair verdict handed down to her saintly husband, it's likely that Mrs. Hughes would try to comfort her with some soothing tea and these chocolate crumpets.

YIELDS 8–10 SERVINGS

1 cup all-purpose flour
2 tablespoons high-quality cocoa powder
2 tablespoons white sugar
2 tablespoons packed dark brown sugar
2 teaspoons baking powder
1 teaspoon kosher salt
¾ cup whole milk
½ tablespoon vegetable oil
1 large egg
2 teaspoons vanilla extract
1½ cups high-quality milk-chocolate chips

1. In a large bowl, thoroughly whisk together the flour, cocoa powder, white sugar, brown sugar, baking powder, and salt.
2. In a small bowl, mix together milk, vegetable oil, egg, and vanilla extract. Whisk with a fork until egg is thoroughly incorporated.
3. Make a small well in the center of the dry ingredients, then slowly pour in wet ingredients. Whisk together thoroughly, then add chocolate chips.
4. Chill mixture for 30 minutes in refrigerator.
5. On a slightly greased nonstick skillet over medium heat, add dollops of the crumpet mixture in the size of crumpets you desire. Once crumpets start to bubble, flip over and cook the other side. Repeat until you use up the entire batch of crumpet dough. Serve warm, perhaps with heated Nutella and sliced strawberries.

TIMES GONE BY

In British slang, calling someone "a bit of crumpet" means she is an attractive woman. It appears that the British like their food slang, as the term "tart" refers to a prostitute.

Tea Time Chocolate-Covered Strawberries

With the fresh strawberries Mrs. Patmore would purchase at the market, these chocolate-covered strawberries are a must for any berry lover in possession of a sweet tooth and a solid pot of tea. Additionally, strawberries are traditionally associated with desire and lust, so if Lady Mary felt like giving off subliminal messages to Matthew Crawley, she would simply have to request these zesty chocolate strawberries.

YIELDS 4 CUPS

10 ounces high-quality semisweet chocolate, chopped

6 ounces high-quality milk chocolate, chopped

8 ounces high-quality white chocolate, chopped

1 pound fresh strawberries (with stems), rinsed and dried

1. Line one large cookie sheet with parchment paper. Chill the lined sheet in refrigerator for at least 30 minutes.
2. Place chopped semisweet and milk chocolates in one bowl and the white chocolate in a different bowl. Using a double boiler, melt the semisweet and milk chocolate, stirring occasionally until mixture is smooth and creamy. Do not let the water touch the bottom of the upper pot. The chocolate mixture should actually be cool to the touch while melting.
3. Once chocolate is melted, remove from heat. Holding strawberries by the stem, dip the berries into the melted chocolate mixture, then place on chilled parchment-lined cookie sheet.
4. Melt white chocolate in the double boiler. Spoon melted white chocolate into a small, sturdy zip-top bag (the kind that holds sandwiches). Cut the bottom corner edge of the bag and drizzle white chocolate over the semisweet and milk chocolate–covered strawberries.
5. Place strawberries aside and allow to set at room temperature at least 1 hour, and serve.

TIMES GONE BY

If at all possible, use chopped chocolate bars or chunks instead of chips for melting. Chocolate chips are made with less cocoa butter so as to keep their shape for chocolate-chip cookies, which makes them harder to melt and less useful for this purpose. Also, it would be historically inaccurate to use chocolate chips, as they did not exist until 1937. Before then, cooks like Mrs. Patmore would have to chop their own chocolate.

A Custard Tart For Isobel's Tea

Even after the death of her son, Isobel frequently hosts lunch for the Crawley daughters. This custard tart—a classic British treat—would likely find its way to Isobel's table. Hopefully Ethel can learn to bake this treat!

YIELDS 6–8 SERVINGS

For Pastry

⅔ cup unsalted butter

2 cups all-purpose flour

Zest of 1 lemon

Kosher salt

½ cup caster sugar

1 large egg, beaten

1 tablespoon whole milk

For Custard

1 cup heavy cream

1 cup whole milk

½ teaspoon high-quality vanilla extract

¼ teaspoon lemon zest

2 teaspoons nutmeg, plus some for garnish

8 large egg yolks

½ cup caster sugar

A Custard Tart For Isobel's Tea

(continued)

1. **For pastry:** Using your fingertips, massage butter into the flour, adding lemon zest and a sprinkle of salt. Knead with your fingertips until it resembles bread crumbs. Mix in sugar, egg, and milk, forming pastry dough.

2. Roll pastry dough out on a lightly floured surface. Use pastry to line an 8-inch nonstick tart tin, leaving a little less than an inch of pastry hanging over the edge. Chill in fridge for at least 30 minutes.

3. Preheat oven to 350°F. Once oven is hot, place pastry in oven and bake for 20 minutes, or until the pastry base resembles a biscuit. Remove from oven and lower oven temperature to 300°F.

4. **For custard:** In a small saucepan, whisk together cream, milk, vanilla, lemon zest, and nutmeg. Bring mixture to a boil.

5. In a heavy bowl, beat together egg yolks and sugar until well combined. Slowly pour hot milk mixture over yolk-sugar mixture, thoroughly beating as you do so. Once combined, strain your custard into another heavy bowl. Allow custard to settle for 1–2 minutes, then remove any froth.

6. Carefully pour custard into tart pan and sprinkle with nutmeg. Bake custard for 35–40 minutes, or until just set with a slight jiggle in the middle. Remove from oven, trim the edges, and allow to cool completely before serving.

TIMES GONE BY

In Britain, custard tarts are often referred to as "egg custards" to differentiate them from corn flour–based custards. A classic variation of this dessert is the "Manchester tart," where jam is spread across the pastry prior to adding custard. Unlike most egg tarts, a custard tart is served at room temperature.

Part 2

SUSTENANCE
FOR THE STAFF

The aristocrats of Downton Abbey aren't the only inhabitants of the great house who eat well! After all, the staff would need a hearty base to keep their energy going during their incredibly strenuous 10- to 12-hour days. While the dishes you'll find in this part aren't nearly as decadent as those in Part 1, these recipes are just as filling and, for many palates, infinitely more delectable! Here you'll uncover recipes for many classic British dishes such as Pub Grub Bangers and Mash, Spicy Pub Fish and Chips, Shepherd's Pie, and Treacle Tart! Be careful, though—the Downton Abbey staff had a vigorous day to work off the calories from these filling meals … if you eat three (or four) of these dishes a day, you too might want to clean a house with more rooms than people!

Chapter 9

HEARTY
BREAKFASTS
TO START
THE WORK DAY

While the masters and mistresses of the house slept until a reasonable hour, the staff would wake early to start their preparations for the day: opening drapes, lighting fires, dusting, and sweeping the floors. Using the servants' back staircases, they would proceed to wake the family around 9 A.M. But before they started all of their work, the servants needed to eat so they had energy to greet their day. Whether it be a simple plate of baked beans, deviled kidneys, or a bowl of porridge, the following breakfast recipes are sure to put a little extra pep in anyone's step—including yours!

Kipper, Fried Egg, and Rosemary Potatoes Surprise

At Downton Abbey, where the staff must wake up hours before sunrise just to make sure that everything is running in perfect condition for the Downton Abbey aristocrats and their guests, a hearty breakfast is key. After all, many of the staff won't have even a moment to eat until much later in the afternoon. As kipper is a traditional breakfast and snack food in England, serving it with fried eggs and rosemary potatoes guarantees a filling dish sure to please even the snobbiest of staff members, including footman Thomas.

YIELDS 4 SERVINGS

1½ pounds small red bliss potatoes, quartered

1 tablespoon chopped rosemary

¼ cup chopped white onion

2 teaspoons crushed garlic

2 teaspoons sea salt

½ teaspoon freshly ground black pepper

¼ cup extra-virgin olive oil

2 tablespoons unsalted butter

2 kippered herring fillets

4 large eggs

Oregano, to taste

1. Preheat oven to 350°F.
2. In a pot of boiling water, cook potatoes until just barely tender. Drain.
3. Toss potatoes with rosemary, onion, garlic, sea salt, black pepper, and olive oil. Evenly transfer potato mixture to a large baking sheet and roast for 30–35 minutes until browned, cooked through, and very fragrant.
4. Melt 1 tablespoon of the butter in a large skillet over medium-low heat. Once melted, add kippered fillets, cooking about 5 minutes per side. Remove and set aside.
5. In a small skillet over medium heat, melt the remaining tablespoon of butter. Once simmering, crack eggs over skillet, one right next to the other. Cook sunny-side up. Once eggs are cooked to your liking, season with oregano, then serve immediately while kippers and potatoes are still warm.

TIMES GONE BY

A kipper is a split, salted, and smoked herring. A *red herring*, a phrase often used in mystery novels, is a purposely misleading object or fact. The phrase came about in the 1800s when British fugitives would rub herring across their trail to divert and confuse the bloodhounds chasing after them.

Spicy Classic Kedgeree

Another import from colonial India, Spicy Classic Kedgeree—often a mix of flaked fish, boiled rice, onions, and hard-boiled eggs—was a commonly enjoyed breakfast dish, especially during the Victorian era when the Dowager Countess grew up. Before it was possible to refrigerate leftover food, this dish was a great way to rid oneself of pesky leftovers. That said, both the staff and the Crawleys would enjoy starting their day by eating this meal.

YIELDS 4–6 SERVINGS

1½ pounds haddock fillets
4 fresh bay leaves
1½ cups long-grain
   basmati rice
Kosher salt
2 tablespoons unsalted
   butter
2 teaspoons grated fresh
   ginger
1 large yellow onion,
   chopped
1 clove garlic, chopped
2 heaping tablespoons
   curry powder
2 medium-sized tomatoes,
   chopped
Juice of 2 lemons
4 large hard-boiled eggs
½ cup fresh coriander,
   chopped
2 tablespoons finely
   chopped chives

1. Place haddock and bay leaves in a shallow pan with just enough water to cover. Bring mixture to boil, then cover and simmer for 5–10 minutes or until cooked through. Remove fish from pan and allow to cool. If skin is on fish, remove it and then flake fish into bite-sized chunks and set aside.
2. In a medium-sized pot, boil rice in salted water for 15 minutes. Drain hot water, then rinse rice in cold water, draining again. Place rice in refrigerator to cool until needed.
3. Melt butter in a medium-sized sauté pan on low heat. Add ginger, onion, and garlic. Allow to cook, stirring frequently, for 5 minutes, then stir in curry powder. Cook for an additional 3–5 minutes, then add in chopped tomatoes and lemon juice.
4. Quarter the eggs. Add haddock and rice to sauté pan and gently heat through. Add eggs, followed by the coriander and chives. Serve in a warm bowl.

Etiquette Lessons

If breakfast is offered to guests late, it is custom to precede the meal by sending coffee, tea, and even some eggs and rolls with jam or butter to the bedrooms of the esteemed family. If this is the case, it is likely that some family members will choose to not come down until much later, perhaps not until lunchtime. As breakfast is supposed to be a less restrained and less formal meal, this is perfectly acceptable and even polite.

Deviled Kidneys

A popular breakfast for the English upper class, this dish would be a staple at the Grantham household breakfast table. And if the Crawleys were feeling particularly benevolent, perhaps there would be room in the budget for the staff to enjoy this meal too.

YIELDS 4 SERVINGS

8 lamb kidneys

4 tablespoons all-purpose flour

1 teaspoon kosher salt

½ teaspoon freshly ground black pepper

½ teaspoon cayenne pepper

2 tablespoons butter

2 teaspoons Dijon mustard

2 teaspoons Worcestershire sauce

1 tablespoon red wine

1½ cups chicken stock

Kosher salt and freshly ground black pepper to taste

8 slices whole-wheat bread, toasted

Finely chopped parsley, for garnish

1. Using a sharp knife, remove gristle and internal membrane from each kidney.
2. In a medium-sized bowl, combine all-purpose flour, salt, black pepper, and cayenne pepper. Coat each kidney in this flour mixture, then shake well to remove excess.
3. Melt butter in a large skillet over medium-high heat. Once melted, add kidneys and cook until each side is browned, about 3 minutes per side.
4. Add Dijon mustard, Worcestershire sauce, red wine, and chicken stock to skillet, whisking thoroughly to combine ingredients. Lower heat and simmer kidneys for another 3 minutes per side.
5. Still simmering the stock, place kidneys on a wooden cutting board. Allow to cool. Once stock has thickened, remove skillet from heat and season to taste.
6. Slice each kidney into 3–4 pieces and place on toast. Serve drizzled with chicken stock mixture and top with parsley.

TIMES GONE BY

For a stronger flavor, try substituting pig kidneys for lamb kidneys. While both provide a tender cut, the lamb kidney has a much more subtle flavor than the pig kidney. This perhaps explains why today lamb kidneys are the most readily available type of kidney to purchase.

Working-Class Porridge

A popular breakfast dish imported from Northern Europe, this would be a common meal offered to the staff of Downton Abbey. Porridge was also a popular prison food, so dear Mr. Bates would likely eat this while awaiting trial for the murder of his wife.

YIELDS 4 SERVINGS

1 cup rolled oats

2½ cups water

1 teaspoon kosher salt

¼ cup raisins

2 bananas, sliced

2 teaspoons cinnamon

¼ teaspoon vanilla extract

1 tablespoon packed light
   brown sugar

1 tablespoon white sugar

2 teaspoons honey
   (optional)

½ cup cold milk (optional)

1. In a saucepan, combine the rolled oats, water, salt, raisins, bananas, cinnamon, and vanilla.
2. Bring to a brief boil, then reduce heat and simmer until the liquid has been absorbed, stirring frequently.
3. Add both sugars. Pour into bowls, then top each with milk and honey, if desired.

TIMES GONE BY

While this porridge might not appear something for which the staff of Downton would give hearty thanks, in London during the Edwardian period, out-of-work families spent as little as a penny per day per person on food, resulting in a greatly shortened lifespan. However, this led to a lowered birthrate, which helped women, who began to experience improved health as a direct result of a reduction in family size.

Boiled Beef Tongue

While perhaps foreign to many American palates, beef tongue was a popular breakfast (or even lunch) dish for the Victorian and Edwardian English. It's likely that many of the Downton Abbey staff felt they would swallow their own tongues in their attempts to stay silent at some of the gross misbehavior of their employers. Boiled beef tongue is a very lean and very fine-grained meat, thus making it not just extremely tender, but very nutritious.

YIELDS 4 SERVINGS

1 fresh beef tongue
2 medium onions, chopped
2 large carrots, chopped
4 celery stalks, chopped
4 sprigs parsley
¼ cup Dijon mustard
2 tablespoons capers,
   drained

1. In a medium-sized pot, add beef tongue, vegetables, and parsley. Cover ingredients with water. Boil uncovered for 3½–4 hours.
2. Remove tongue from pot; don't worry if it appears discolored. Remove the skin from tongue, slicing the skin lengthwise and peeling it back. Though you shouldn't find any gristle or small bones, if you do, remove them as well.
3. Slice tongue. Serve cooled with mustard and capers.

TIMES GONE BY

Before the British discovered the joy of beef tongue, the Paleolithic hunters sought it out—along with its fatty counterparts such as trotters (feet), brains, or marrow. Although tongue is mainly a dish served to the middle and lower classes, even the upper class would have enjoyed this delight.

Breakfast Baked Beans

No full English breakfast is complete without baked beans in tomato sauce served on toast! It's easy to imagine Mr. Bates or Mr. Carson slathering these beans on a piece of bread before hurrying to help their masters. Baked beans on toast continued to be a European breakfast staple over the years and is still enjoyed today.

YIELDS 6–8 SERVINGS

2 tablespoons extra-virgin olive oil

2 medium onions, chopped

2 cloves garlic, chopped

1 tablespoon minced fresh rosemary

1 teaspoon chili flakes

1 tablespoon light brown sugar

1 teaspoon honey

½ cup tomato paste

1 (15-ounce) can crushed tomatoes

2 cups chicken stock

1 teaspoon kosher salt

½ teaspoon freshly ground black pepper

4 (15-ounce) cans Great Northern or cannellini beans, drained and rinsed

1 loaf sourdough bread, sliced and toasted

1. Preheat oven to 350°F. In a 4-quart ovenproof dutch oven, heat olive oil over medium-high heat. Add chopped onions, stirring often, until they begin to brown. Using a wooden spoon, scrape any browned onion bits from side of pot.
2. Add garlic, rosemary, and chili flakes, and let cook for 2 minutes. Mix in brown sugar, honey, and tomato paste, stirring thoroughly to combine. Add crushed tomatoes and chicken stock, followed by salt and pepper.
3. Stir in beans. Cover pot and cook in oven for 1 hour or until beans are softened to desired consistency. Serve over toast.

TIMES GONE BY

While this recipe requires you to make your own beans, most English folk would make breakfast easy on themselves by using a can of Heinz Baked Beans or Branston Baked Beans. Heinz Baked Beans were originally made with pork, a practice that stopped due to rationing during World War II. Nonetheless, during *Downton Abbey*'s time, canned beans, while likely acceptable for the staff to eat, would not be chosen over Mrs. Patmore's own special recipe.

O'Brien's Black Pudding

Also known as Blood Pudding, this British dish—traditionally consisting of pork blood, oatmeal, and sometimes onions—would normally be served for breakfast but could also be offered at lunch or even dinner. It's not hard to imagine the spiteful O'Brien (who perhaps has more of a heart than she's willing to let on) enjoying this dish as she harbors ill will toward the Countess of Grantham . . . feelings that would eventually vanish after the horrible accident with the misplaced soap.

YIELDS 4 SERVINGS

4 cups fresh pork blood

1 tablespoon kosher salt

1 cup whole milk

2 large onions, chopped

12 ounces suet, shredded

½ cup oatmeal

1 teaspoon nutmeg

¼ teaspoon oregano

¼ teaspoon basil

¼ teaspoon rosemary

½ teaspoon cayenne
  pepper

Prepared sausage skins
  (optional)

½ cup unsalted butter
  (optional)

¼ cup vinegar (optional)

1. Preheat oven to 300°F.
2. Pour blood into a deep pan, keeping cool. Stir in salt.
3. Slowly stir in milk, onions, suet, oatmeal, herbs, and spices. Pour blood mixture into prepared sausage skins, or else pour into a large, ovenproof dish such as a dutch oven.
4. Bake sausage skins or dish, covered, in a water bath for 1½–2 hours. Alternatively, cover and steam blood mixture in a large saucepan for the same amount of time.
5. Allow sausages to cool, then slice. Fry sausages in butter if desired, or serve with vinegar.

TIMES GONE BY

This dish is considered a delicacy in the English Black Country (hence the name) and in the English North West, especially in Lancashire, which is also the home of the World Black Pudding Throwing Championships. While this dish is incredibly popular in England, variants can also be found throughout Europe in Germany, Austria, and even France. Asia and Spain also offer a type of black pudding, though their versions use rice instead of the oatmeal found in most European versions.

Not Your Typical English Breakfast: American Johnnycakes

While Thomas might enjoy the dinners served in America, he likely would have looked unfavorably upon this filling American breakfast staple, a form of cornmeal flatbread reminiscent of a pancake. In New England, where Thomas was staying, these would be referred to as "Johnnycakes"; in the South these would be known as "Hoecakes." Neither name would much suit the snooty Thomas, though here's hoping a touch of sugar will help!

YIELDS 12 SERVINGS

2 cups finely ground cornmeal

1½ tablespoons sugar

1 tablespoon light brown sugar

2 teaspoons kosher salt

2 cups boiling water (should really be boiling)

½ cup whole milk

4 tablespoons unsalted butter

1. In a medium-large bowl, whisk together cornmeal, sugars, and salt. Carefully pour in boiling water and mix until it reaches a paste-like consistency.
2. Gradually stir in milk. Batter should be moist yet firm, like mashed potatoes.
3. Melt 1 tablespoon of butter on a hot griddle. Drop batter by tablespoons onto griddle, spreading them so they reach about a 2-inch diameter. Cook on each side until golden brown, about 4–6 minutes, then remove from heat. Repeat with rest of batter, adding more butter as necessary to keep griddle well greased. Serve warm with syrup, jam, and/or butter.

TIMES GONE BY

By the early 1920s, a desire for all things "modern" and "American" swept through Britain. No meal felt this more than breakfast, as the rise of "fast" yet "healthy" breakfast cereals (mainly invented and marketed by brothers Will and John Kellogg) crossed the Atlantic to tempt British housewives who could quickly feed their families with them for cheap and without guilt.

Lady Mary's Scrambled Eggs

After Lady Mary and Charles Blake get stuck out in the farm saving the pigs, she sheepishly admits of her cooking prowess: "I can scramble eggs. That's about it." There's a chance that Lady Mary used a recipe similar to this one. If so, Charles was a lucky man because these scrambled eggs, thanks to the help of butter and cream cheese, are delicious! Nonetheless, this dish is a bit too "plebeian" for the upper crust, and would more likely be enjoyed by the Downton Abbey staff. After all, it's hard to imagine Lord Grantham munching on his daughter's version of scrambled eggs!

YIELDS 6–8 SERVINGS

½ cup (1 stick) unsalted butter

10 large eggs, room temperature

½ teaspoon kosher salt

2 teaspoons freshly ground black pepper

4 tablespoons water

4 ounces cream cheese

1 teaspoon chopped chives

1. Melt butter over medium heat in a large, heavy skillet.
2. In a medium-sized bowl, whisk together eggs, salt, pepper, and water until slightly frothy. Pour into hot skillet and immediately turn the heat to very low.
3. When eggs begin to thicken, stir in cream cheese. Continue to stir eggs until they reach desired consistency. Scoop scrambled eggs onto plates; sprinkle with chives for garnish.

TIMES GONE BY

As demonstrated by poor Molesley's plight after the death of Matthew, there was mass unemployment in Britain in the 1920s. This was due to a variety of reasons, including the lack of jobs available to servicemen after the war, lack of demand for goods, and deflation. Poor Molesley would consider himself lucky to have Lady Mary's Scrambled Eggs for breakfast, lunch, *or* dinner! Though he'd consider himself even luckier to have Ms. Baxter in his life!

Chapter 10

A QUICK LUNCH BETWEEN BUSINESS

The servants would take their lunch—which they referred to as dinner—at midday, long after the aristocrats ate their own lunch. This would be the most filling meal of the servants' day. Whereas lunch for the upper class was not a large or formal affair, the servants' own lunch (also known as dinner) had a rigorous etiquette. The staff would stand around the table until their superiors sat down; the butler (Mr. Carson) and housekeeper (Mrs. Hughes) would sit at the heads of the table. Men would be allowed to drink three pints of beer with their dinner, while women were not allowed more than two. Nonetheless, this would be a great period of respite (and likely, venting) for the servants before the rest of the long workday.

Classic Cornish Pasty

It is likely that at least one of the many workers at Downton Abbey hails from Cornwall, and that this pasty—often lauded as Cornwall's national dish—would be beloved by any of the Downton Abbey servants, Cornish or not. The pasty, British slang for a pie made with meat, dates all the way back to the 1300s, and was actually originally a dish meant for the wealthy. By the 1600s, however, members of the working class were also enjoying this dish, as it could be easily eaten while on the go.

YIELDS 6 CORNISH PASTIES

For Pastry

2¼ cups all-purpose flour

1 teaspoon kosher salt

4 ounces cold, unsalted butter, cut into pieces

4 ounces lard, cut into pieces

1 large egg yolk

6 tablespoons cold water

For Filling

1¼ pounds rump roast, diced

2 small yellow onions, finely chopped

1 potato, cut into ¼-inch dice

2 teaspoons kosher salt

1 teaspoon freshly ground black pepper

1 large egg, lightly beaten

2 tablespoons whole milk

Classic Cornish Pasty

(continued)

1. **For pastry shell:** In a large bowl, sift together the flour and salt. Using your fingers, knead the butter and lard into the dry ingredients until the mixture resembles coarse bread crumbs.
2. In a small bowl, whisk together egg yolk and water, then add to flour mixture. Mix thoroughly until dough just forms. Knead until pastry is smooth. You should be able to manipulate dough without breaking it, but the dough should also retain its texture. Press into a flattened disc shape and wrap in plastic. If pastry breaks while rolling it out, add a bit more water. Refrigerate for at least 30 minutes.
3. Unwrap dough and roll out until it is ¼ inch thick. Cut out six circles, each about 5–6 inches in diameter. Stack the pastry rounds onto pieces of parchment paper (with pieces between each round to prevent sticking) and refrigerate while you prepare the filling.
4. Preheat oven to 400°F.
5. **For filling:** In a medium to large mixing bowl, combine meat, onions, potato, salt, and pepper until thoroughly mixed.
6. Remove pastry shells from refrigerator. Place on a clean surface, then place about ¼–½ cup of filling to one side of the center of each

pastry. Using the beaten egg, brush the edges of the pastry and then bring the unfilled side over to cover the filled side so edges meet. Press edges together and seal, then crimp with a fork. Repeat with remaining pasties.
7. Brush all pasties with remaining egg. Cut several slits into the top of the pasties. Bake for 25 minutes or until pasties are golden brown around edges. Reduce heat to 350°F. Continue baking until pasties are completely golden brown. Remove from oven and allow to cool for 15 minutes before serving.

TIMES GONE BY

On July 20, 2011, the Cornish pasty was given the "Protected Geographical Indication" status by the European Commission. According to the commission's strict guidelines, an authentic Cornish pasty should be shaped like a *D* and crimped on one side, but not on the top. Ingredients must include uncooked beef, turnip, onion, and potato, along with a seasoning of salt and pepper. This status also means that Cornish pasties must be prepared (but not baked) in Cornwall, causing a major change for many supermarkets and cafés that offered their version of a "Cornish Pasty" outside of this locale.

Yorkshire Pudding

Yorkshire Pudding was an excellent and affordable way to fill up on a meager budget. Often, Yorkshire Pudding was served before a less-than-filling meal as a way to stave off hunger. While not enjoyed by the upper crust, Yorkshire Pudding—along with a side of jam or cream—is the kind of snack that Mr. Mason would serve to Daisy during her after-Christmas visit.

YIELDS 6–8 SERVINGS

1½ cups all-purpose flour
1 teaspoon kosher salt
¾ cup whole milk, room temperature
3 eggs, room temperature
½ cup water
½ cup unsalted butter, cut into pieces

1. In a large bowl, combine the flour and salt. Make a well in the dry mixture, then pour in the milk, whisking thoroughly. Beat in eggs one at a time.
2. Pour dry mixture into a blender, then add water. Blend until the mixture is light and frothy. Chill in the refrigerator for at least 3 hours, covered.
3. Let batter warm up to room temperature before using. While batter warms up, preheat oven to 400°F.
4. Place butter in a 9×12-inch baking pan in oven and cook until sizzling, at least 5 minutes. Pour the batter over the melted butter and bake for 30 minutes or until the sides have risen and are golden brown. Cut into 6–8 portions and serve immediately.

TIMES GONE BY

The history behind this dish is long and storied. When wheat became a viable option for cooking cakes and other batter-related dishes, cooks up in Northern England, fans of the "waste not, want not" philosophy, developed a way to use the fat drippings from roasting meat to make a batter pudding. The Yorkshire Puddings served at Downton Abbey were flatter than they are today, though the Royal Society of Chemistry issued a proclamation that a Yorkshire Pudding was not a true Yorkshire Pudding if it was less than 4 inches tall. While this recipe does not use beef drippings, beef drippings can easily be substituted for the butter.

Tom Branson's Guinness Corned Beef

Even the Earl of Grantham—who is likely not the biggest fan of the Irish, thanks to Tom Branson running off with his daughter—would enjoy this Irish classic every now and then. That said, this dish is likely to be eaten more by Tom Branson and his coworkers than by the Crawleys, as it is unlikely the aristocrats of *Downton Abbey* would want to be seen eating something as plebeian as a sandwich.

YIELDS 16 SERVINGS

4 pounds corned beef brisket, rinsed and patted dry

1 cup packed light brown sugar

2–3 (12-ounce) bottles Guinness stout (or other Irish stout beer)

1. Preheat oven to 300°F.
2. Place corned beef brisket on a rack in a large dutch oven. Rub brown sugar all over the corned beef, coating completely. Pour Guinness stout all over and around beef, until beef is thoroughly soaked and submerged in beer.
3. Cover dutch oven and gently place in preheated oven. Bake for 2½–3 hours and serve hot.

TIMES GONE BY

Perhaps the most obvious time to cook this dish would be St. Patrick's Day, which was celebrated by the Irish as early as the ninth and tenth centuries. However, St. Patrick's Day would not become the festive holiday that we now know and love until many, many years later. The United Kingdom did not declare St. Patrick's Day an official holiday until 1903, and Britain's first St. Patrick's Day parade was not held until 1931.

Spicy Pub Fish and Chips

This classic British dish dates back to the 1800s, with the first "chippy," or fish and chips shop, appearing in the early 1930s. Fish and chips was one of the most popular meals during World War I, as it was available to all regardless of wealth. Nonetheless, it was lower- and middle-class families more than the aristocracy who ate this dish. It is likely that Mr. Bates partook in a version of this dish in the pub where he hid out for a few days.

YIELDS 4 SERVINGS

For Chips (Fries)
1 gallon safflower or vegetable oil

4 large Russet potatoes, or any floury potatoes

For Batter
2 cups all-purpose flour

1 tablespoon baking powder

2 teaspoons kosher salt, plus more to taste

1 teaspoon freshly ground black pepper

¼ teaspoon lemon pepper

Dash cayenne pepper

1 bottle dark beer, such as Manns Brown Ale or Sierra Nevada Brown Ale

Dash Tabasco sauce

1½ pounds firm, white-fleshed fish such as cod, cut into 1-ounce strips

Cornstarch, for dredging

Malt vinegar, for serving

Spicy Pub Fish and Chips

(continued)

1. Heat oven to 200°F.
2. Heat the oil in a 5- to 6-quart dutch oven over high heat until it reaches 320°F.
3. Slice potatoes with skin on using a V-slicer. Place in a large bowl of cold water.
4. In a separate large bowl, make batter: Whisk together the all-purpose flour, baking powder, salt, black pepper, lemon pepper, and cayenne pepper. Slowly whisk in the beer and Tabasco sauce until the batter is smooth and free of lumps. This may take a while, just keep whisking. If the batter feels too thick, thin with water. Refrigerate for 15–30 minutes.
5. Drain potatoes, removing any excess water. When oil in dutch oven reaches 320°F, submerge potatoes in the oil. Working in small batches, fry potatoes for about 3 minutes or until edges are just golden. Remove from oil, drain, and cool to room temperature.
6. Increase oil temperature to 375°F. Fry potatoes again, in batches, and cook until crisp and golden brown, about another 3 minutes. Remove from oil and drain on a roasting rack. Season with kosher salt while still hot, then hold in oven.
7. Allow oil to turn back down to 350°F. Dredge fish strips in cornstarch, then again working in small batches, dip the fish into batter and immerse into hot oil. When batter is set, turn pieces of fish over and cook until golden brown, about 2 minutes. Drain fish on roasting rack or paper towel, and serve with malt vinegar and salt.

TIMES GONE BY

Before safflower oil or vegetable oil were used for frying, it was common to make fish and chips using beef drippings or plain old lard. While Americans would likely flavor this dish with mayonnaise or tartar sauce, the English would choose to stick with malt vinegar and salt. This dish would typically be served with Mushy Peas (see Chapter 11).

Pub Grub Bangers and Mash

This traditional English dish, composed of mashed potatoes and sausages, is often found at British pubs. While the Crawley sisters likely wouldn't be familiar with such food, most of the staff that keeps Downton Abbey running would know this filling dish quite well and would perhaps partake on their days off.

YIELDS 6–8 SERVINGS

8 large Russet potatoes, peeled and quartered

2 tablespoons unsalted butter

¼–½ cup whole milk

Kosher salt and freshly ground black pepper to taste

1½ pounds beef sausage

½ cup diced onion

1 teaspoon rosemary

1 teaspoon oregano

1 clove garlic, minced

¼ cup sliced mushrooms

1 (.75-ounce) packet dry brown gravy mix

1 cup water

Pub Grub Bangers and Mash

(continued)

1. Preheat oven to 350°F. Place potatoes in a saucepan with just enough water to cover. Bring to a boil, then lower heat and cook potatoes until tender, about 25 minutes. Drain, then mash with 4 teaspoons of the butter and enough milk to reach a creamy consistency. Continue mashing until smooth. Season to taste with salt and pepper.

2. In a large skillet over medium heat, cook sausage until heated through, about 3–5 minutes. Remove sausage from skillet and set aside. Add remaining butter to skillet, and add onion, rosemary, oregano, garlic, and mushrooms. Stir until tender. Whisk together gravy mix and water as directed on packet, then add to skillet with onion and mushrooms. Simmer, stirring constantly, to form a thick gravy.

3. Pour half of the gravy mixture into a medium-sized casserole dish so that the bottom is coated. Place sausages in a layer over the gravy, then cover with remaining gravy. Top with mashed potatoes.

4. Bake bangers and mash uncovered in preheated oven for 25 minutes or until potatoes are evenly browned.

TIMES GONE BY

According to the *Oxford English Dictionary*, while many believe that the term "bangers" had its origins in World War II, the phrase was in use at least as far back as 1919. Apparently, before World War I, "bangers" were referred to by upper-crust Victorians as "little bags of mystery" because people suspected the sausages were filled with horsemeat. Once World War I began, however, there was a dramatic reduction in the production and farming of meat due to war rationing, so producers stuffed their sausages with cereal and water, which caused them to pop, hiss, and "bang" when cooked over fires in open trenches—hence their name.

Thomas's Salted Cod Cakes

Due to the United Kingdom's prime location, fish has always been a major part of the English diet. Indeed, there would be an abundance of sole, haddock, and cod for Mrs. Patmore to choose from when it came to cooking meals for the family and staff. Even perpetually ill-willed Thomas would tone down his salty attitude when served these delicious salted cod cakes for lunch!

YIELDS 6–8 SERVINGS

1 pound salted cod
2 large Russet potatoes,
  peeled and cubed
4 teaspoons seafood
  seasoning
2 teaspoons sea salt
1 teaspoon freshly ground
  black pepper
½ cup fresh parsley,
  chopped
½ cup fresh cilantro,
  chopped
2 large eggs, beaten
1 large onion, finely
  chopped
½ cup all-purpose flour
½ cup extra-virgin olive oil
1 lime, sliced, for garnish
1 lemon, sliced, for garnish
Tabasco, for garnish

1. Place salted cod in a large bowl and cover with cold water. Refrigerate cod for at least 8 hours, pouring off the water and replacing with fresh cold water every 2 hours. Once fish has soaked in water for 8 hours, rinse off fish and cut into 3 sections.
2. Place potatoes and cod in a large pot and cover with water. Bring water to boil over high heat, then reduce heat to medium-low, cover, and let simmer until the potatoes are tender and the cod flakes easily, about 30 minutes. Drain and let cool for 10 minutes.
3. Place potatoes and cod into a large mixing bowl. Season with seafood seasoning, salt, pepper, parsley, and cilantro. Roughly mash with a potato masher, then add eggs and onion until evenly combined. Do not over-mash—there should still be pieces of cod and potato in the mixture. Form mixture into golf ball–sized balls, then roll balls in flour. Flatten slightly between palms.
4. Heat olive oil in a medium skillet over medium-high heat. In batches, fry cod cakes in oil until golden and crispy on both sides, about 3–4 minutes per side. Drain on a plate lined with paper towels, then serve with sliced lime, lemon, and Tabasco.

TIMES GONE BY

As readily available as seafood was for those with money to spend, poorer families in Edwardian England would only eat seafood once a week, and usually the cheapest seafood at that, such as kipper. These poor families were lucky to get one solid meal a day, and would not complain at the lack of protein (much less taste) in their diet.

Downstairs Toad in the Hole

This dish—consisting of meat smothered in Yorkshire Pudding batter—would have been a diet staple of most of Downton Abbey's servants, as it was both cost-effective and easy to make. While not the healthiest of dishes, even cranky O'Brien would stop complaining once this moist delicacy was placed before her.

YIELDS 4 SERVINGS

8 links pork sausage

½ cup chopped and cooked onion

1½ tablespoons vegetable oil

2 cups all-purpose flour

4 large eggs, room temperature

1 cup milk

1 teaspoon Worcestershire sauce

½ teaspoon mustard powder

¼ teaspoon garlic powder

1 teaspoon kosher salt

½ teaspoon freshly ground black pepper

1. Preheat oven to 400°F.
2. Spread oil over the bottom of a metal baking dish, then arrange sausages on oiled dish in a single layer. Sprinkle with cooked, chopped onion. Bake for 10 minutes in preheated oven.
3. While baking sausages, whisk together flour, eggs, and ½ cup of the milk in a medium-sized bowl until smooth. Gradually whisk in the rest of the milk until smooth, then thoroughly stir in Worcestershire sauce, mustard powder, garlic powder, salt, and pepper.
4. Remove sausages and onions from oven. Pour batter over them until almost completely and evenly covered. Return pan to oven and bake for 30–35 minutes or until the center has risen and browned. It is normal for the underside to be slightly soft.

Suggested Pairings

Toad in the Hole is commonly served with a heaping helping of onion gravy and a small side of vegetables. Cookbooks in the late 1800s recommended making this dish with "pieces of any kind of meat, which are to be cheapest at night when the day's sale is over," rather than with the sausage listed here. In Hannah Glasse's 1747 cookbook *The Art of Cookery*, she included a variation of this dish called "Pigeons in a Hole," which used pigeons as the meat. No wonder past English cooks found it necessary to smother this dish in gravy!

The Lancashire Hot Pot

It's not surprising that the male servants at Downton Abbey such as Thomas or William might require a day away to air their troubles, and it's quite likely that they would get hungry while doing so. Luckily, this filling, traditional meat-and-potato casserole was available at almost any pub at the time, so the servants wouldn't have to worry about filling their gullets if Mrs. Patmore wasn't around to cook for them.

YIELDS 4 SERVINGS

½ cup unsalted butter, softened

2 pounds stewing lamb, cut into large chunks

2 medium onions, chopped

4 carrots, chopped

3 tablespoons all-purpose flour

2 teaspoons Worcestershire sauce

2 cups lamb stock

2 cups chicken stock

Kosher salt and freshly ground black pepper to taste

2 bay leaves

2½ pounds potatoes, peeled and thinly sliced

½ cup unsalted butter, melted

1. Preheat oven to 350°F.
2. In a large, ovensafe dutch oven, melt softened butter over high heat until hot but not smoking. Heat lamb chunks on all sides until colored, then remove lamb chunks and drain on a paper towel.
3. Add onions and carrots to hot dutch oven and sprinkle with flour. Sauté, stirring constantly, until vegetables are softened but not colored. Stir in Worcestershire sauce, lamb stock, chicken stock, and salt and pepper to taste. Bring mixture to a boil, then stir in meat and add bay leaves.
4. Turn off heat. Arrange sliced potatoes on top of meat, then cover with half of the melted butter. Cover dutch oven, then place in preheated oven for 1½ hours or until potatoes are cooked.
5. Brush potatoes with more butter, then turn up oven to 375°F. and add rest of melted butter. Cook until potatoes are brown, about 5 minutes.

TIMES GONE BY

While this recipe might include what seems like a lot of lamb for one dish, it is nothing compared to what Victorian royalty might have been served. At Buckingham Palace, in fact, there were daily deliveries of 200 necks of mutton and 250 shoulders of lamb, among other groceries. It seems that next to ruling, the most important part of the day for the royals was eating!

Bubble and Squeak

A convenient use for leftover Christmas food, Bubble and Squeak is often served on Boxing Day (usually the day after Christmas, a holiday celebrated by the Commonwealth of Nations countries), though this dish can be made any day of the year. While Mrs. Patmore would never dream of serving this downstairs dish to her superiors, it's likely that at some point or another the staff enjoyed this recipe. The Boxing Day holiday tradition began in the United Kingdom, when the wealthy would give a box containing a gift to their servants.

YIELDS 6 SERVINGS

1 medium head cabbage, chopped

8 slices bacon, diced

2 teaspoons extra-virgin olive oil

1 yellow onion, thinly sliced

2 large carrots, diced

¼ cup peas

2 tablespoons unsalted butter

4 cups baked and thinly sliced Russet potatoes, cooled

½ teaspoon paprika

2 teaspoons kosher salt

1 teaspoon freshly ground black pepper

1. In a large saucepan, cook cabbage in a small amount of water for 10 minutes or until very tender. Drain and set aside.
2. In a nonstick cast-iron skillet, cook bacon in olive oil for 3 minutes, then add onion, carrots, and peas. Cook until bacon is cooked and vegetables are soft; then add butter and cooked cabbage and potatoes. Season with paprika, salt, and pepper. Add more spice to taste. Cook mixture until browned on bottom, then turn over and cook again.

TIMES GONE BY

The first mention of this dish can be found in Thomas Bridges's 1770 *A Burlesque Translation of Homer*: "We therefore cooked him up a dish/ Of lean bull beef with cabbage fried,/And a full pot of beer beside:/ Bubble, they called this dish, and squeak. . . . " Collaborator Francis Grose goes on to define the dish in his 1785 *A Classical Dictionary of the Vulgar Tongue*: "Bubble and squeak, beef and cabbage fried together. It is so called from its bubbling up and squeaking whilst over the fire." While this dish traditionally calls for meat, due to rationing during World War II, meat came off the ingredients list.

Pork Pie Balls

Pork pie, also known as porkie, is Cockney slang for "lie," a term Thomas would be well-acquainted with as he has a tendency to fib in order to increase his own influence at Downton Abbey. Perhaps whenever he chews one of these traditional British bites he is full of remorse for his misdeeds, though that seems unlikely. Nonetheless, the rest of the staff of Downton (other than perhaps O'Brien) could eat these with a clear conscience.

YIELDS 4–6 SERVINGS

For Filling

2 pounds finely chopped pork, preferably ½ pork shoulder and ½ pork belly

2 tablespoons Worcestershire sauce

4 tablespoons Dijon mustard

1 small bunch parsley, chopped

1 small bunch sage, chopped

2 teaspoons ground nutmeg

3 teaspoons ground white pepper

For Crust

2 cups all-purpose flour

1 teaspoon kosher salt

1 cup lard

¾ cup water

4 large egg yolks, beaten

Pork Pie Balls
(continued)

1. **For filling:** In a large metal bowl, thoroughly mix together pork with Worcestershire sauce, Dijon mustard, parsley, sage, ground nutmeg, and white pepper. (The more black pepper, the spicier and better the pie.) Divide the mix into four equal-sized balls and chill in refrigerator.

2. **For crust:** In a separate large bowl, mix together flour and salt. Set aside.

3. In a medium-sized saucepan, heat lard and water to a boil over medium-high heat. Stir into the flour with a wooden spoon to form a smooth dough. Let cool until it's not too hot to handle.

4. Preheat oven to 400°F. Cover large or medium-sized baking sheets with parchment paper.

5. Roll out dough onto a floured surface about 5mm (0.2 inches) thick and place the meatballs onto the pastry. Cut large circles around each ball, at least double the size of the ball, to make sure that the dough can thoroughly cover the meat.

6. Wrap the dough around the meat, smoothing the pastry to create a ball of dough and meat. There should be no meat peeking through.

7. With a biscuit cutter, cut a small circle in extra dough. Brush with egg yolk and place on top of ball to create a sort of lid. Place pie balls on parchment paper–covered baking sheets, then brush each ball all over with egg yolk. With a knife, make a small hole through the lid of the ball to allow steam to escape while baking.

8. Place pork pie balls in preheated oven for 30–35 minutes or until balls are golden and oozing juice. Remove from oven, then let sit for 5 minutes before placing on a cooling rack. Eat hot or cold, depending on taste.

TIMES GONE BY

The most traditional of pork pies is the Melton Mowbray pork pie from the late 1800s, which originated in the town of Melton Mowbray in North Leicestershire. The uncured meat is gray in appearance and chopped rather than ground. Also, as the pie crust is molded by hand and baked freeform, the sides bow out, forming an uneven circle not found in most other pies.

Coq au Vin

While not the fanciest of dishes, this French dish would be a filling entrée that would warm even the coldest soul. Perhaps this warming meal would be served when O'Brien let down her cold exterior after feeling remorse for testifying against Mr. Bates.

YIELDS 4–6 SERVINGS

2 cups pearl onions

½ cup all-purpose flour

Kosher salt and freshly ground black pepper to taste

4 chicken thighs, cut into serving pieces

4 chicken legs, cut into serving pieces

8 slices bacon

3 cloves garlic, crushed

2 medium carrots, chopped

2 cups button mushrooms

1 tablespoon unsalted butter

2 (750 ml) bottles red wine (such as Burgundy)

¼ cup Cognac

¼ cup tomato paste

2 cups chicken broth

5 sprigs fresh thyme

1 tablespoon Herbes de Provence

4 cloves garlic

1 bay leaf

Coq au Vin

(continued)

1. In a large pot, bring 3 cups of water to a boil. Add pearl onions and boil for 1 minute. Remove onions, cool, then peel. Set aside.

2. In a large zip-top bag, mix together flour, salt, and pepper. Add chicken and shake to thoroughly coat each piece. Remove chicken from bag and set aside.

3. In a large dutch oven over medium heat, fry bacon until crisp. Remove bacon to a paper towel and let drain. Then set aside and chill in refrigerator.

4. In the same dutch oven, using leftover bacon fat, add pearl onions, garlic, carrots, mushrooms, and butter; sauté until onions are lightly browned, about 10–12 minutes. Remove vegetables from pan and set aside.

5. Next, brown the chicken pieces in the same dutch oven with remaining juices. Brown until chicken is golden brown. Remove chicken pieces and set aside; chill covered in refrigerator overnight.

6. Pour red wine, Cognac, tomato paste, and chicken broth into dutch oven, stirring thoroughly over medium heat. Mix in thyme, Herbes de Provence, 4 cloves garlic, and bay leaf. Stir in pearl onions, carrots, and mushrooms. Simmer for 10 minutes, then remove from heat. Cover and refrigerate overnight.

7. Remove from refrigerator, then reheat over medium-low heat, covered, for 1½–2 hours until chicken is tender. Remove chicken, then place in a heatproof container and keep warm in oven.

8. Turn heat up to medium-high and remove cover from dutch oven. Simmer sauce for 45 minutes or until it is reduced by a third. Once the sauce has thickened, remove from heat. Pour over chicken and serve.

TIMES GONE BY

This dish has its roots in France, where each region of France braises the chicken in its local wine. The French phrase *coq au vin* means "rooster with wine," yet it is more common to cook this dish with chicken instead of rooster.

Chapter 11

DOWNSTAIRS SUPPER

For most of us, supper hints at the end of a long day, but for the staff of Downton Abbey suppertime was just another brief break before doing their evening chores. Nonetheless, this would be the most relaxed meal of the day, and the staff would be allowed to supplement their meals with leftovers from the meals served upstairs. In the end, what Mrs. Patmore cooked up would really depend on the amount of time and energy required for the upstairs inhabitants. After all, a servant's life revolves around her master's!

Mushy Peas

While the Crawley family might not eat this dish, it would be well known among the servants at Downton Abbey as an accompaniment to fish and chips. Mrs. Patmore might whip this up on nights when the staff is too tired to properly eat after a full day of tending to Downton's regulars and their guests.

YIELDS 4 SERVINGS

1½ cups (12 ounces) dried
　marrowfat peas
4 cups water
2 teaspoons baking soda
2 tablespoons butter
¼ cup heavy cream
1 tablespoon sugar
1 teaspoon kosher salt
½ teaspoon freshly ground
　black pepper

1. Soak dried peas overnight in a large bowl full of water and baking soda. The baking soda is important because it helps break down the peas. The next day, drain peas, then place them in a medium-sized saucepan and just cover with water. Simmer for 25 minutes; the peas should break up without mashing.
2. Remove peas from heat. Stir in butter until it melts, followed by cream, sugar, salt, and black pepper. If desiring a thinner consistency, add more cream.

TIMES GONE BY

Upon hearing the phrase "mushy peas," the Crawley sisters might haughtily refer to it as "Yorkshire caviar," a reference to the stereotype that Yorkshiremen are unwilling to spend money on luxuries. Ladies Mary, Sybil, and Edith, however, would know that their family could afford—and would purchase—buckets of caviar if so desired.

Downstairs Mashed Potatoes

Just because this isn't the most regal of dishes doesn't mean it isn't one of the more delicious ones! Anyone—regardless of personal wealth—would enjoy the creamy, not to mention buttery taste of well-mashed potatoes. Whether Lady Mary and her sisters could bear to be spotted eating such a lowly and unattractive dish is debatable, which means that mashed potatoes are more likely to be enjoyed by the servers of Downton Abbey than by those served.

YIELDS 4–6 SERVINGS

8 medium Russet potatoes, peeled and cubed

½ cup heavy cream, warmed

½ cup whole milk, warmed

½ cup unsalted butter, softened

2 teaspoons kosher salt

1 teaspoon freshly ground black pepper

1. Place potatoes in a large saucepan and cover with water. Cover pot and bring water to a boil. Cook for 30–35 minutes or until extremely tender. Drain well.
2. Add cream, milk, butter, salt, and pepper to potatoes. Mash until light and fluffy.

Suggested Pairings

Tom Branson would expect these mashed potatoes to be served with Tom Branson's Colcannon or the Shepherd's Pie (see both recipes in this chapter) as potatoes are a sturdy, not to mention predictable, side dish to most lower- to middle-class meals.

Walnut and Celery Salad with Pecorino

This dish, while likely enjoyed by the Downton Abbey staff, would be considered too plebeian for the aristocrats of Downton due to its lack of fancy French ingredients.

YIELDS 10–12 SERVINGS

1½ cups whole walnuts

2 small shallots, minced

2 tablespoons sherry vinegar

2 teaspoons fresh lemon juice

1 tablespoon walnut oil

2 tablespoons extra-virgin olive oil

Kosher salt and freshly ground black pepper

2 pounds celery, thinly sliced

4 ounces dry Pecorino cheese, thinly shaved

1. Preheat oven to 350°F. Evenly spread walnuts in a medium-sized pie dish and toast for 10–15 minutes, until lightly golden and fragrant. Let cool, then coarsely chop.
2. In a small bowl, combine the shallots with the sherry vinegar. Then whisk in the lemon juice, walnut oil, and olive oil. Season with salt and pepper.
3. In a large bowl, toss together the celery and Pecorino cheese. Add in the dressing and nuts, then toss. Serve immediately.

Etiquette Lessons

There's a whole language in just how one places his fork on his plate at the end of the meal. To show when you're finished in England, your fork and knife may rest either straight up and down on the middle of the plate with the handles resting on the rim of said plate, or the fork and knife may be angled between the 10 and 4 o'clock positions—handles still on the rim. And whatever you do, *do not* place your napkin on the plate!

Tom Branson's Colcannon

If there's one thing that chauffeur Tom Branson is proud of it's his Irish heritage. Thus, it's likely that he'd ask Mrs. Patmore to make this dish for him during a particularly lonesome evening after Lady Sybil rebuffs another one of his advances. That said, convincing Mrs. Patmore to cater to such a request from an impertinent servant would be another thing altogether.

YIELDS 6 SERVINGS

3 pounds Yukon Gold potatoes, scrubbed

1 cup butter, chopped into tablespoons

½ cup heavy cream, heated

¾ cup whole milk, heated

Kosher salt to taste

Freshly ground black pepper to taste

1 head green cabbage, cored and finely shredded

1 pound ham, cooked

1 clove garlic, minced

4 green onions, sliced, white parts and green tops separated

1. In a large pot, steam the potatoes in their skins for 30 minutes. Peel them using a fork, then chop with a knife before mashing. Mash until all lumps are removed. Add ½ cup of the butter, then gradually pour in heated cream and heated milk, stirring constantly. Season with salt and pepper.
2. Boil the cabbage in water until it turns a darker shade. Add 2 tablespoons of the butter to help tenderize it. Cover with lid for 3–5 minutes. Drain cabbage thoroughly, then return it to pan and chop into small pieces.
3. In a large saucepan, cover the ham with water. Bring ham to a boil and let simmer for 45 minutes or until tender. Then drain the ham and chop it into small pieces.
4. In a medium-sized skillet, heat remaining butter over medium-high heat. Stir in garlic and white parts of the green onions. Cook until the garlic has softened and mellowed. Add it to mashed potatoes, followed by the chopped ham and cabbage.
5. Serve in individualized soup bowls, topped with 1 tablespoon extra butter (if desired), and sprinkle with green-onion tops to serve.

TIMES GONE BY

It's an Irish tradition to serve this dish on Halloween with small coins or rings concealed inside, similar to the way the Downton Abbey aristocrats would serve Mrs. Patmore's Christmas Pudding (see Chapter 7) with treats within. Maybe if Tom asks Mrs. Patmore really nicely, she'll do this for him on the festive day!

Classic Steak and Kidney Pie

Even though the poorer classes—such as those that make up the staff at Downton Abbey—were allowed the least choice meats (such as the chuck steaks and the lamb kidney used in this recipe), this Steak and Kidney Pie would still be a sumptuous meal for anyone, regardless of their riches.

YIELDS 4–6 SERVINGS

2 tablespoons vegetable oil

1½ pounds chuck steaks, cut into 1½-inch cubes

½ pound lamb kidney

Kosher salt and freshly ground black pepper to taste

1 tablespoon unsalted butter

2 medium onions, chopped

1 clove garlic, minced

4 medium carrots, diced

4 large mushrooms, sliced

2 tablespoons all-purpose flour

3 teaspoons tomato purée

3 bay leaves

1 cup beef stock

1 cup Guinness beer (or any stout or lager)

1 teaspoon Worcestershire sauce

14 ounces puff pastry

1 large egg, beaten (for glaze)

Classic Steak and Kidney Pie
(continued)

1. Heat vegetable oil in a large pan over medium-high heat. Season chuck steaks and lamb kidneys with salt and pepper. Place steaks and kidneys in skillet and fry until fully colored.

2. Remove steaks and kidneys from pan and place in a large saucepan. Add butter to original pan and melt over medium heat. Add onions, garlic, and carrots, stirring frequently, and sauté for 3–5 minutes. Then add the sautéed vegetables to saucepan with meat.

3. Next add mushrooms to pan. Sauté the mushroom slices for an additional 3 minutes, adding more butter if necessary. Turn mushrooms repeatedly, then remove from heat.

4. Heat the saucepan with the meat over medium heat. Add the flour, stirring for 3 minutes. Add tomato purée, sautéed mushrooms, and bay leaves. Pour in beef stock and beer, bringing mixture to a simmer. Skim off any excess impurities from top of stock. The meat should just be covered; if not, add more stock or beer. Simmer gently, partially covered, for 2 hours. Check every half hour for potential skimming needs.

5. After 1½–2 hours, check meat for tenderness. If the meat has cooked properly, the sauce will have reduced, both thickening its consistency and increasing its flavor.

6. Add Worcestershire sauce. Transfer to a pie dish and allow meat to cool until it is lukewarm.

7. Preheat oven to 400°F.

8. Roll the pastry until it's about ¼-inch thick. Cut a strip of pastry to sit around the rim of the dish; this will help the top to stay put. Brush the rim of the pie dish with beaten egg before applying the strip. Then brush strip again with egg. Taking care that the pastry top is larger than the dish, sit it on top. Push down around the sides, trim, and crimp for a neat finish. Brush completely with egg wash and place in the preheated oven. Bake for 40–45 minutes or until golden brown.

TIMES GONE BY

Any of the Granthams might read about this dish while browsing their Charles Dickens books. The famous author discusses steak and kidney pie and the changing culinary market in his famous first novel *The Pickwick Papers*.

Soupe à l'Oignon

A popular dish from Roman times, this French onion soup was, throughout time, considered a peasant dish because onions were easy for the poor to grow and eat. Nonetheless, the nice cheeses add a taste of formality to this informal treat. Thus, while not likely served to the guests of Downton Abbey, the staff would highly enjoy this soup.

YIELDS 4–6 SERVINGS

1 cup unsalted butter

6 sweet onions, sliced

3 cloves garlic, peeled and chopped

2 bay leaves

2 sprigs fresh thyme

Kosher salt and freshly ground black pepper

1 cup quality red wine

3 heaping tablespoons all-purpose flour

8 cups beef broth

2 tablespoons brandy

1 baguette, sliced

¼ cup unsalted butter, melted

½ pound freshly grated Gruyère cheese

⅓ pound freshly grated Parmesan cheese

Soupe à l'Oignon

(continued)

1. Melt butter in a large pot over medium-high heat. Stir in onions, garlic, bay leaves, fresh thyme, salt, and pepper. Cook, stirring often, until the onions are mushy and caramelized, around 20–25 minutes.

2. Slowly pour in wine, then increase heat until mixture reaches a brief boil. Then reduce heat and simmer until all the wine has evaporated, about 10–15 minutes. Discard bay leaves and thyme. Sprinkle flour over the onion mixture and stir, making sure heat is low so flour does not burn. Cook, stirring every 3–5 minutes, for 15 minutes.

3. Slowly pour in beef broth and brandy, then increase heat to a low simmer and cook for 20 minutes. Season soup with salt and pepper.

4. Turn on oven's broiler. Arrange baguette slices on a baking sheet in one long layer. Do not overlap slices. Using a spoon, dab melted butter over baguette slices. Evenly cover baguettes with Gruyère and Parmesan cheeses, then broil until toasts are bubbling and golden brown, about 5 minutes. Cut into four to six strips.

5. Pour soup into bowls and float several of the Gruyère-Parmesan croutons on top. Serve.

Suggested Pairings

While Mrs. Patmore would need to perfectly time the release of this dish to her staff in between their many upstairs obligations, the longer she cooks this soup, the more complex and delicious the flavors. Try this with a glass of good red wine and perhaps some crusty bread slathered with Brie.

Stubborn Oxtail Soup

The Earl and Countess of Grantham would never dream of serving this dish at a dinner party due to the poor quality of its meat. Mrs. Patmore, however, would have no qualms about serving this to her staff, especially during a particularly busy day when all she could use for the staff meal would be leftovers. This dish is actually best when made one full day prior to serving, which would give the cook time to focus on planning for intricate dinner parties for the Crawleys. Even the most stubborn of staff (such as Thomas or O'Brien) would not turn their back on this filling meal.

YIELDS 6–8 SERVINGS

3 tablespoons vegetable oil

3 pounds meaty oxtails, patted dry

Kosher salt to taste

Ground black pepper to taste

8 cups water

6 (14.5-ounce) cans beef broth

4 cups high-quality dry red wine

¼ cup unsalted butter

4 medium carrots, peeled and finely chopped

2 medium parsnips, peeled and chopped

1 medium onion, chopped

2 medium leeks, chopped

2 tablespoons tomato paste

6 cloves garlic, minced

1 teaspoon dried thyme

1 bay leaf

4 large Russet potatoes, peeled and cut into ¼- to ½-inch cubes

⅓ cup finely chopped fresh Italian parsley

Stubborn Oxtail Soup

(continued)

1. Heat vegetable oil in a large stockpot over medium-high heat. Rub oxtails with salt and pepper, then add them to pot and let brown on all sides, about 20 minutes.

2. Add water, beef broth, and 3 cups of the wine to pot. Bring mixture to a simmer, then reduce heat to medium-low. Cover partially and gently simmer, stirring occasionally, until meat is tender, about 2½–3 hours.

3. Carefully remove oxtails from soup. Place oxtails in a large bowl and set aside.

4. Pour cooking liquid into a separate bowl and freeze until fat separates from liquid, at least 1 hour. Spoon fat off top of cooking liquid.

5. Remove meat from oxtails. Add meat to the cooking liquid with fat removed.

6. Heat ¼ cup butter in same stockpot over medium heat until melted. Increase heat to medium-high, then add carrots, parsnips, onion, leeks, tomato paste, garlic, thyme, and bay leaf. Sauté until vegetables are soft and slightly browned, about 15 minutes. Add meat and liquid mixture to pot, then stir in remaining cup of wine. Bring soup to a boil, then add potatoes and lower heat to a simmer. Cover and cook until potatoes are soft, stirring occasionally, about 30 minutes. Add Italian parsley, then season with salt and pepper to taste. Ladle into bowls and serve.

TIMES GONE BY

According to legend, oxtail soup, while a uniquely British-sounding dish, originated in 1793 during the Parisian Reign of Terror, when many French nobles were reduced to begging for scraps. One day a noble-turned-beggar passed a local tannery and noticed a pile of discarded ox tails, and used them to cook himself oxtail soup. After he claimed the dish gave him good luck, other beggars started making the dish.

Mock Turtle Soup

As turtle was quite pricey to ship to England, most British citizens had to make do with "mock turtle soup," which used brains, organs, or scrap meat such as from a calf's head to replicate the texture and flavor of the soup. Following is an authentic recipe from the early 1900s that ex-housemaid Ethel Parks would likely cook while trying to raise her son without financial help from Major Bryant.

YIELDS 6–8 SERVINGS

1 calf's head

1 gallon water

½ cup unsalted butter

¼ pound ham, cubed

1 shallot, diced

4 celery stalks, diced

1 leek, diced

1 medium yellow onion, diced

1 small turnip, diced

½ teaspoon fresh parsley, chopped

½ teaspoon fresh thyme, chopped

½ teaspoon marjoram, chopped

½ teaspoon fresh basil, finely chopped

1 bay leaf

4 cloves, ground

⅓ cup flour

Kosher salt and freshly ground pepper to taste

Mock Turtle Soup

(continued)

1. Wash the half calf's head thoroughly. Cut all flesh from the bones and tie together in a cheesecloth.
2. Pour water into a large stockpot and bring to a boil, then reduce heat and simmer at medium heat. Place cheesecloth full of meat, along with the calf's head bones, into water. Continue simmering, stirring occasionally, for at least 3 hours.
3. Remove the calf's head meat and bones, then strain stock into a clean pot. Allow stock to get cold, then remove all of the excess fat.
4. Heat butter in a large skillet, adding ham, shallot, celery stalks, leek, onion, and turnip. Then add spices and continue to cook.
5. When ham and vegetables are fried, add flour and continue to cook until mixture is a light brown, stirring constantly to keep from burning.
6. Reheat stock in a large stockpot. Heat to a boil, then allow to simmer. Add ham-vegetable-flour mixture, then allow to simmer for 15 minutes. Season with salt and pepper and let simmer for an additional ½ hour.
7. Remove all fat as it rises. Strain stock into another pot, then cut calf's head meat into medium-sized pieces, about three bite's worth. Add this meat to stock.
8. Increase heat to a boil, then let cool. Best if served, reheated, 24 hours later.

Etiquette Lessons

If served at a house of repute, mock turtle soup would be served, if possible, in a turtle shell, so as to give the semblance of being actual turtle soup. However, those who were serving actual turtle soup could be lax on appearances and would plate their soup in a tureen, since they possessed the real deal.

Split Pea Soup

In classic English literature, eating pea soup is considered a sign of poverty. Thus, this would be a dish the staff and townsfolk of Downton Abbey would eat, but not the lords and ladies. No doubt Mrs. Patmore would make a hearty and delicious split-pea soup to warm her staff on cold winter nights. If Mrs. Patmore wanted to offer this classic soup with a bit of variety, she only needs to cook this soup with yellow split peas, as it would thus be called a "London particular" after the thick yellow smogs for which London was famous until the passing of the Clean Air Act in 1956.

YIELDS 6–8 SERVINGS

4 cups chicken or vegetable stock

4 cups water

1 (1-pound) ham bone

2½ cups green split peas

1 cup diced onions

1 teaspoon kosher salt

½ teaspoon ground black pepper

1 large clove garlic, chopped

2 bay leaves

1 pinch thyme

2 cups chopped celery stalks

2 cups chopped carrots

1 cup diced potato

1. Pour stock and water into a large stockpot and bring to a boil. Add ham bone, then lower heat to simmer stock for 1 hour, stirring every 15 minutes.
2. Add peas to stockpot and allow to soak, liquid still simmering, for 15 minutes. Then add onions, salt, pepper, garlic, bay leaves, and thyme. Cover, bringing soup to a boil, then simmer for 1½–2 hours, stirring occasionally.
3. Remove bone from soup and cut off meat. Dice the meat into bite-sized pieces and return to soup. Discard the bone. Add celery, carrots, and potato to soup. Then cook slowly, uncovered, for 30–45 minutes or until vegetables are tender.

Etiquette Lessons

When you are finished with your soup, it is polite to leave your soup spoon on the soup plate or saucer, handle to the right, over the edge of the plate, parallel to the table's edge. The spoon should *never* be left in the soup bowl or in any bowl or cup.

Magnificent Mutton Stew

Mutton, a popular meat in Edwardian England, comes from a fattened sheep at least two years in age. While wealthy Edwardians served mutton with a variety of fancy sauces created by the famous Chef Escoffier, the servants at Downton Abbey would be happy to eat their mutton in this filling stew.

YIELDS 4–6 SERVINGS

½ cup grapeseed oil

4 carrots, diced

4 celery stalks, diced

2 white onions, diced

6 cloves garlic, diced

6 sprigs rosemary

1 (4-pound) leg of mutton, diced off the bone

1 bottle red wine

½ cup tomato paste

4 cups low-sodium vegetable stock

6 Yukon Gold potatoes, diced

Kosher salt and freshly ground black pepper to taste

½ cup unsalted butter

1. In a large dutch oven, heat grapeseed oil over medium heat until it begins to glisten. Stir in carrots, celery, onions, garlic, and rosemary, and sauté until onions are translucent, about 5–7 minutes.
2. Add mutton pieces and stir until all sides have browned. Lower heat, then stir in wine and tomato paste; simmer for 10 minutes. Increase heat and add vegetable stock, bringing mixture to a boil for 3 minutes. Reduce heat to medium-low and cover, cooking for 4–5 hours. Be careful to not let liquid completely dissipate by adding extra stock or water if necessary.
3. Meanwhile, in a medium-sized bowl, thoroughly mix potatoes with salt and pepper.
4. Once meat starts to show signs of tenderness, add seasoned potatoes. The stew is ready to be eaten once the meat is extremely tender. Whisk in butter to thicken sauce before serving.

Suggested Pairings

Try this dish with a large glass of red wine, some crusty bread, and Asparagus with Hollandaise Sauce or with Daisy's Noisette Potatoes (see both recipes in Chapter 6).

Rejuvenating Beef Stew

Mrs. Patmore would be well aware of the rejuvenating effects of a solid meal, and would likely have made this filling stew for the staff during a particularly busy week full of houseguests. Perhaps, for example, when Mr. Pamuk and all the other guests are in town for the hunt, Mrs. Patmore would offer this dish as a way to soothe the servants' tired souls and feet.

YIELDS 8 SERVINGS

2 pounds sirloin steak, trimmed and cut into ¾-inch cubes

2 tablespoons vegetable oil

½ pound red potatoes, cubed

½ pound small white boiling potatoes, cubed

1 cup beef broth

1 cup water

1 tablespoon Worcestershire sauce

1 yellow onion, sliced

2 cloves garlic, peeled

2 bay leaves

1 teaspoon kosher salt

1 teaspoon white sugar

2 teaspoons brown sugar

½ teaspoon freshly ground pepper

1 teaspoon lemon juice

1 teaspoon orange juice

1 teaspoon oregano

1 teaspoon paprika

1 teaspoon cayenne pepper

1 teaspoon allspice

3 large carrots, sliced

3 stalks celery, chopped

3 tablespoons butter

1 medium turnip, peeled

2 tablespoons cornstarch

Rejuvenating Beef Stew

(continued)

1. In a large skillet, brown meat in hot vegetable oil.
2. Boil both sets of potatoes until soft. Set aside.
3. In a large pot, add browned steak, beef broth, water, Worcestershire sauce, onion, garlic, bay leaves, salt, white and brown sugars, pepper, lemon juice, orange juice, oregano, paprika, cayenne pepper, and allspice. Cover and simmer for 90 minutes. Remove bay leaves and garlic cloves. Add carrots, celery, and cooked potatoes. Cover and cook for 45 minutes. Remove 2 cups hot liquid and set aside.
4. In a medium-sized skillet, melt butter. Sauté turnip in butter until crusty and brown. Add turnip to stew.
5. In a separate bowl, combine ¼ cup of water with the cornstarch until smooth. Mix with reserved hot liquid and return mixture to pot. Cook, stirring frequently, until bubbling. Serve by ladling into bowls.

Suggested Pairings

For extra spice, try adding 2 teaspoons of garlic salt or a packet of dry onion soup mix.

Shepherd's Pie

While this might not be a familiar dish to the aristocrats of Downton Abbey, all the staff would know this dish all too well—and much to their dismay. Traditionally, shepherd's pie would be made with leftover roast lamb that has been put through a mincer. However, this recipe suggests regular ground sheep or ground beef. On an off day, Mrs. Patmore would cook this dish since it was quite an easy way to feed a large number of people.

YIELDS 6–8 SERVINGS

2 pounds ground sheep or ground beef
3–4 tablespoons extra-virgin olive oil
2 cloves garlic, minced
1 onion, chopped
1 red bell pepper, chopped
½ cup mushrooms, sliced
4 tablespoons (½ stick) unsalted butter
4 tablespoons all-purpose flour
2 cups chicken broth
2 teaspoons Worcestershire sauce
Kosher salt and freshly ground pepper to taste
1 (9-inch) unbaked pastry crust

1. Preheat oven to 450°F. Grease a 2-quart baking dish.
2. Sauté ground meat in 3 tablespoons olive oil until cooked through and browned. Transfer meat to baking dish. Add 1 more tablespoon of oil to pan if needed. Sauté garlic, onion, red pepper, and mushrooms until tender, about 4–5 minutes. Spoon over meat in baking dish.
3. Pour off excess oil from pan. Melt butter and add flour to form a roux. Cook for 3–4 minutes over medium-high heat. Slowly add the chicken broth, stirring to keep smooth. Cook until bubbly and slightly thickened.
4. Remove sauce from heat and add Worcestershire sauce. Season to taste with salt and pepper. Pour over meat and vegetables.
5. Roll out pastry crust to fit over casserole dish. Crimp edges to seal. Prick with a fork to allow steam to escape. Bake until crust is well browned, about 25–30 minutes. Serve hot.

TIMES GONE BY

This dish would be served frequently at the prison that Mr. Bates would find himself in at the end of Season 2. His shepherd's pie, however, would not be nearly as delicious as this dish.

Mrs. Patmore's Downstairs Pork Pie

A take on Shepherd's Pie (see recipe in this chapter), this pork pie would be a frequent dinner offering for the staff as it is both filling and relatively inexpensive to make. Mrs. Patmore would be likely to serve this often during the war, when the kitchen is particularly sensitive to the lack of ready ingredients.

YIELDS 12–14 SERVINGS, OR 2 PIES

1½ pounds lean ground pork

1 pound ground hamburger

1 large onion, chopped

2 stalks celery, chopped

¼ teaspoon ground cloves

½ teaspoon ground cinnamon

1 teaspoon kosher salt

1 bay leaf

3 cups water

4 Russet potatoes, peeled and cubed

2 (15-ounce) packages refrigerated pie crusts

1. In a large saucepan, mix together the pork, hamburger, onion, celery, cloves, cinnamon, salt, bay leaf, and water. Simmer over medium-low heat for 3½ hours or until the water has fully evaporated. Discard bay leaf, then remove mixture from heat.
2. Near the end of those 3½ hours, place the potatoes in a separate saucepan and cover with water. Bring mixture to a boil, cooking until tender, about 15 minutes. Drain, then mash potatoes. When the meat mixture is ready, stir in mashed potatoes until meat and potatoes are evenly blended.
3. Preheat oven to 375°F. Line two 9-inch pie plates with bottom crusts. Spoon equal amounts of meat-and-potato mixture into each crust. Cover with top crusts and seal edges.
4. Bake pies until crusts are golden brown, approximately 45 minutes.

TIMES GONE BY

If Mrs. Patmore was feeling particularly proud of her pork pie, she could enter a pork pie competition in Yorkshire for the best pork pie. That said, she would have to be familiar with their colloquialism, as in Yorkshire pork pies are known as "growlers." Considering the way Mrs. Patmore can growl at Daisy, she shouldn't have any problem with this!

Chicken, Leek, and Caerphilly Cheese Pie for St. David's Day

There would most certainly be Welshmen amongst Downton Abbey's staff, and they would likely request this Welsh entrée for dinner on St. David's Day—a holiday honoring St. David, the patron saint of Wales, and Welsh heritage—every March 1. This dish incorporates the national emblem of Wales—leeks—and the Welsh Caerphilly cheese.

YIELDS 1 PIE, OR 4–6 SERVINGS

2 tablespoons unsalted butter

1 large onion, chopped

4 cloves garlic, sliced

2 teaspoons sugar

4 chicken thighs, chopped

2 cups sliced leeks, white parts only

2 tablespoons all-purpose flour

1 cup dry white wine

1½ cups low-sodium chicken stock

1 cup plus 2 tablespoons heavy cream

2 teaspoons Dijon mustard

Kosher salt and freshly ground black pepper to taste

½ cup halved prunes

⅔ cup crumbled Caerphilly cheese

1 tablespoon chopped parsley

1 tablespoon chopped tarragon

1 pound ready-rolled puff pastry

1 large egg yolk

Chicken, Leek, and Caerphilly Cheese Pie for St. David's Day

(continued)

1. Preheat oven to 350°F.
2. In a large saucepan over medium heat, melt butter. Add onion, garlic, and sugar, and sauté until onions are translucent and garlic starts to color, about 10–15 minutes.
3. Add chicken pieces to onions and garlic, and cook for an additional 5–7 minutes until chicken is seared.
4. Stir in leeks and flour, stirring constantly until ingredients are well combined. Slowly add wine and chicken stock to mix, stirring until sauce has thickened.
5. Add in 1 cup cream and the mustard, then salt and black pepper to taste.
6. Remove from heat, then stir in prunes, cheese, parsley, and tarragon.
7. Evenly distribute pie filling into a medium-sized pie dish.
8. In a small bowl, stir together 2 tablespoons cream and the egg yolk. Brush around edge of pie dish, then cover filling with puff pastry and cut around the sides with a knife. Brush remaining egg wash over pie. Poke holes all over pastry top to let out steam, then bake in preheated oven for 25–30 minutes or until golden brown.

TIMES GONE BY

Welsh people would also celebrate St. David's Day by wearing a daffodil or leek lapel pin. Perhaps Mrs. Hughes and Mr. Carson might even allow them to hang a flag of St. David, the patron saint of Wales, in their rooms for the holiday.

Mr. Bates's Chicken and Mushroom Pie

A variant of the Warm Chicken Pot Pie (see recipe in this chapter), this dish is one of the most popular types of savory pie served in Britain. Mr. Bates's pub would definitely offer this warm, creamy pie to its patrons.

YIELDS 4 SERVINGS

2 tablespoons extra-virgin olive oil

3 boneless chicken breasts, skinned and chopped

1½ cups quartered button mushrooms

1 medium onion, chopped

½ cup frozen green peas

2 cloves garlic, finely chopped

4 tablespoons unsalted butter

2 tablespoons all-purpose flour

¼ cup heavy cream

½ cup whole milk

1 cup low-sodium chicken stock

1 teaspoon freshly grated nutmeg

1 teaspoon kosher salt

½ teaspoon white pepper

½ teaspoon dried thyme

1 (11-ounce) frozen puff pastry, thawed

1 large egg, beaten

Mr. Bates's Chicken and Mushroom Pie

(continued)

1. Preheat oven to 375°F.
2. In a medium frying pan, heat olive oil over medium-high heat. Add chopped chicken and fry until it just barely begins to color.
3. Add mushrooms and continue to fry until chicken turns golden brown. Remove chicken and mushrooms from pan. Add onion, peas, and garlic to same pan and fry for an additional 5–7 minutes until soft. Remove from heat and set aside in the same bowl as chicken and mushrooms.
4. In a medium-sized saucepan, melt butter over medium heat. Stir in flour and cook for an additional 3 minutes or until roux is formed. Keep stirring.
5. In a small bowl, mix together cream, milk, and chicken stock. Then stir in nutmeg, salt, white pepper, and thyme. Pour liquid slowly into roux, whisking constantly until smooth. Simmer over low heat, still stirring constantly, until sauce has thickened.
6. Pour sauce over chicken and mushroom mixture. Mix well, then spoon into a pie dish and leave until completely cooled.
7. Roll out pastry onto a clean, lightly floured surface. Brush edges of pie dish with beaten egg, then lay pastry on top. Brush top of pie with beaten egg, then make 3–4 slits in the top of pie to allow steam to escape. Bake in preheated oven for 20–25 minutes or until golden brown on top and bubbly inside.

Suggested Pairings

While this pie is a meal unto itself, many a heartier staff member might request a vegetable such as Baked and Buttery Balsamic Asparagus with Sea Salt (see Chapter 6) or even Downstairs Mashed Potatoes (see recipe in this chapter) as a side accompaniment.

Warm Chicken Pot Pie

There's something about warm chicken pot pie that heals the soul and, since this dish is an excellent type of comfort food, it's likely Mrs. Patmore would have offered it not just to her fellow employees but even to the Countess of Grantham after her unfortunate miscarriage.

**YIELDS 1 PIE,
OR 8 SERVINGS**

1 pound skinless, boneless
   chicken breasts, shredded
2 cups sliced carrots
1 cup sliced celery
1 cup frozen green peas
3½ cups low-sodium
   chicken broth
½ cup unsalted butter
1 cup chopped onion
⅓ cup all-purpose flour
1 teaspoon kosher salt
½ teaspoon freshly ground
   black pepper
½ teaspoon garlic powder
1 teaspoon poultry
   seasoning
1½ cups whole milk
2 (9-inch) unbaked pie
   crusts
1 large egg white

1. Preheat oven to 375°F. In a large saucepan, mix together chicken, carrots, celery, and green peas. Add 1 cup of the chicken broth and then enough water to cover and boil for 20 minutes. Remove from heat and set aside.
2. In a separate saucepan, heat butter and onion over medium heat, cooking until chopped onion is translucent. Slowly stir in flour, salt, pepper, garlic powder, and poultry seasoning. Add in the remaining 2½ cups chicken broth and the milk. Simmer over medium-low heat until thick. Remove from heat and set aside.
3. Place 1 pie crust in a deep pie dish, then brush with egg white. Cover with pastry weights and bake in preheated oven for 5 minutes. Remove from oven, then remove pastry weights from pie.
4. Evenly pour chicken mixture into baked pie crust, then pour hot butter-onion mixture over chicken mixture. Cover with unbaked pie crust, then seal edges and cut away excess dough. Be sure to make several small cuts on pie top to allow steam to escape.
5. Bake pie in oven for 45 minutes or until pastry is golden brown and filling is bubbly. Cool for 10 minutes before serving.

TIMES GONE BY

British pot pies differ from American pot pies, which often lack a bottom crust and are more of a casserole than a pie. Also, British pot pies tend to have a thicker, heavier crust—some are even made with shortcrust!

Nothing to Sneer At Osso Buco for Thomas

While snooty Thomas might first raise his nose at this traditional Italian "farmhouse" dish, once Martha Levinson's staff serves him hearty Italian Osso Buco (Italian for "bone with a hole") he'll certainly change his mind! Osso Buco goes especially well with Lord Grantham's American Italian: Risotto alla Milanese (Chapter 3), so feel free to pair these dishes to impress your guests.

YIELDS 6 SERVINGS

2 sprigs fresh rosemary

1 sprig fresh thyme

2 cloves garlic, peeled

1 bay leaf

Cheesecloth

Kitchen twine

3 (1-pound) whole veal shanks,, trimmed

Sea salt and freshly ground black pepper to taste

All-purpose flour, for dredging

½ cup extra-virgin olive oil

1 large yellow onion, chopped

2 medium carrots, chopped

2 cloves garlic, thinly sliced

2 tablespoons tomato paste

1 cup red wine

3 cups beef stock

3 tablespoons chopped fresh flat-leaf Italian parsley

Zest of 1 lemon

Nothing to Sneer At Osso Buco for Thomas

(continued)

1. Form a bouquet garni by placing the rosemary, thyme, garlic cloves, and bay leaf in a cheesecloth, then secure it with kitchen twine.
2. Pat veal shanks dry; using kitchen twine, secure meat to the bone. Season shanks with salt and pepper, then dredge in flour. Shake off excess.
3. In a large dutch oven, heat olive oil over high heat. Add meat to pot, browning on each side for about 3 minutes. Remove shanks from pot and set aside.
4. Using the same pot, combine chopped onion, carrots, and sliced garlic. Season with salt, then sauté over medium-high heat until onions and garlic are translucent and carrots are soft, about 10 minutes. Mix in tomato paste. Return shanks back to pot, followed by red wine. Reduce liquid by half, then add bouquet garni and 2 cups beef stock and bring to a boil.
5. Reduce heat to low, cover pot and let simmer for 1½–2 hours, or until meat is falling off the bone. Be sure to check shanks every 20 minutes, adding extra stock as necessary. Stock should *always* be up about ¾ of the shank.
6. Remove cooked shanks from pot. Cut and discard kitchen twine. Discard bouquet garni. Stir together all the juices left over in the dutch oven, then pour over shanks. Garnish with parsley and zest.

Etiquette Lessons

David, Prince of Wales, later Edward VIII, introduced some updated fashion options for the men during his reign—including the ability to wear "midnight blue" and not just black with evening-wear attire. Midnight blue, unlike its predecessor black, did not give off a greenish cast under certain light or show dust. Though first worn by just self-proclaimed "dandies" and aristocrats, by the end of the 1920s, midnight blue was worn by all.

Chapter 12

DESSERTS FOR THE SERVANTS' SWEET TOOTH

Although it wasn't incredibly common for the chef to cook up a special dessert for her fellow staff, it wasn't unheard of. After all, after a long work day, the maids and footmen would all deserve a treat—but whether they would be allowed one is another question entirely. In this chapter you'll learn how to whip up desserts that every member of the Downton Abbey staff would be well acquainted with, from Tweeny's Tipsy Cake to Treacle Tart to Classic Vanilla Rice Pudding. These desserts might be served after supper (see Chapter 11) or with dinner/lunch (see Chapter 10).

Mrs. Patmore's No-Knead Sally Lunn Bread with Warm Honey Butter

In a pinch, Mrs. Patmore could quickly and easily make this bread for teas or lunches. It requires less preparation than most breads, but is nonetheless warm, slightly sweet, and delicious—especially with the addition of the warm honey butter! This would be a hit not just with the aristocrats of Downton Abbey but the busy staff as well (if they were lucky enough to get a piece).

YIELDS 1 LOAF, OR 10–12 SERVINGS

For Bread

1 (¼-ounce) package active dry yeast

½ cup warm water (110°F–115°F)

1 cup warm whole milk (110°F–115°F)

¾ cup unsalted butter, softened

½ cup sugar

2 teaspoons kosher salt

3 eggs, room temperature

1 teaspoon lemon juice

5½ cups all-purpose flour

For Honey Butter

½ cup unsalted butter, softened yet still warm

¼ cup honey, slightly warmed

½ teaspoon sugar

1 teaspoon sea salt

Mrs. Patmore's No-Knead Sally Lunn Bread with Warm Honey Butter

(continued)

1. In a large bowl, dissolve yeast in warm water. Mix in the milk, ¾ cup butter, sugar, salt, and eggs. It does not matter if the butter is not completely melted. Whisk in lemon juice, then slowly pour in flour and beat until smooth. If mixture is not a soft dough, add up to an extra ½ cup flour.

2. Place dough in a thoroughly greased bowl. Do not knead dough. Turn dough once so it becomes thoroughly greased. Cover bowl with a moist towel and let dough rise in a warm place until doubled, about 1–1½ hours.

3. Punch dough down, then spoon into a greased and lightly floured 10-inch bread pan. Cover and let rise until once again doubled, about 1 hour. Preheat oven to 375°F.

4. Place bread in middle rack of oven and bake for 30–35 minutes or until golden brown and a toothpick inserted comes out clean. Remove bread from pan to a wire rack and let cool.

5. In a small bowl, mix together softened ½ cup butter, honey, sugar, and sea salt. Chill butter in refrigerator until butter reaches a spreadable consistency or until needed. Spread over sliced bread.

TIMES GONE BY

There's a great deal of debate over the origins of this bread. Some say the recipe was brought to Bath, England, by a French immigrant in the seventeenth century, and that a Mrs. Sally Lunn sold her "Sally Lunn Buns" as a means of making money. Others claim that the name is derived from the French phrase *soleil et lune*, "sun and moon," due to the color and shape of the traditional buns: the "sun" referring to the golden top and the "moon" referring to the white, spongy interior. At any rate, any Edwardian visiting Bath on holiday would know this bread well.

Treacle Tart

A classic British dessert that most of the staff at Downton Abbey would be well acquainted with, "treacle tart" is Cockney slang for "sweetheart." Perhaps even the Ladies Crawley would give this dessert a try, though it's just as likely the traditional Earl of Grantham might turn his nose up at a supposedly lower-class sweet. Nonetheless, this dessert would be well-known to the staff and all their family, many of whom likely originated from working-class London, where Cockney slang and all its associations originated.

YIELDS 6–8 SERVINGS

For Pastry
2 cups all-purpose flour

1 teaspoon kosher salt

2½ teaspoons sugar

1 cup unsalted butter, chilled and cut into ½-inch cubes

6 tablespoons ice water

For Filling
1½ teaspoons lemon zest

½ cup rolled oats

½ teaspoon ground ginger

1 cup golden syrup (1 part sugar to 1 part water)

2 tablespoons lemon juice

For Topping
Whipped cream, for garnish

Treacle Tart

(continued)

1. **For pastry:** Thoroughly mix together flour, salt, and sugar in a large bowl. Add butter, and mix until mixture resembles coarse meal. (You might need a blender to do this; otherwise use your hands.) Add ice water, a tablespoon at a time, until mixture just begins to clump together. Make sure the dough holds together when pinched.

2. Place dough on a clean surface. Gently shape the dough mixture into two discs. Work the dough just enough to form the discs, but do not overknead. Sprinkle a little flour around each of the discs, then wrap in plastic wrap and refrigerate for at least 90 minutes.

3. Remove one disc from the refrigerator. Let soften for 10 minutes in order to help with rolling. Then, with a rolling pin on a lightly floured surface, roll out disc to a 12-inch circle about ⅛-inch thick. Carefully place on a 9-inch pie plate, gently pressing pie dough down so it lines up with bottom and sides of pie dish.

4. Preheat oven to 400°F.

5. **For filling:** In a large bowl, mix together the lemon zest, oats, and ginger. Place half of it into the pastry, then pour golden syrup and lemon juice on top of the pie. Cover with rest of oat mixture.

6. Roll out the second disc following previous directions. Cut into strips to lay a trellis over the tart.

7. Bake in preheated oven for 30 minutes, then serve hot or cold with whipped cream.

Suggested Pairings

No treacle tart would be complete without a hearty serving of Clotted Cream (see recipe in Chapter 8)!

Tweeny's Tipsy Cake

Similar to the English trifle, Tipsy Cake, the name given to an old-fashioned English sweet dessert cake, was originally made by soaking sponge cake in high-quality sherry and brandy. This soul-warming alcoholic cake would certainly be enjoyed by the Downton Abbey staff and by the "tweeny," or kitchen maid—in this case, Daisy—most of all, as it would serve as a delicious snack after a hard night of scrubbing dishes.

**YIELDS 2 CAKES,
OR 8–10 SERVINGS**

6 ounces unsweetened chocolate squares, preferably Guittard

¼ cup instant espresso powder, such as Megdalia d'Oro or Café Bustelo

¼ cup boiling water

1¼ cups cold water

¾ cup whiskey

1 cup unsalted butter

1½ teaspoons vanilla extract

2¼ cups sugar

3 eggs

2 cups self-rising flour

Confectioners' sugar, for garnish (optional)

1. Preheat your oven to 350°F.
2. Melt chocolate over low heat, stirring frequently.
3. Dissolve espresso in boiling water. Once dissolved, stir in cold water and whiskey, then set aside.
4. Cream together butter, vanilla extract, and sugar. Add eggs one at a time, beating well after each addition. Add melted chocolate.
5. Alternately add flour and espresso/whiskey mixture. The mixture will be incredibly runny and thin, but do not be alarmed.
6. Pour batter into two 6×9-inch loaf pans.
7. Place pans into preheated oven and bake until a toothpick inserted in cakes comes out clean, about 1 hour. Cool. Sprinkle with confectioners' sugar when serving (optional).

Etiquette Lessons

Dessert is served to your guests in the same order as dinner was presented. Though you might crave it, black coffee is *never* served at a truly fashionable dinner table until after dessert is finished and cleared away. Should a lady wish for a second glass of wine at this time, the gentleman nearest her may serve it—she may *not* serve herself. However, please note that it is considered unseemly for a lady to require another glass of wine with dessert, so drink responsibly. Not that Lady Mary would pay any attention to such rules, much to her parents' chagrin and the servants' amusement.

Mr. Bates's Bread and Butter Pudding

It's likely that when Mr. Bates's lovely wife, Anna, dreams of his prison release, part of that dream involves baking Mr. Bates a celebratory dinner. This homey and classic British pudding dish, while not nearly as sweet as Anna, would nonetheless be on the list of desserts to serve Mr. Bates after his diet of prison food!

YIELDS 4–6 SERVINGS

1 large baguette
½ cup unsalted butter, melted
¾ cup whole milk
2 cups heavy cream
4 large eggs, beaten
1 tablespoon maple syrup
1 cup sugar
2½ teaspoons cinnamon
1 teaspoon nutmeg
1 teaspoon kosher salt
2 teaspoons vanilla extract

1. Preheat oven to 350°F.
2. Cut enough of the baguette into 1-inch cubes to measure 4 cups.
3. In an 8-inch square pan, toast cubed bread in the middle of the oven until bread is crisp but not golden, about 5–7 minutes. Mix melted butter in with bread, tossing to coat bread completely.
4. In a medium-sized bowl, thoroughly whisk together milk, cream, eggs, maple syrup, sugar, cinnamon, nutmeg, salt, and vanilla. Pour over bread, stirring to coat. Cover and chill pudding for at least 1½ hours.
5. Bake pudding in the middle of oven until it just sets but still trembles slightly, about 50–55 minutes. Serve warm or at room temperature.

TIMES GONE BY

Most bread-and-butter pudding dishes include raisins, so it would be historically accurate to add ½–1 cup raisins to this dish. The earliest bread-and-butter puddings were called "whitepot," and either bone marrow (yikes!) or butter could be used. They could also be made with rice instead of bread, which led to the rise of rice puddings such as Classic Vanilla Rice Pudding (see recipe in this chapter). At any rate, a bread pudding such as this one or the Dark Chocolate Bread Pudding with Salted Caramel Sauce (see Chapter 7) is an excellent way to make use of stale bread!

William's Bilberry Pie

This pie, a particular favorite of those residing in Northern England, would likely be greatly appreciated by William on his last days. Whether he is well enough to enjoy this sweet concoction of bilberries—found in North and West England and also known as European blueberries—is unlikely, but perhaps Daisy would appreciate the comfort food.

YIELDS 1 PIE, OR 6–8 SERVINGS

For Pastry
2 cups all-purpose flour

2 teaspoons sugar

1 teaspoon kosher salt

1 teaspoon baking powder

½ cup shortening

½ cup lard

⅓ cup water

1 large egg yolk

1½ teaspoons vanilla extract

1 teaspoon distilled white vinegar

For Filling
½ cup plus 2 tablespoons superfine white sugar

1 pound tart cooking apples, peeled, cored, and quartered

⅔ cup unsalted butter

1¼ cups bilberries (or blueberries for American chefs)

1 large egg, lightly beaten

William's Bilberry Pie

(continued)

1. In a medium-sized bowl, mix together flour, sugar, salt, and baking powder. Cut in shortening and lard until mixture resembles coarse bread crumbs.

2. In a small bowl, whisk together water, egg yolk, vanilla extract, and white vinegar. Slowly pour into dry ingredients, then knead dough briefly until just smooth. Allow to rest for 15 minutes at room temperature.

3. Preheat oven to 400°F.

4. Divide dough in half, then roll out ½ of the pastry dough into a circle to line a 9-inch pie dish. Place in pie dish, then cover and chill for 15 minutes. Meanwhile, roll out other pastry dough half so it is large enough to cover pie dish. Set aside.

5. To make filling, place ½ cup sugar in a large mixing bowl. Thinly slice apple quarters and add to sugar. Mix apples and sugar together well.

6. In a large saucepan over medium-heat, melt butter. Add the sugar-apple mixture and cook for 5–7 minutes, then stir in bilberries and cook for an additional 5 minutes. Remove from heat and let cool.

7. Fill pie dish with bilberry mixture. Lay the pastry circle on top of bilberry pie and seal by crimping edges together. Cut a tiny circle in the center of pie to let steam escape.

8. Brush pastry with lightly beaten egg, then sprinkle with remaining 2 tablespoons sugar. Bake pie for 20–25 minutes or until pie top is golden brown and the fruit tender.

Suggested Pairings

Just like the Treacle Tart (see recipe in this chapter), no bilberry pie is complete without a hefty side of Clotted Cream (see Chapter 8).

Meatless Mince Pie

Dating back to the thirteenth century, meatless mince pie is a traditional Christmas dish enjoyed by both lower- and middle-class British. During the Christmas ball held for Downton Abbey's servants, it is likely that at some point the staff would find the time to enjoy this delicious dessert. Originally made with meat, mince pies were gradually made with the more palatable mincemeat—a combination of dried fruits, sugar, spices, and brandy.

YIELDS 6–8 SERVINGS

For Crust
½ cup cold unsalted butter, cut into ½-inch cubes

1½ cups all-purpose flour

1 teaspoon kosher salt

½ cup cold water

For Filling
1½ cups raisins

6 red apples, peeled, cored, and chopped

⅓ cup orange juice

½ cup apple cider

½ cup white sugar

½ cup packed brown sugar

1 teaspoon cinnamon

¼ teaspoon ground ginger

½ teaspoon ground nutmeg

1 graham cracker, crushed

For Topping
½ cup white sugar

¾ cup all-purpose flour

6 tablespoons unsalted butter, cut into ½-inch cubes

1 graham cracker, crushed

Meatless Mince Pie

(continued)

1. Preheat oven to 400°F.
2. **To make crust:** In a large bowl, mix together the cold butter, flour, and salt with a fork until the mixture resembles bread crumbs. Mix in the cold water, a little at a time, until the mixture just holds together. Mix again, then turn out onto a lightly floured surface. Roll into a 10-inch circle, and invert a 9-inch pie dish onto the dough. Flip the dough over. Fold the dough over the edge of the pastry dish and set aside.
3. **To make filling:** In a large saucepan, combine raisins, apples, orange juice, and apple cider, and bring to a simmer over medium heat, stirring occasionally, until the apple pieces are soft, about 20 minutes. Stir in white and brown sugars, cinnamon, ginger, nutmeg, and crushed graham cracker. Mix well, then pour into prepared pie crust.

4. **To make topping:** Mix together ½ cup white sugar, flour, butter, and graham cracker in a large bowl until the mixture resembles bread crumbs. Sprinkle over mince pie.
5. Bake pie in the preheated oven for 15 minutes, then lower temperature to 350° F and bake until pie topping is lightly browned, about 35 more minutes. Cool before serving.

TIMES GONE BY

Mince pies were originally made in an oval shape to represent the manger that Jesus slept in as an infant, with the toppings symbolizing his swaddling clothes. A custom from the Middle Ages had it that if you ate a mince pie every day from Christmas to Twelfth Night, you would have good luck and happiness for the whole year.

English Eccles Cake

It's likely that Mrs. Hughes and Mr. Carson were raised on this popular Victorian dessert, and Mrs. Patmore would have no problem reintroducing this to her staff. It's likely that, when enjoying this dish, Mrs. Hughes and Mr. Carson, usually so stoic, would experience intense nostalgia for their childhoods. Of course, they'd be careful to shield their intense feelings from the rest of the staff!

YIELDS 6–8 SERVINGS

4 tablespoons unsalted butter

1 cup dried currants

2 tablespoons chopped candied mixed fruit peel

½ cup white sugar, plus extra for decoration

½ cup dark brown sugar

½ teaspoon allspice

¼ teaspoon nutmeg

¼ teaspoon cinnamon

½ (17.5-ounce) package frozen puff pastry, thawed

¼ cup whole milk

1 large egg, beaten

English Eccles Cake

(continued)

1. Preheat oven to 400°F. Thoroughly grease a large baking sheet.
2. Melt butter in a small saucepan over medium heat. Stir in currants, fruit peel, white sugar, brown sugar, allspice, nutmeg, and cinnamon. Mix thoroughly until sugar is dissolved and fruit is coated. Remove from heat.
3. Roll out thawed pastry on a clean, lightly floured surface until it is ¼-inch thick. Cut out eight circles, each roughly 5 inches in diameter; set aside remaining pastry dough for use in other recipes. Divide currant mixture evenly between circles, then moisten edges of pastries with a little bit of milk, fold together, and pinch to seal.
4. Turn pastries upside down onto floured surface and carefully roll out to make a wider and flatter pastry. Be careful not to break the dough.
5. Brush cakes with beaten egg, then sprinkle with white sugar. Make three parallel cuts across the top of each cake, then place on greased baking sheet.
6. Bake pastries in preheated oven for 15–20 minutes or until golden brown. Remove and sprinkle with a little more sugar, then serve.

Times Gone By

English Eccles Cake is named for the town of Eccles in Lancashire, and was a popular pastry in the seventeenth century. However, these cakes were banned—along with mince pies—by the Puritans in 1650. In fact, Oliver Cromwell decreed in an act of Parliament that anyone found eating a currant pie would be imprisoned. Luckily, by the time of the Restoration, the cakes were once again popular.

Classic Vanilla Rice Pudding

Everyone at Downton Abbey would have had rice pudding at least once in his or her life. However, as rice pudding is an affordable dessert that the staff and their families could easily afford to make on their own, this dish is more likely to be enjoyed by the downstairs dwellers of Downton Abbey than by the Crawleys.

YIELDS 6–8 SERVINGS

1½ cups water
¾ cup basmati rice
1 teaspoon kosher salt
3 cups whole milk
1 cup heavy cream
¼ cup sugar
2½ teaspoons vanilla paste
Nutmeg, for garnish

1. In a large saucepan over medium-high heat, bring water, rice, and salt to a simmer. Reduce heat to low and cover. Simmer for 10–15 minutes or until water is absorbed.
2. Add milk, cream, and sugar to mixture. Stir in vanilla paste, then increase heat to medium and cook uncovered, stirring occasionally, for at least 35 minutes or until rice is tender and mixture thickens to a soft, creamy texture.
3. Remove rice pudding from heat and divide among small bowls. Sprinkle with nutmeg and serve.

TIMES GONE BY

Rice pudding is a very "literary" dessert—it frequently pops up in some of the greatest of literature. Charles Dickens mentions it in his tale "The Schoolboy's Story." In her novel *Emma*, Jane Austen also describes a meal including rice pudding, while poets Walt Whitman, T.S. Eliot, and A.A. Milne also all lent their pens to describing this traditional treat.

Pineapple Upside Down Cake for a Topsy Turvy World

In the 1920s, the explosion in canned and prepared foods meant that more women could cook at home—without the help of a domestic staff they couldn't afford. Pineapple used to be considered an exotic delicacy, but the advent of canned pineapple allowed those in the upper-middle and upper classes in America to serve this treat as a show of wealth. And while this cake might first make an appearance in Martha Levinson's kitchen, as the 1920s roared on it would certainly soon make frequent appearances in the kitchens of the British middle class—and eventually upper class—as well!

MAKES 1 (10-INCH) ROUND CAKE

½ cup unsalted butter

1 cup packed dark brown sugar

1 (20-ounce) can sliced pineapple

10 maraschino cherries, halved

1 cup cake flour

1 teaspoon baking powder

½ teaspoon kosher salt

4 large eggs, separated

1 cup white sugar

2 tablespoons pineapple juice

¼ cup sour cream

1 teaspoon almond extract

Pineapple Upside Down Cake
for a Topsy Turvy World
(continued)

1. Preheat oven to 325°F.
2. In a 10-inch cast-iron skillet, melt butter over low heat. Remove from heat, then sprinkle evenly with brown sugar. Arrange pineapple slices so they cover bottom of skillet, then distribute cherries around pineapple and set aside.
3. Sift together flour, baking powder, and salt.
4. In a large bowl, beat together egg yolks and sugar thoroughly. Gently fold in flour mixture, followed by the pineapple juice, sour cream, and almond extract.
5. Beat egg whites in a small bowl until soft peaks form. Fold egg whites into flour mixture, stirring until blended.
6. Spread batter evenly over sliced pineapple in skillet, then place skillet in oven and bake for 30–35 minutes, until surface springs back gently when pressed with fingertip. Remove from oven, then loosen the edges with a butter knife and let cool. Wait 10–15 minutes before inverting onto a serving platter.

TIMES GONE BY

While an "upside down cake" might sound strange, this method of cooking cakes has been around for centuries. Back before ovens, it was easy for more primitive cooks to make their cakes by adding fruit and sugar to the bottom of the pan and adding a relatively simple cake batter on top. All the cook needed to do was place the skillet over the fire for it to cook, and then she could flip it over to show the pretty fruit and let the fruit juices sink into the batter. It wasn't until 1911 when one of James Dole's engineers invented a machine to slice pineapple into rings, however, that this cake became at all easy (and downright fun) to make!

Reference List

Archbold, Rick, and Dana McCauley. *Last Dinner on the Titanic: Menus and Recipes from the Great Liner.* New York: Madison Press/ Hyperion, 1997. Print.

Broomfield, Andrea. *Food and Cooking in Victorian England: A History.* Westport, CT: Praeger, 2007. Print.

Burnett, John. *Plenty & Want: A Social History of Diet in England from 1815 to the Present Day*, 3rd edition. London: Routledge, 1989. Print.

Garmey, Jane. *Great British Cooking: A Well-Kept Secret.* New York: William Morrow Cookbooks, 1992. Print.

Hattersley, Roy. *The Edwardians.* New York: St. Martin's, 2004. Print.

La Falaise, Maxime de. *Seven Centuries of English Cooking.* Edited by Arabella Boxer. New York: Barnes & Noble, 1992; Grove Press editions, 1973, 1994. Print.

Mennell, Stephen. *All Manners of Food: Eating and Taste in England and France from the Middle Ages to the Present.* Oxford: Basil Blackwell, 1985; Illini Books edition, 1995. Print.

Slater, Lydia. "Dinner Is Served . . . Upstairs and Down: The Recipes from the Original TV Series Are as Irresistible Today as They Were in the Seventies." *MailOnline. Daily Mail UK*, 15 Jan. 2011. *www.dailymail.co.uk/femail/food/article-1347092/BBCs-Upstairs-Downstairs-recipes-original-TV-series-irresistible-today.html.*

Visser, Margaret. *The Rituals of Dinner: The Origins, Evolution, Eccentricities, and Meaning of Table Manners.* New York: Grove Weidenfeld, 1991. Print.

Standard U.S./Metric Measurement Conversions

Volume Conversions

U.S. Volume Measure	Metric Equivalent
⅛ teaspoon	0.5 milliliters
¼ teaspoon	1 milliliters
½ teaspoon	2 milliliters
1 teaspoon	5 milliliters
½ tablespoon	7 milliliters
1 tablespoon (3 teaspoons)	15 milliliters
2 tablespoons (1 fluid ounce)	30 milliliters
¼ cup (4 tablespoons)	60 milliliters
⅓ cup	90 milliliters
½ cup (4 fluid ounces)	125 milliliters
⅔ cup	160 milliliters
¾ cup (6 fluid ounces)	180 milliliters
1 cup (16 tablespoons)	250 milliliters
1 pint (2 cups)	500 milliliters
1 quart (4 cups)	1 liter (about)

Weight Conversions

U.S. Weight Measure	Metric Equivalent
½ ounce	15 grams
1 ounce	30 grams
2 ounces	60 grams
3 ounces	85 grams
¼ pound (4 ounces)	115 grams
½ pound (8 ounces)	225 grams
¾ pound (12 ounces)	340 grams
1 pound (16 ounces)	454 grams

Oven Temperature Conversions

Degrees Fahrenheit	Degrees Celsius
200 degrees F	95 degrees C
250 degrees F	120 degrees C
275 degrees F	135 degrees C
300 degrees F	150 degrees C
325 degrees F	160 degrees C
350 degrees F	180 degrees C
375 degrees F	190 degrees C
400 degrees F	205 degrees C
425 degrees F	220 degrees C
450 degrees F	230 degrees C

Baking Pan Sizes

U.S. Size	Metric
8 × 1½ inch round baking pan	20 × 4 cm cake tin
9 × 1½ inch round baking pan	23 × 3.5 cm cake tin
11 × 7 × 1½ inch baking pan	28 × 18 x 4 cm baking tin
13 × 9 × 2 inch baking pan	30 × 20 × 5 cm baking tin
2 quart rectangular baking dish	30 × 20 × 3 cm baking tin
15 × 10 × 2 inch baking pan	30 × 25 × 2 cm baking tin (Swiss roll tin)
9 inch pie plate	22 × 4 or 23 × 4 cm pie plate
7 or 8 inch springform pan	18 or 20 cm springform or loose bottom cake tin
9 × 5 × 3 inch loaf pan	23 × 13 × 7 cm or 2 lb narrow loaf or pate tin
1½ quart casserole	1.5 liter casserole
2 quart casserole	2 liter casserole

INDEX

About the Author

Emily Ansara Baines is also the author of *The Unofficial Hunger Games Cookbook*. She has also worked as a professional baker and caterer throughout the East and West Coasts, most recently in her native Los Angeles. When Emily isn't busy writing, baking, or trying to learn French, she's watching her favorite series, *Downton Abbey*, in hopes of one day being as poised and elegant as the ladies of Downton.